At The Chalkface

Practical Techniques in Language Teaching

**Edited by Alan Matthews,
Mary Spratt and
Les Dangerfield**

GW00703390

Edward Arnold

A division of Hodder & Stoughton

LONDON   MELBOURNE   AUCKLAND

© 1985 Alan Matthews, Mary Spratt, Les Dangerfield

First published in Great Britain 1985
Reprinted 1986, 1988, 1989, 1990

British Library Cataloguing in Publication Data

At the chalkface.
  1. English Language——Study and teaching——
  Foreign speakers
  I. Matthews, Alan   II. Spratt, Mary
  III. Dangerfield, Les
  428.2'4'07   PE1128.A2
ISBN 0 7131 8177 X

Typeset in 10/11 pt Compugraphic Baskerville by Colset Private Ltd,
Singapore
Printed and bound in Great Britain for Edward Arnold,
a division of Hodder and Stoughton Limited,
Mill Road, Dunton Green, Sevenoaks, Kent TN13 2YA
at The Bath Press, Avon

Contents

Introduction

At The Chalkface is a collection of down-to-earth articles on the theory and practice of teaching English as a foreign language in secondary schools and to adult students. It comprises edited articles from the British Council's Newsletter for Portuguese Teachers of English and others which have been specially commissioned. All the articles have been written by teachers and teacher-trainers with experience in both the private and state school systems.

At The Chalkface will be of particular use to native and non-native-speaker teachers of English working with students from the age of 11–12 upwards in secondary schools. It will also be a useful resource for teachers working in private language schools in Britain and other countries. A distinctive feature of the book is that the writers have borne in mind the needs of less trained teachers, especially those working with large classes and without the support of sophisticated equipment or teaching aids.

At The Chalkface is intended for use as general background reading and a fund of teaching ideas for individual teachers, and also as the basis for group discussions on pre- and in-service teacher-training courses.

At The Chalkface may be worked through systematically or dipped into as and where most relevant. The book consists of four sections, the first two of which—*Oral Lessons* and *The Listening, Reading and Writing Skills*—are divided into (i) background articles linking practice to underlying theory (ii) articles on relevant classroom techniques and (iii) a number of lesson plans and practical teaching ideas exemplifying points made in (i) and (ii). The third section—*Achievement Testing*—has three similar divisions but in this case the third consists of complete sample tests with marking guides and notes. The final section—*Other Areas*—contains practical articles on a variety of topics.

A glossary is provided at the end of the book with simple, clear explanations of the ELT terms used throughout.

Acknowledgements

The editors would like to thank the following for their collaboration: the British Council for their permission to use a number of articles from the Newsletter for Portuguese Teachers of English; David Cranmer, John McDowell and Eddie Williams for their comments on the articles; and Teresa Nunes da Silva for typing the draft manuscript.

The publishers would like to thank the following for permission to include copyright material:
Bell and Hyman Limited for Alan Matthews and Carol Read: *Tandem*; Thomas Nelson & Sons Ltd for W S Fowler et al: *Incentive Themes*; Oxford University Press for B Hartley and P Viney: *Streamline — Departures* and the Press Association for the 'Conteh, the driver, banned for a year' article from The Guardian of July 7 1979.

Abbreviations

The following are the abbreviations used throughout the book.

BB	blackboard
FL	foreign language
L_1	first language, mother tongue or native language
L_2	the first foreign language learnt
OHP	overhead projector
RP	Received Pronunciation (see Glossary)
S	student (or pupil)
Ss	students (or pupils)
STT	Student Talking Time
S – S	one student speaks to another student
Sq – Sa	one student asks a question to another student who answers
T	teacher
Tq – Sa	the teacher asks a question to a student who answers
T – S	the teacher speaks to a student
TTT	Teacher Talking Time

Section A
Oral Lessons

Background

1

The teacher's role in the oral lesson—a reminder

David Cranmer

In the thick of day-to-day teaching, trying to cram a seemingly endless syllabus into all too few hours, let us sit back a moment and try to remember what roles, in addition to 'getter-through-of syllabus', we should aim to fulfil. Here are a few notes.

1   Motivator

The teacher-as-motivator is to my mind the single most important role for, whatever technical virtues a teacher possesses, however good at the language the teacher is, without motivation the students will never learn. The following are motivating factors.

Personality of the teacher

—overall attitude: sensitivity, sympathy, encouragement, openmindedness, flexibility;
—avoidance of sarcasm and ridicule aimed at the student;
—appropriate personality role according to the situation:
  a) paternal (authority figure)
  b) maternal (affectionate figure)
  c) fraternal (permissive figure).
The last of these personality roles is more appropriate to teaching older children and adults.

Competence and confidence of the teacher

The teacher must be seen by the students to be both competent and confident, even if in a limited area. The teacher must be competent in the following:
—clarity of thought—muddled thinking in the teacher creates confusion in the student;
—care in preparation and efficiency in execution (see **conductor** role below);

—the language being taught—this does not mean teachers must know everything, merely be competent within the limitations required by their teaching.

Teacher's ability to interest students

If the students are bored they will:
—not pay attention → not learn;
—be easily distracted → get up to mischief → prevent others from learning.
The teacher must provide interest through:
—identifying and catering to the students' interests in terms of topics, e.g. themselves (the most interesting topic of all!), their hobbies, ambitions, dreams;
—variety of language points, skills practised, interaction T→S, S→T, S→S, pair/group activities;
—humour (in visual aids e.g. cartoons; anecdotes and jokes as reading or listening passages; mime);
—inherently interesting tasks, e.g. problem-solving.
Remember that students are more likely to be interested in you and what you are doing if you show an interest in them. No matter how big your class, you must try and get to know your students as people and not just as numbers in a register. Do not regard time in class spent on learning about your students as wasted teaching time. On the contrary, the extra motivation generated through this will more than compensate.

Showing the need

Students who do not see the point of what they are meant to be learning will not learn well. Show the need in terms of:
—the syllabus and tests;
—what the students do not know (language areas where the students cannot function) whether because they have never learnt it or because they have forgotten;
—situations/roles in which the students may indeed need to function.

2   Informant

Perhaps the most obvious role of the teacher is as an informant. This can be in the following contexts:
a) new input (initial presentation);
b) extension of already presented material;
c) revision (reminding students of forgotten points);
d) explanation—during a)–c), but also in remedial work.
   The teacher needs to bear in mind what and how much information to give, when and how—to take a ridiculous example, do not teach the students all the uses of the past perfect (including 3rd conditional and regrets with *if only*) from a native speaker's grammar book when they cannot yet handle *is* and *are*!

3   Conductor

By 'conductor' is meant the person who conducts the lesson. This role is concerned with the practical things a teacher needs to be able to do in the lesson. The teacher must be able to:
—elicit (draw words/sentences from the students instead of simply giving them);
—initiate rules and check that the students have grasped the concepts involved;
—explain things and answer students' queries;

—handle aids;
—provide a model for students to imitate;
—give cues (for instance in drills);
—establish linguistic and situational contexts;
—give instructions for activities (especially important in setting up and managing pair and group work);
—monitor (check whether the students are doing the activity in the way required, whether they are getting the language points right, whether there are any problems);
—correct (see below).

All these things must be efficiently executed.

Remember: it is better to be competent in a few things and expand the techniques later than to be incompetent in many and, through the sheer quantity, unable to improve any.

4 Diagnoser

The teacher must be able to diagnose what should be taught by:
—showing the need to learn an item (because of lack of knowledge) — for instance, by trying unsuccessfully to elicit it;
—evaluating the learners' errors in terms of the need for remedial work.

Never forget to *praise* what the students do know.

5 Corrector

The teacher must come to a decision about what, how much, when and how to correct.

What?   Could be recently taught items, commonly recurring errors, what a student has asked to have corrected, errors just too horrible to leave uncorrected (e.g. *mans* instead of *men*).

How much? Depends on the confidence of the student (according to level, age and character) and on the aim of the activity—more correction if the aim is accuracy, less if it is fluency.

When?   In accuracy-orientated activities (e.g. drills), as soon as possible. In fluency-orientated activities (e.g. role-plays, discussions), later. You can note down the errors and tell the students afterwards or, if possible, it is better still to record the activity and play it back afterwards, correcting it.

How?   Remember that 'No!' or 'That's wrong' plus a correct version is not the only way. You can use gestures (shaking your head) or expressions (a grimace). You can react authentically (interpreting the remark/question as actually spoken rather than as obviously intended). Try to let the students correct themselves before giving the correct version—or let other students help.

6 Conclusion

Above all the teacher must seek to encourage the students. This encouragement involves all aspects of the teacher's role—a sympathetic attitude, not demanding beyond the students' capabilities, not overcorrecting, praising what has been well done. Maybe a little humility helps—even teachers are not perfect!

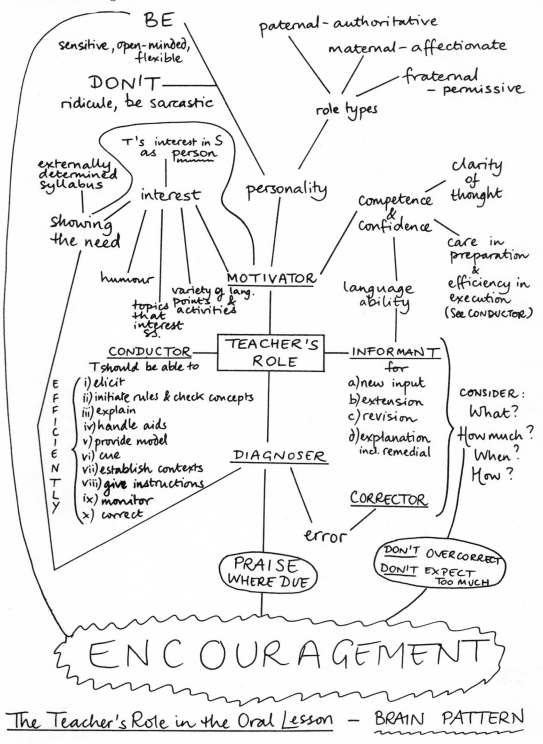

BE
sensitive, open-minded, flexible

DON'T
ridicule, be sarcastic

paternal - authoritative
maternal - affectionate
fraternal - permissive

role types

T's interest in S as person

externally determined syllabus

interest

personality

clarity of thought

competence & confidence

care in preparation & efficiency in execution (see CONDUCTOR)

showing the need

humour

topics that interest ss.

variety of lang. points & activities

MOTIVATOR

language ability

CONDUCTOR
T should be able to

EFFICIENTLY

i) elicit
ii) initiate rules & check concepts
iii) explain
iv) handle aids
v) provide model
vi) cue
vii) establish contexts
viii) give instructions
ix) monitor
x) correct

TEACHER'S ROLE

INFORMANT
for
a) new input
b) extension
c) revision
d) explanation incl. remedial

CONSIDER:
What?
How much?
When?
How?

DIAGNOSER

CORRECTOR

error

PRAISE WHERE DUE

DON'T OVERCORRECT
DON'T EXPECT TOO MUCH

ENCOURAGEMENT

The Teacher's Role in the Oral Lesson — BRAIN PATTERN

The teacher's role in the oral lesson — 'brain pattern' (An explanation of this type of 'brain pattern' diagram is given in the author's three articles *Notes, Summaries and Compositions* on pages 75, 98 and 106.)

2

The presentation stage

Mary Spratt

An oral lesson which aims to teach new structures or functions is often divided into three stages, commonly known as the presentation stage, the practice or accuracy practice stage, and the production, freer or fluency practice stage.

In this and the following two articles, I will look at each of these stages separately but, before that, it would be useful to see how the three operate together. Comparing them to steps in learning to drive a car gives a clear idea of their relationship. Learner-drivers first watch what the instructor does and listen to his/her explanations (the presentation stage). They then copy the instructor and practise by repeating the same operation under the instructor's close supervision (the practice stage). Finally the instructor puts the learners in a situation in which they must make their own restricted choices, decisions and actions (the production stage).

This analogy does not extend, however, to the learners' perceptions of their learning situation; very often learner-drivers have high motivation to learn and a clear appreciation of the relevance of each new learning point. Also, in spite of passing frustrations, they bring these attitudes to each driving lesson, so they invariably realise why they are learning what they are learning and why they need to learn it. For this reason, they participate actively and interestedly.

Most teachers know that the same cannot always be said for language students. And yet success in language learning depends not only on going through the mechanics of learning, but also on *wanting* to learn, and a teacher can do much to generate student motivation. Therefore, to teach a new language point, a teacher needs both to establish the mechanics of a lesson efficiently and to choose contexts and activities that will increase students' motivation and their perception of their need to learn.

Bearing these points in mind, we can now take a closer look at the presentation stage and particularly at four aspects of it:
1. The language items to present
2. The purpose of the presentation stage
3. Contexts for presentation
4. Procedures for presentation

1 The language items to present

The presentation stage may focus on any of the following:
—one or several exponents of a function e.g. *would you mind if . . ., could I . . ., do you think I could . . ., would it be all right if I . . .*, as exponents of 'asking for permission';
—exponents of different functions grouped together in a natural

sequence e.g. inviting → refusing an invitation → giving an excuse
→ inviting again → accepting;
—a structure e.g. the impossible or third conditional;
—one use of a structure e.g. the present perfect simple with *since* or *for*

2   The purpose of the presentation stage

The presentation stage aims to give students the opportunity to:
—realise the usefulness and relevance of the new language and their need to learn it;
—concentrate on the meaning of the new language and, where appropriate, its degree of formality;
—pay attention to the pronunciation, stress, intonation and spelling of the new language;
—focus on the grammar (morphology and syntax) of the new language.
Clearly, students have much to do at the presentation stage. Let us now see how the teacher can be of help.

3   Contexts for presentation

To convey the form of the new language as well as the full force of its meaning and relevance, the teacher will have to introduce the language to students within the wrap of two kinds of context: situational and linguistic. Since much of the success of the presentation stage and of the ensuing lesson depends on these contexts being well chosen, it is worth having a closer look at them.

Situational context

A situational context is simply the situation language occurs in or, with reference to the presentation stage, the situation the teacher chooses to allow the new language to occur in e.g.

	Situation	Language
Example 1	buying quantities of food	countable and uncountable nouns
Example 2	talking with a bank manager for advice on financial problems	exponents of advice
Example 3	a husband and wife arguing about a minor car accident he has just had	should/shouldn't have + past participle

In a well-chosen situational context, the elements of that situation bring out the meaning (and degree of formality) of the new language and capture the students' attention by being relevant to their world. For example, to present 'suggesting and accepting suggestions', teachers could choose the situation of two imaginary friends trying to decide what to give another friend as a birthday present but if, instead, they made suggestions about what birthday present the class could give to one of its members, they would no doubt bring home the usefulness, relevance and meaning of the language more strongly. Similarly, although the meaning of the language of 'giving directions' could be brought out clearly by showing a map and a picture of a person asking a policeman the way, students might well relate much more quickly to and identify better with a map of their own town and a picture of a foreign tourist asking a student the way.

Textbooks, videos or tapes can often provide ready-made situational contexts, but when these are unavailable or unsuitable for any reason, teachers must devise their own by building on the classroom situation, the outside world or the inside world of shared imagination. What then becomes important is to make the contexts transparent and involving. Striking magazine pictures, realia or OHP transparencies can help greatly to achieve this, though on occasions, such as in story-telling, it can be fruitful to leave visualization to the students' imagination, feelings and experience.

Linguistic context

A linguistic context is the language surrounding a particular piece of language. For example, in the previous sentence *is* is surrounded by two noun phrases containing a certain number of lexical items. For the presentation of new language, linguistic contexts should be meaningful, clear and free from unnecessary language items. This involves a delicate balance, as the context must be simple enough to reveal form but rich enough to reveal meaning and remain a sample of authentic language. Teaching a new structure in the midst of a large number of new vocabulary items, for example, would only divide the students' attention between the new structure and the new vocabulary. However, simplifying the linguistic context to such an extent that little but the new language remains (as was often done in the audio-visual and audio-lingual methods), deprives students of the linguistic clues to the meaning and the operation of the grammar of the new language, runs the risk of making the language artificially simple and not authentic and often creates a boring and unrealistic situational context.

4 Procedures for presentation

The context a teacher chooses for the presentation of a new item of language differs with each item, but the procedure used for presentation is by contrast fairly standard. It usually includes the following points in this order:

— Build up the situational context. This can be done through the use of pictures, a dialogue, a tape, chatting, a board story etc.
— Elicit the new language from the students or tell it to them. Elicitation involves trying to encourage students to produce language they have never been taught; they may well not be able to produce it correctly, but can nevertheless make guesses or call on outside knowledge. If they do so successfully, they will be pleased. If not, they will realise their need to learn it and become more receptive. In other words, this procedure makes students less dependent on the teacher, more adventurous with the language and more confident, and increases their motivation and involvement in learning the new language item.
— Focus the students' attention on the marker sentence. A marker sentence is the first example of the new language that students focus on and use as a model for producing other similar sentences. Get the students to repeat the new language. This can be done chorally and individually.
— Check the students' understanding of the concepts behind the new language. A teacher does concept checking to find out whether the

students have really grasped the meaning and form of the new item. For example, when teaching the past tense of regular verbs for unrepeated actions that happened at a stated moment in the past, the teacher will need to check that the students understand at least the 'pastness' of the tense and the situation, and the role of the *-ed* suffix. If the marker sentence was *Martians landed in Australia yesterday* within the context of a newspaper report of an apparent sighting of Martians, concept work might involve a dialogue between teacher and students with the teacher asking questions such as *When did this take place?, Is 'yesterday' in the past or the present? What tense do you think 'landed' is? What shows you it is the past tense? How do you think we form the past tense?* Similarly, when teaching *Excuse me*, the teacher will need to check that the students realise that this expression is used to catch the attention of strangers and is not an equivalent of *please* or *hello*. Concept work might here involve these questions: *Why does he say 'excuse me'? Would you say 'excuse me' to a friend? Is 'excuse me' the same as 'please'? What's the difference? When would you say 'excuse me' to someone?*

The amount and type of concept work required vary with the age, knowledge, interests and mentality of each class; for example, it may or may not be useful to employ grammatical terms or do concept work in the L_1, or to have more than one concept check during a lesson. A teacher must make this decision based on knowledge of the class.

This background article has looked at the procedures involved in the presentation stage and the rationale that lies behind them. For practical lesson plans relating to this stage see Section A, 'Lessons and practical teaching ideas' and, for further reference to some of the above points, *Lesson Planning* on page 18.

3

The practice stage

Mary Spratt

The rationale behind the practice or accuracy practice stage is that of giving students the opportunity to use the newly presented language in a controlled framework so as to allow them to memorise its form and assimilate its meaning more fully.

Traditionally, this stage of the lesson was dominated by teacher-led drills. Recently, however, it has also come to include interactive communicative activities between students, on the grounds that student interaction provides greater and more authentic practice for each student and that communicative activities increase students' interest, understanding and retention of the new language.

We need now to look at both drills and activities in some detail to see how they can most help the student to achieve the aims of the practice stage.

1 The features of practice stage work

What is the difference between a drill and an activity? One difference is that a drill is normally paced, cued and conducted by the teacher, with the class responding either chorally or individually, while an activity is paced and controlled more by the students themselves as they talk to one another, prompted by visual or written cues. Over the years, drills have received much criticism, especially for the lack of genuine communication that is inherent in the way they are conducted. A distinction has in fact been made between mechanical and meaningful drills. A mechanical drill focuses on the form of the new language by getting students to repeat or manipulate the form of the marker sentence provided by the teacher. At worst, to get the drill right, students need not even understand the meaning of what they are saying. For example:

T: The man is swimming.
S: The man is swimming.
T: running
S: The man is running.
T: blimping
S: The man is blimping.
T: trooling
S: The man is trooling.

Blimp and *trool* are, of course, nonsense words which serve to illustrate the point that students can be minimally involved in the meaning of what they are saying in this kind of drill. Mechanical drills have the restricted aim of giving students an opportunity to get their tongues round and begin to memorise the form of the language—an important aim nonetheless.

Meaningful drills, unlike mechanical ones, require students to understand the cues they hear. They are meaningful because they give students an element of meaning-based choice as to what they reply, as in the following example:

T: I've got a headache.
S1: You should take an aspirin.
S2: You should lie down.
S3: You should go for a walk.
T: I'm starving.
S1: You should eat something.
S2: You should have a meal.
S3: You should think of something else.
T: I'm so hot.
S1: You should have a drink.
S2: You should take your jersey off.
S3: You should open the window.

In the above drill, each student may respond in more than one way, provided the answer is appropriate to the teacher's cue sentence.

But there is another level of 'meaningfulness' which needs to be taken into consideration. Here is some further practice stage work, based this time on a series of pictures:

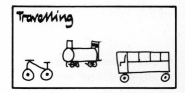

Example 1 (to practise comparatives of short and long adjectives). Teacher-led drill.

T: more expensive
S: A bus is more expensive than a bike.
T: faster
S: A train is faster than a bike.
T: more interesting
S: The cinema is more interesting than TV.
T: healthier
S: Oranges are healthier than ice cream.
T: more tiring
S: A bike is more tiring than a bus.
T: dirtier
S: A city is dirtier than the seaside.

Example 2 (to practise *I'd rather* + infinitive without *to*). Pair work student dialogues: 'finding out your partner's preferences'.

S1:   I'd rather eat ice cream than oranges.
S2:   Me too, and I'd rather read a book than go to the cinema.
S1:   Oh, really? I'd rather go to the cinema. What about travelling?
S2:   Well, I'd rather travel by bus than by train. *etc.*

In my opinion, this second example is more 'meaningful' than the first. In the first, the students are merely supplying known information and stating the obvious, whereas in the second they are supplying unknown personal information about themselves. They are thus involved in a communicative exchange which they can both find interesting and identify with. This kind of exchange, which provides students with reasons for talking other than that of simply learning the language, increases motivation and memorisation.

What is important to realise is that 'meaning' in this instance is operating not only on the level of meaning-based choice, but also on the level of personal relevance and involvement by allowing students to talk about situations they can identify with, find out from and contribute to

Another characteristic of the second example is that, unlike the first one, it looks like 'real language'; it contains exclamations, agreements, hesitations, etc. as well as the structure that is being practised, thus giving students practice in important social language too. It also contains a degree of unpredictability, as one student cannot predict exactly what a partner is going to say. As a result of this, students have a reason for listening, and listening attentively, because they will later have to respond quickly and appropriately to the unpredictable language. Social language and unpredictability are, of course, also features of real language; in normal conversation we never know exactly what the people we are talking to are going to say, but once they have said it we normally reply appropriately and to the point. We could say that this activity therefore not only practises new language, but also trains certain other skills that are required in real communication. It is a truly communicative activity.

We have so far isolated three features of a good practice stage activity: it must be meaningful in the involving sense defined above; it must provide students with practice in some of the unpredictable features of real language; and it must allow for genuine social language reactions. Another feature is that it must offer everyone opportunities for sustained controlled practice, as this is one of the main reasons for the practice stage. The participation patterns which allow students to participate most are obviously those in which the teacher participates least on the verbal level i.e. pair work, group work or mingles.

2 Controlling language at the practice stage

Teachers may wonder how pair work, group work or mingles can be sufficiently controlled to provide students with relatively mistake-free practice of the new language. To do this, practice stage activities have to be set up in the way illustrated below:

Example (model on the blackboard)

Invite: Would you like to . . .? + time and place
Refuse: I'm sorry, I'm afraid I can't.
Give reason: . . .
Invite again: Could you . . . instead?
Accept: Yes, thanks very much. That would be nice.

Students are given a handout of a page from a diary showing the seven days of the week. They are then asked to fill in the four days on which they are busy by writing in what they are going to do and when, i.e. day or evening, using either invented or real information. In pairs, the students then invite one another out and accept or refuse by consulting their diaries. The activity allows students to make mistakes in the prepositions of time and place, for example, but not in their practice of the new language of 'inviting' because this is given to them in the model.

Students will also be prevented from making mistakes if the procedure and language involved in their practice stage activity are made absolutely clear to them. A short demonstration of the activity between the teacher and a good student, or between two students in open pairs, serves this purpose very well.

3   Practice stage procedures

At the practice stage the teacher has to consider not only how to make the tasks both sufficiently controlled and purposeful for the students, but also in what order to carry them out. This order, which of course follows on from presentation stage work, normally operates on the principle of gradually easing the teacher out as model so as to let the students take over. A typical practice stage might therefore follow this pattern:

— one or two brief drills to allow practice with the form of the language;

— one or two controlled communicative activities to consolidate the meaning of the new language and provide opportunities for real language use.

We can conclude by saying that at the practice stage each student must be helped to apply the new language to interesting and relevant situations that illustrate its form, meaning and usefulness. This should take place in controlled but interesting conditions that include aspects of real communication. For examples of practice stages, see articles 11 and 12 (pages 40 and 45).

4

The production stage

Mary Spratt

1   The role of the production stage

The role of the production stage in the presentation, practice, production sequence can be illustrated by returning briefly to the learner-driver analogy of the presentation stage article. After learner-drivers have been shown how to do certain tasks and have carried them out with the instructor's help and guidance, they finally have to perform them independently. At this moment, while the instructors, maybe even reluctantly, withdraw their guidance, the learner drivers try on their own, consolidate their experience and learning and even correct their own mistakes when these stop them carrying out their task effectively. This is the role of the production stage.

Experimentation

This analogy helps us to realize that full learning does not take place until learners become free of their teacher and do things for themselves and by themselves. Language learning is no exception to this. One of the aims of the production stage is to give learners the opportunity to experiment on their own and to allow them to see how much they have really understood and learnt of the language that, until now, has been practised under controlled conditions. They may well make mistakes but, like the learner driver, they will try to correct any mistakes that prevent them from achieving their aim.

Feedback

Learners need feedback on their learning and, similarly, teachers need feedback on their teaching. If teachers do not give their students a free rein, they can never know how much the students have really learnt. Another aim of the production stage is to provide teachers with the opportunity for checking just this.

Integrating new language with old

A third aim of the production stage is to give learners the opportunity to integrate the newly-learnt language into previously-learnt language in an unpredictable linguistic context, on both the receptive and productive levels. We can once again usefully compare this process to learning to drive. Learner-drivers may first, for example, learn to change gear, then learn how to brake. At a later stage, however, road conditions will demand that they learn to combine gear changing and braking. In other words, they must co-ordinate two previously separate activities and integrate them into one main one, that of driving, because unforeseen and unforeseeable circumstances on the road will always require that of them. In communication, language speakers never know what functions or mixtures of function, for example, they will be required to produce or interpret in a particular situation.

Motivation

A further very important aim of the production stage is that of providing motivation, of giving students the pleasure of success and of achieving goals in a foreign language. How satisfying it is when they can at last try things out by themselves. Even though it may initially be worrying for them, eventually it can only be rewarding and even exhilarating to see the result of their learning and see themselves doing something well and usefully all alone.

Creating the right conditions

The production stage thus clearly gives priority to experimentation, creative language use, spontaneity, motivation, confidence-building and fluency. These are not necessarily always easy to achieve in the classroom, so we will turn now to look at how the teacher can help create conditions in which these attitudes and use of language can come about. Particular participation patterns, certain types of activity and atmosphere are important ingredients in these conditions.

The most suitable participation patterns for the production stage are pair work, group work and mingles, as they give everyone many opportunities to speak. They also favour relaxation because, while they are in progress, the teacher's eye and ear can no longer be on everyone. A relaxed atmosphere encourages use of language and expression of personality, so communication becomes freer, more creative, more personally involving and more unpredictable, and thus more motivating—providing the task is not beyond the students' abilities.

2 Types of activity

The kinds of activity which are appropriate at the production stage are, among others, role-plays, discourse chains, discussions, communication-gap activities and games. What is important is that the teacher constructs these activities in such a way that they promote communication and yet ensure that the new language occurs unprompted, naturally, and frequently in the context of other previously learnt language. The unguided manner in which the new language occurs is what distinguishes a production stage activity from a practice stage activity. Role-plays, games and questionnaires, for instance, are not necessarily production stage activities in themselves. The difference between a practice stage game and a production stage game, for example, is the degree of linguistic guidance the students are given. They will receive a model of the new language at the practice stage but at the production stage they will have to create the new language themselves.

Let's look at an example. Imagine the aim of a lesson is 'Asking for and giving information at the railway station'. At the practice stage, students could work in pairs, each student with one of the cards below, and produce dialogues orally:

Student 1—Passenger
London to ?
Instructions: find out about travelling to Cambridge, Brighton and Edinburgh. Note down the information you receive so you don't forget.
—Excuse me, what time's the next train to_____?
—How much is the single fare?
—How long does it take?

Student 2—Station Clerk
London to ?
Instructions: answer the questions the passenger asks you by finding the information in this chart.

	Time	Fare	Length of journey
Cam.	18.10	£3	1 ¼ hrs
Bri.	19.05	£5.50	2 ½ hrs
Edin.	18.35	£25	5 hrs

N.B. Students should change cards and partners after the dialogue is complete and start another dialogue. This is so that each student practises the target language. There should therefore be a second set of cards mentioning three other towns so as to maintain the information gap.

At the production stage, students could do pair work developed from the following discourse chain or from the role-play below:

Discourse Chain

Man		*Clerk*
Greet and ask about time of train to X. →		→Reply.
Find out the price ← of a single ticket. →		→ Reply.
Find out how long ← the journey takes. →		→Reply.
Thank and ← say goodbye →		→ Say goodbye.

Role play

> *Passenger*
> You want to go to New York but you don't know the times of the
> trains, the prices of tickets or how long the journey takes. Find out
> all this information from the station clerk.

> *Station Clerk*
> You are a clerk at Boston station. You have to answer all the
> questions about travelling that people ask you.

N.B. The clerk would need an information leaflet with the times,
prices and lengths of journey of different trains for both these
production stage activities.

Instructions

It is clear from these examples that the type of guidance given to the
students at the production stage focuses more on giving information
about a situation and the roles within it than on providing language.
This means that teachers must make their instructions comprehensive
and explicit, even going as far as to include a short dummy run of the
activity if necessary. One of the main reasons why production stage
activities go amiss is because students are unclear as to what is expected
of them. As a result, they either branch off in unintended language
directions, start using their mother tongue or simply start chatting and
thinking of other things.

Atmosphere

The atmosphere appropriate for a good production stage is clearly going
to be both relaxed and purposeful, so that students feel confident enough
to try out the new language and have a reason for and interest in
communicating and using this language. Teachers can do much to create
this relaxed yet purposeful atmosphere. They can organize concrete tasks
clearly so that students feel no doubts or uncertainties about what is
required of them or their ability to carry out the tasks. Also, and very
importantly, teachers can keep well out of the limelight, thus
withdrawing any constraining influence their presence may have on the
students' willingness and ability to communicate fluently and express
their personalities.

Correction

To be able to keep out of the limelight, teachers need to have a
particular attitude to the students' mistakes, for mistakes there will often
be. They must learn to stand back, and let the students correct their
own and one another's mistakes. Should they notice that mistakes are
really impeding communication, they may choose to intervene if the
students' discomfort is evident or if a student asks for help. Otherwise
they can best use this time, in which students are gaining valuable
fluency practice, to listen out for, diagnose and maybe take note of any
mistakes that do occur in a discreet and unthreatening way. With such a
record of mistakes, they can then do correction work once the activity is
over, or further work on the same point in following lessons. If there are
no mistakes the teacher can simply feel satisfied.

3 Value of the production stage

Teachers and students alike may well be wary of the kind of free work mentioned in this article if they have done little or none of it before. This worry comes, I believe, from the strangeness of the new roles that both students and teacher are expected to play in these activities. As with all new roles, they may not be easy to assume at the first go but, with perseverance, everyone in the classroom will become used to them and come to see the great value of the activities: students will much appreciate success and expression in the new language, teachers will welcome the opportunities provided for discovering what remedial or revision work needs to be done in future and, finally, teachers and students alike will realize the value of the production stage as a tool for fluency-practice and confidence building. For examples of lesson plans for this stage of the lesson see Section A, *Lessons and practical teaching ideas*.

5

Presentation, practice and production at a glance

Carol Read

	Presentation	Practice	Production
Purpose	— to give Ss the opportunity to realise the usefulness and relevance of a new language item — to present the meaning and form — to check understanding	— to provide maximum practice within controlled, but realistic and contextualised frameworks — to build confidence in using new language	— to provide the opportunity for Ss to use new language in freer, more creative ways — to check how much has really been learnt — to integrate new language with old — to practise dealing with the unpredictable — to motivate Ss — can be used for revision or diagnostic purposes
Important Features	— clear, motivating, natural and relevant context — model (or marker) sentence(s) — concept checking — grammatical explanation if necessary	— framework provides guidance for utterances, reduces scope for errors — clear and realistic prompts — Student Talking Time maximised	— purposeful tasks — Ss work together at their own pace — clear instructions — allowance of possibility of making mistakes
Typical Activities	— build-up of appropriate situational and linguistic contexts for new language — listening to and initial repetition of model sentences	— drills (choral and individual) — 2, 3, 4 line dialogues — information and opinion gap etc.	— games, role plays, discourse chains, discussions, information and opinion gaps etc.
Role of Teacher	— informant	— conductor — corrector	— monitor, adviser, encourager, mistake-hearer, consultant

Type of Interaction	— T→Ss choral
	— T→S individual
		— T→S
		— S→S (open pairs)
		— S→S (closed pairs)
			— S→S pairs
			    groups
			    mingles

Degree of Control	— highly controlled, T model	— very controlled, Ss have limited choice	— greater element of freedom
Correction	— important to correct so that Ss have correct grasp of form	— T, other Ss or self-correction	— generally non-interference by T
Length and Place in Lesson	— short — usually at the beginning	— depends on Ss' needs and difficulty — follows presentation, or at the beginning for revision	— depends on level of Ss and type of activity — after presentation and practice — within or across lessons

6

Lesson planning

Les Dangerfield

The effectiveness of a teacher in the classroom can be decisively influenced by the preparation which has gone into a lesson. Beyond the collection or production of appropriate materials and aids, planning can involve anything from a series of mental notes to a detailed written procedure for the lesson.

1 What a lesson plan should provide

1.1 A clear and explicit presentation of aims and of the procedure by which they are achieved. The first thing to decide is what should be achieved within a lesson. By making this an explicit, written statement, teachers provide themselves with simple basic guidelines from which the lesson can be planned and in terms of which it can be judged. The fundamental questions a teacher should ask of a lesson plan are:
—Are the aims of the lesson valid in terms of the students' needs?
—Can these aims be realistically achieved with this group of students and in the time allowed?
—Do the activities in the procedure for the lesson match and achieve the stated aims?

1.2 A reminder of: the order of events in the lesson; aids to be arranged and collected immediately before the lesson; page numbers and cassette counter numbers; details, such as vocabulary to pre-teach, which could otherwise be easily overlooked once the lesson is in progress.

1.3 An at-a-glance check of: the projected rough timing of each stage of the lesson; the balance, for example, of practice of the four skills, of variation in activities and in interaction patterns.

1.4 A record for future reference and re-use. Teachers may rarely use precisely the same lesson on any two occasions but, if post-lesson comments are added (see below), then a past lesson plan will at least provide a useful starting point the next time they have the same aims in mind with a similar group of students.

2 Suggestions for the content of a lesson plan

Once teachers have decided on the information and format for a lesson plan which best suit their needs, it is advisable to draw up a model proforma with the appropriate subheadings and/or columns which can then be photocopied and put on file ready for use. Some useful sections for any lesson plan could be as follows.

2.1 'Level' or 'Year'—for reference purposes.

2.2 Overall time for the lesson.

2.3 Aims. The inclusion of a clear statement of aims has already been justified. Several points have to be borne in mind when this is being formulated:
— Does the lesson involve revision, presentation, practice, production or a combination of these?
— If a structure is being taught, for example a verb tense, which form of this structure is to be practised—the negative, the question, the short answer, etc.?
— Which function of the structure is being taught. For example, if teaching the *will* future, is it being taught in the function of prediction, of new decision on future action, or some other use?
— Which exponents of a function are going to be taught and will these involve making students aware of level of formality/informality or of firmness/tentativeness of the different exponents?
— Will it also be necessary to teach co-functions, i.e. responses to the main function? For example, when teaching 'inviting', it is advisable to teach students how to accept and refuse an invitation too.
— Will the lesson focus on lexis, pronunciation, stress and intonation too?
— If the lesson aims to practise the reading, listening or writing skills, then the sub-skills to be practised should be specified in the aim of the lesson, e.g. does a reading lesson practise skimming, scanning, intensive reading and/or extensive reading?

2.4 Aids. Whether they be books, handouts, realia or whatever, a list for quick reference before the lesson can avoid moments of embarrassment and interruptions to the lesson, as when the teacher forgets the cassette and then has to collect and cue it during lesson time.

2.5 Anticipated problems. This is a useful section of the lesson plan because its existence requires teachers to think of problems that students are likely to have during the course of the lesson and thus build in means of tackling them in advance, rather than coming to the problems unprepared. For example, an elementary/intermediate oral lesson in which structural or functional items are to be taught, will commonly involve problems of:
— concept, for example students may have problems in separating the conceptual differences between the various forms referring to the future;
— form, for example the common problem which students have in forming the negative and interrogative of the present simple, and in producing the third person of the same tense;
— pronunciation, for example problems involving the pronunciation of contracted forms and of stressed v. unstressed forms, e.g. *I was there* (*was* unstressed) v. *Yes, I was* (stressed).

2.6 Procedure. Here this article will restrict itself largely to format, referring to content only in very general terms. For details on content, the reader is referred to the articles on presentation, practice, production and listening, reading and writing skills.

   The procedure for the lesson can perhaps be laid out in a column format with columns for the following:

—stage of the lesson, e.g. presentation, fluency practice, freer oral practice, written practice, production,

—the details of each stage, containing such information as the context of the activity, the model dialogue or sentence to be used and reference to aids and page numbers of books. (This should be a broad column.)

—timing of each activity. They should not be finely timed down to each minute, which would not be practical, but approximate times for each section of the lesson allow the teacher to monitor overall timing as the lesson proceeds.

—interaction pattern, e.g. open pairs or groups. This provides an at-a-glance check on the balance of interaction patterns within the lesson and can show what the teacher and students are doing at any one point.

2.7 Comments. These can be added after the lesson for future reference; they would refer to weaknesses in the lesson and perhaps suggest alternative strategies.

3   Influences on the content of the lesson

Despite the enormous variety of published materials and teaching aids at the disposal of language teachers, there are a number of factors which can severely restrict their freedom of choice of techniques and materials for a particular lesson. In general terms, these stem from the physical teaching situation, the nature of the students, the influence of an organisation in determining a syllabus and the way in which people are understood to learn or acquire language. In this last section of the article these factors will be looked at more closely.

3.1 Practical constraints. In a number of ways, time has an important influence over lesson content. First, and most obviously, the length of the lesson will determine how much can be done in that lesson. Secondly, frequency of lessons must be considered. If lessons are held only weekly, then each lesson is more likely to need a revision component. If, at the other extreme, students have several classes a day, then some of those lessons, probably the later ones, will necessarily involve less intensive activities and less input of new language than if the lessons were less frequent. Too frequent an input of new language only serves to overload the students' capacity to assimilate it. Finally, the time of day often makes a difference to what can be done in a lesson. Evening students often progress less quickly than others simply because they usually come to classes after work and are often tired before the lesson begins.

The number of students in a class is another basic influence on lesson planning as, in general, the larger the class, the longer any activity takes. Class size will also affect the type of activity appropriate; for example, the larger the class, the more important it becomes to maximise each student's opportunity to speak through pair and group work.

The size of the classroom and the nature of its furnishing will often determine whether an activity is practical or not. In a small room with twenty students and heavy immobile desks, it would be unwise to embark upon anything involving any significant student movement.

The final area to mention in connection with purely practical constraints is the availability of aids. It can be easier to plan a lesson if a school has, for example, no cassette players at all, than if it has a small number of them among a large staff. To plan a listening comprehension around a recorded text only to find that another teacher is already using the school's cassette player can be a frustrating experience.

3.2 The teacher. Lesson planning is a complex procedure of selection which the teacher goes through, drawing on experience and knowledge. However, over and above this, there is a further element which would cause two teachers with the same lesson objectives, the same students in the same environment and the same knowledge of methodology to devise two quite different lesson plans, and that is the personality of each teacher. A majority of teachers spend a certain amount of time experimenting with new ideas, but for a great deal of their teaching time they still resort to methods which are well-tried and of which they feel sure.

So for one teacher, role play is part of a well-tried methodological repertoire, whereas for another it is an unknown area full of risks. What has come to be included in each teacher's repertoire will depend very much on his or her attitudes and personality. Attitude will affect selection of method through the way each teacher sees the students best learning. Personality affects selection through the style of teaching with which the teacher feels most at ease.

3.3 The students. Firstly, the needs of the students should be considered. Those wishing only to read professional journals in English should spend much of their lesson time practising the reading skills, to take one example. Students' needs are often in reality rather difficult to specify. Even if the needs of each individual in a class can be identified, there is very often no homogeneity of need among those individuals.

Secondly, the students' present level of English will influence not only the teacher's choice of achievable objectives within the lesson, but also the length of time spent on each activity, the length of comprehension texts, the amount of new vocabulary introduced and, to an extent, the amount of freedom of production the students are allowed in the lesson.

Two further factors which are closely linked are the age and interests of the students. Both will affect the choice a teacher makes of the context in which language is to be practised and of the topics chosen as the subject of comprehension texts and discussion. A text about university life in Britain is likely to be of greater interest to university age students than to classes of either children or businessmen, for instance.

The students' language learning background will influence the choice of techniques and even that of lesson objectives. If students are not used to pair and group activities, they will need to be gradually educated in the usefulness of such techniques rather than being plunged straight into a series of lessons based largely around them. If the students' previous experience of language learning has involved purely grammatical labelling of items, then once again they will need a certain amount of training to see language analysed into a functional framework.

As in the case of the teacher, the attitudes and personalities of students have to be taken into consideration when selecting techniques for a lesson. Will students be inhibited by role play? Will some students consider some activities childish or offensive in some way?

Finally, but by no means of least importance, there is a further factor, which tends to be a problem felt by state school teachers of English rather than those in specialist language schools, and that is the problem of mixed-ability classes. In state schools, where membership of a class often depends on age rather than level of attainment in language, there can frequently be a tremendous range of student ability within the same class. If the teacher is to avoid taking a middle road and thus overstretching one half of the class whilst boring and holding back the other half, then clearly some very special lesson planning strategies will be required, ideally placing a greater emphasis on self-paced activities, such as reading and writing tasks, and group work.

3.4 Motivation and the maintenance of interest. If a lesson is not relevant to the needs, at least self-perceived, of the students and if the contexts used are not meaningful because they are inappropriate to the students' age group or cultural background, then there will inevitably be a loss of interest and thus of motivation. Relevance and meaningfulness are starting points from which lessons can be made motivating.

Motivation and interest are much more likely to be maintained if the students can recognize the aims of a lesson and the relevance of those aims to their language-learning needs. If lack of a meaningful context means that students cannot see why they are learning something and how it could be useful to them, they are unlikely to be motivated by or interested in the lesson.

Creating meaningful and relevant practice activities in a lesson can go only so far towards maintaining interest, however. If the activity, however initially enjoyable, is made to continue for too long a period in the lesson, then interest will flag. This must be a matter for teacher judgement through experience and will depend very much on factors such as the age and language level of the class—but variety in the lesson is vital. This variety applies to a number of variables within the lesson: variety of skills practised, variety of aids used to change the focus of the lesson, variety of interaction from teacher-student to pairs and to groups, seated or standing, and variety of pace between different phases of the lesson.

3.5 The influences of syllabus and exams. In the same way that a lesson can be said to be part of a course, then a single lesson plan is more often than not a teacher's interpretation of a small part of the syllabus for that course. To the extent that a lesson can be judged largely in terms of the validity of its objectives and the effectiveness with which the chosen procedure achieves these objectives, the syllabus that is laid down by the education authority, school or individual teacher is bound to have a fundamental influence on these elements of the lesson structure. To sum up this point and make clear its ramifications for lesson planning: a syllabus should reflect perceived student needs; the aims of any one lesson should reflect a part of the overall objectives of that syllabus; and the procedure followed by the lesson plan should be so devised as to ensure that the aims of the lesson are achieved.

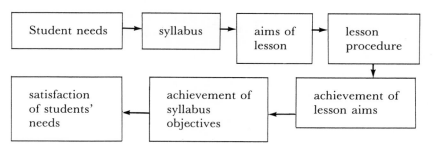

Examinations can also have an important effect on lesson planning in that the teachers' familiarity with the formats used in the anticipated examination, whether public or internal, will influence their choice of practice activity. To illustrate this point, if teachers know that the students' grasp of grammar is going to be tested through grammar transformation exercises, they are much more likely to use this form of practice in lessons. Not to do so would disadvantage students in the examination, as they would then be encountering unfamiliar exercise types.

It would be wrong to say that any planning style is markedly superior to another. This article has, therefore, not attempted to do this, but to think through the process of lesson planning and to provide a checklist for teachers' preparation.

Techniques

7

Information-gap activities for oral/aural practice

Alan Matthews and Carol Read

Communication is a two-way process: what A says helps to shape B's reply, which in turn influences A's answer and so on. But A, however accurately he may think he can predict what B will say, never knows for sure what exactly will be said. Often big jumps are made which could in no way have been predicted. It is this spontaneity and unpredictability of oral/aural communication which is hard to simulate in the classroom, especially at the elementary level and in large classes. Yet we need to give our students practice in handling the unknown if we want to prepare them properly for real communicative situations.

Traditionally, dialogue practice was provided in such a way that students A & B were fully aware of what each would say before the dialogue began. Although this type of language practice has some value, it does not go far enough. Information-gap activities are designed to take the students one stage further towards being able to handle more realistic communication.

At the start of an information-gap activity, each pair of students is provided with similar but different information, usually on handouts labelled A and B. They exchange information by using relevant language (not by looking at each other's handouts!) so that by the end of the interchange they are both in possession of the total amount of information. They do not know in advance what information they are going to receive in reply to their questions, i.e. new information is being given and received.

1 Points to bear in mind

There are a number of points to bear in mind when using information-gap activities.

Careful preparation

The students cannot be expected to do this type of activity successfully without very careful preparatory work. Information-gap exercises can be devised to give tightly controlled or freer practice of exponents of one or more functions. The exponents first need to be presented or revised and the students given sufficient controlled practice: this lays the necessary foundations for the information-gap activity that is to follow.

Pre-teaching of vocabulary

When students are working in closed pairs, they should be allowed to get on with the task in hand without unnecessary interruption. If the teacher is aware that some of the vocabulary needed for the activity is likely to be unfamiliar to all or some of the students, then it should be taught beforehand. This ensures that the flow of the activity is not interrupted.

Clear instructions

Students unused to doing pair work of this type need training in the mechanics of the activity. Instructions need to be crystal clear to ensure that all students know what to do (e.g. it is best if each pair swivels round to face each other; they should know who is A and who is B; they should not look at each other's handouts; it should be clear whether they have to jot something down and where). In a monolingual class, the instructions might well be given in the mother tongue.

Demonstration

It is wise, especially with a class that is unfamiliar with this type of activity, to demonstrate a part of it to the whole class. The teacher can play A and a good student B, and the first part of the task can be worked through. This should provide a clear model for all the other students before they set to work in their closed pairs.

Mixed ability

Most teachers, especially those working in secondary schools, have large groups of students with different aptitudes for learning languages, different degrees of motivation and very different levels of ability. There exists no magic solution to these problems. It helps, however, to foster, as far as possible, a cooperative atmosphere whereby better students are encouraged to help the less competent ones. This particularly applies to pair work. The teacher needs, however, to be sensitive to the students' wishes and not dictatorially impose unpopular pairings which will be counter-productive.

Use of the mother tongue

In monolingual classes, it is natural for the students to break into their own language, either during an activity, (e.g. when a difficulty arises) or more especially when they have finished an activity before other students. It is helpful if the teacher gently insists over a period of time on only English being used; also, a silent extension activity, e.g. a follow-up writing task, ensures that students who finish first have something else to do.

The teacher's role

After carefully setting up the activity, the teacher should first quickly check that each pair is in fact doing the activity in the way intended, and then circulate again, listening to samples of the oral work of as many pairs as possible. On-the-spot correction should be cut down to a minimum as it is usually interpreted as an unwelcome interruption, but a mental note should be made of the recurring errors for later attention.

2   An example

The following example of an information gap activity and accompanying teacher's notes is taken from *Tandem* by Alan Matthews and Carol Read (published by Bell & Hyman).

Describing People

Student A

Which three people must you meet?

Tell your friend to meet:

David: tall
      slim
      short dark hair
      glasses
wearing: jeans and a
         sweater
carrying: bag and
         newspaper

Sheila: short
       slim
       long dark hair
wearing: dress and a jacket
carrying: handbag

Steve: tall
      fat
      short fair hair
      glasses
wearing: jacket and trousers
carrying: suitcase

Student B

Which three people must you meet?

Tell your friend to meet:

Susan: tall
      slim
      short dark hair
      glasses
wearing: skirt and striped
         jacket
carrying: suitcase and
         umbrella

John: not very tall
      short fair hair
      beard
wearing: suit and tie
carrying: briefcase

Jean: short
      fat
      long fair hair
wearing: shirt and trousers
carrying: jacket and handbag

TEACHER'S NOTES

LANGUAGE

What's (s)he like?	*(S)he's . . .*
	(S)he's got . . .
What's (s)he wearing/carrying?	*(S)he's wearing/carrying . . .*
What'll (s)he be wearing/carrying?	*(S)he'll be wearing/carrying . . .*

Steps

1. Divide the class into pairs. Tell one student to look at **A** and the other at **B**. Remind them not to look at each other's books.

2. Tell the PP to imagine that they have agreed to go to the airport to meet three of their partner's friends who are arriving from London. Explain that the three people they must meet are among the pictures on the left side of the page. Point out that as they don't yet know the three people, they need to ask their partner for a good description of them so that they don't make a mistake at the airport.

3. Explain to the PP that on the right side of the page are notes describing the three people their partner is going to meet. Point out that the notes include details of physical appearance and information about what each person will be wearing and carrying.

4. Tell the PP to take it in turns to use the notes to describe the people who their partner must meet at the airport. Tell the PP to listen to each description carefully and decide which of the people in the pictures on the left is being described. Tell the PP to write the names of the three people they must meet under the appropriate pictures.

5. To check that their choices are correct. tell the PP to use the pictures they have chosen as a basis for describing to their partner the three people they will meet. Their partner can compare this description with the original notes and check that it is correct.

NB. For the T's information. the correct choices for both **A** and **B** are as follows:

6. Once the PP are sure their choices are correct. tell them they may compare the pictures and descriptions in each other's books.

Extension Work

Ask the PP to choose someone in the class and write a short description of their physical appearance and what they are wearing. Tell the PP to read each other's descriptions and see if they can guess who is being described in each.

NB: PP = Pupils

8

Discourse chains

Mary Spratt

1   What they are   **Meeting someone**

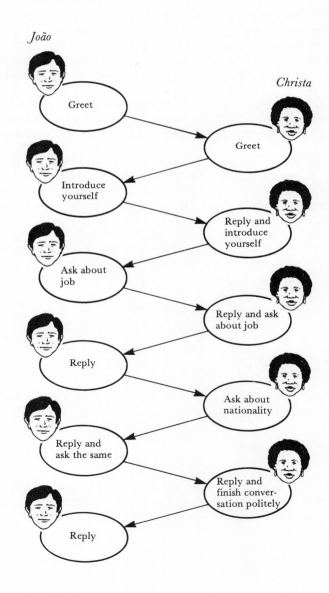

Invitations

A	B
Catch attention.	Reply.
Invite to the cinema tonight.	Refuse politely, give reason.
Invite to a party on Saturday.	Accept gladly.
Propose a time and place.	Agree.
Say goodbye.	Say goodbye.

Above are two examples of discourse chains. These are dialogues reduced to the names of functions and presented diagramatically with the functions placed in order of occurrence, as indicated by arrows, under headings showing who says what.

A discourse chain can produce various versions of a dialogue. For example, the following is just one of the dialogues that the 'Invitations' discourse chain could generate.

A: Margaret.
B: Yes.
A: Would you like to come to the cinema tonight?
B: Sorry, I'm afraid I can't, I'm going out.
A: Oh, well, what about coming to a party on Saturday?
B: O.K., that'd be nice.
A: Good. Shall we meet outside the Town Hall at 7?
B: O.K. Fine.
A: Bye then, see you on Saturday.
B: Bye.

2   When to use them

As they allow for a variety of exponents of the same functions, discourse chains provide an excellent means of practising language within a controlled situational framework, while giving students a considerable degree of choice as to which exponents to use. For this reason, they can be used for various purposes:

a) to provide freer work after more controlled forms of practice have taken place and to lead in to even freer activities;

b) to bring together for revision purposes items previously taught separately;

c) to revise the language of a particular situation;

d) to diagnose students' language needs. One could, for example, ask students to supply the conversations indicated in one of the above discourse chains; if the students made lots of mistakes as they did this, it would become clear that this was an area in which they needed help;

e) to provide a framework for dialogue writing;

f) to provide practice in appropriate language use;

g) to test students' knowledge of the language connected with particular situations.

The functional labels in a discourse chain are what generate the conversation; it is therefore vital to keep them simple to make sure that students, particularly at elementary level, understand them. Besides the name of the function, information about register can also be included, e.g. 'greet casually', 'accept formally', thus providing students with practice in using language appropriately (as mentioned in (f) above). Parallel discourse chains on the same situation but involving different levels of formality can also be used for this purpose.

3   How to use them

There is no one fixed way of using discourse chains, but a fairly standard one which meets the purposes of points a–e above is the following:

—Establish the situational context of the discourse chain, e.g. for 'Invitations', the teacher can show the students a picture of a man and a woman in an office, establish their names, their relationship and any other interesting or useful information.

—Present the discourse chain on the blackboard or OHP transparency. The teacher can either reveal the whole chain at once or only one exchange at a time, eliciting the relevant language as the dialogue progresses. Appropriate explanations can be given at this stage if the students are unfamiliar with the technique and/or with any of the functional labels.

—Choose two students on opposite sides of the class, allot each of them the role of one of the speakers in the chain, and then ask them to go through their parts. This provides an example for the whole class of what they are required to do.

—Either: divide the class into closed pairs and ask them to practise the dialogue simultaneously;

Or: if the discourse chain is printed on a handout and distributed to each student, use it as a mingling activity.

—Provided the discourse chain has not already been over-exploited on this occasion, students can then write up the dialogue or a parallel one.

A lot of valuable mileage out of such a little creature.

9

Structured conversations

Roger Gower

Many conversation classes fail because
—the students are insufficiently motivated to speak

—too few students participate
—the teacher does most of the talking
Here are some ways of organizing the class to get the students talking.

1 Pyramid discussion

This technique could be used with a wide variety of topics. In this example, I have based the discussion on 'Camping'.

Stage 1

The teacher tells the group they are going to spend 2 weeks camping, say in southern Greece in December. To warm them up and to bring to the foreground all they know about the topic, there is informal discussion about, for example, who has actually been camping, and what the weather is likely to be at that time of year (December is perhaps preferable to July because there is usually more disagreement about what to expect). The teacher then gives out a list of objects they will definitely take.

What you will definitely take:

tent
sleeping bag
clothing (except waterproofs and overcoat)
enough money for travel and basic food supplies
cooking stove
matches
plastic plates/dishes/knives/forks/spoons/cups
a saucepan/a frying pan/a kettle
toilet paper
towel

The teacher also gives out a list of, say, 20–30 objects they *could* take, ranging from borderline necessities such as a compass or a piece of string to, perhaps, less important items, such as a bottle of brandy!
For example:

You can now take ten of the following items with you. Think carefully which you will most need and write out your list:

compass	torch	sun glasses
camera	radio	sun cream
swimming costume	sticking plaster	aspirin
mirror	books to read	map
rope	binoculars	a bottle of brandy
umbrella	overcoat	hot-water bottle
pen-knife	chess set	a piece of string
portable TV	soap	disposable bags
antiseptic	flannel	insect repellant
lamp	raincoat	hammer

Stage 2

Students are then asked to reduce this second list to ten items on their own. They should choose the things they think would be most useful and think of good reasons for their choice. This initial decision-making is important because it forces the students to invest part of themselves in the task.

Stage 3

Students are then put into pairs and asked to compare and combine their lists and produce ten items they both agree on. It is important that each student justifies to the other why they think something should be included or why they are prepared to leave something out. In other words, their earlier decisions may have to be modified by discussion.

Stage 4

The pairs are asked to form groups of four and to reach agreement on a list of ten items. And so on.

This building up of groups can go on at the teacher's discretion but it is possible for a whole class of, say, 20 to argue a compromise on a final list. The activity normally lasts about 45 minutes and, although it starts quietly, it quickly becomes heated. The big advantage is that the teacher says nothing except to give very simple instructions. As with all communication activities, though, it is best not too use it too frequently.

2   Using statements for conversation structures

The topic used in this example is 'Parents'.

Method 1: modifying

The students are given a list of, say, ten controversial statements. For example:

— Parents should teach boys to sew and girls to mend the car.
— Every child needs at least one brother and one sister.
— Children should work in their school holidays and earn money.
— It's better for the whole family (grandparents included) to live under the same roof.
— Parents should not tell their children what to do after they are 16.
— The father is the head of the family.
— Brothers are responsible for their sisters.
— Parents should be strict about what time their children come home, even when they're teenagers.
— Fathers should not help mothers with domestic work.
— Children learn more from their parents than they do from school.

Groups are asked to modify the statements so that they can all agree with them. Groups then compare their modified statements with those of other groups. As in a summit meeting, the aim of the discussion is to argue like blazes and then produce a neutral communiqué that offends no-one!

Method 2: sequencing

The students are given a list of, say, ten non-controversial statements. For example:

— It's important to put children to bed early if they have school the next day.
— Parents should be happily married.
— The family should have a steady income.
— It's good for children to have neighbours with children their own age.
— Children learn a lot from travelling with their parents.
— Parents should encourage their children to play sports.
— Too much television is bad.
— Children learn a lot from their parents reading to them.
— Children should not be spoilt too much.
— Parents should love their children.

They are then asked to sequence them (1–10) in order of priority for the successful bringing up of children in the home. The activity can be organized on an individual → pair → group basis (as in pyramid discussion) or with the students in simple discussion groups. Sharing views and compromise are inevitable.

Method 3: defending

Different controversial statements (e.g. 'Children should be encouraged to leave home at 16') are written on pieces of paper and then put into a box. The students are told to pick out a statement and then spend a few minutes preparing arguments to defend it. One of the students can be made chairperson. All students then have to present their arguments in turn, answer questions and defend themselves from attack! It is likely that free discussion will quickly break out, but possibly in the end there can be a vote as to the most convincing defence. This method is often more effective than formal debates, which can be rather cumbersome.

There are lots of ways of organizing these activities, but the principles of modifying, sequencing and defending ensure that there is plenty of motivation to speak and that all the students say something. The use of pair and group discussion units to compare, refine and combine also keeps the teacher from dominating the discussions. In all cases, it is important to choose topics that your students can relate to.

10

Role play

Les Dangerfield

Published ELT materials use the term 'role play' to refer to a variety of classroom activities, from controlled information-gap activities to complex simulations. This article, however, will consider role play in the sense of an activity for which the context and the roles of the students are determined by the teacher, but in which students have freedom to produce language which they feel appropriate to that context and to their assigned roles.

1   Why use role play?

The arguments in favour of using role play are, by and large, common to other group activities such as games and discussions of various kinds. The students' linguistic performance during role play provides the teacher with essential feedback on how well they have learnt the new language and understand its appropriateness to a given context. Without this feedback, the teacher can never be sure that the new language has been fully assimilated.

Role play is one method of maximising Student Talking Time, ensuring that students get an optimum level of practice during their limited class time. It also provides variety of activity and of interaction, and takes the focus of the class away from the teacher. The increased freedom thus obtained gives the teacher a useful opportunity to deal with individuals and to monitor their performance. Shy students can also benefit from group practice of this kind—they may be more forthcoming in small groups than when faced with the prospect of speaking in front of a whole class.

2   Answers to some problems

Teachers often fight shy of using role play for a number of reasons·

'Students cannot be expected to act.'
This largely depends on the type of role the students are given. If, for example, they are asked to play the parts of a travel agent and a customer, they only need to project their own personalities into the given situation. It is only when the roles specify details of personality ('you are light-hearted and quick-witted') or mood ('you are furious') that any dramatic ability is really needed.

If the students are provided with sufficient context and role information, and if the language needed to fulfill the roles is pitched at the right level, there is no reason why they should not produce the appropriate language. It is this that the teacher is interested in and not a convincing theatrical performance.

'A lot of students are inhibited by role playing.'

This worry springs from the misconception that a role play should be acted out by a group of students in front of the class. If one of the aims of the activity is to give students the maximum opportunity to talk, then clearly this method would not be very efficient. Unless the teacher has specific points to make to the class as a result of their watching a role play by one group, then the whole class, divided into groups, should be doing the role play simultaneously.

'Mistakes cannot be corrected when several groups are talking independently.'

This is, of course, true and is a necessary compromise in return for the increase in Student Talking Time involved. However, one day the students may find themselves in such situations outside the classroom when they will not be prompted and will not have their mistakes corrected, and it is better that they first have experience of this in the protective environment of the classroom.

'It feels insecure or lacking in control when the teacher is no longer the focus of the class's attention.'

This is, however, a situation to be taken advantage of, in that teachers can provide help where it is needed without delaying the rest of the class at the same time. It is not, on the other hand, being suggested that teachers should be constantly correcting mistakes overheard. If a quick word or two at an opportune moment provides effective correction of a significant mistake, or helps a student who is lost for words, then by all means provide those words. If, on the other hand, a correction would involve a lengthy interruption which could destroy continuity and the students' suspension of disbelief, then the mistake, if felt to be important enough, can be noted by the teacher for later mention.

'How should the role play be physically organised?'

This is determined by two factors. First, it depends on the ratio of classroom space to numbers of students and the nature of the classroom furniture—these factors may inhibit student movement. Second, what are the characters in the role play doing? If they are the drivers of cars involved in an accident, they will be standing in the road talking; thus the students should ideally be standing too. Needless to say, whether seated or standing, the students in any one group should be facing each other and the groups should be spread as equidistantly around the class as possible.

'What about role allocation problems?'

The temptation to give the main role to the best student and vice-versa should be resisted—this will only deprive weaker students of much-needed practice.

If a role play depends on the class breaking down into equal groups of, say, four students, work out beforehand which role is most dispensable. Then if, because of student numbers on the day, it is necessary to have four groups of four and two groups of three, there is no delay while the teacher puzzles out how to get around the problem.

3   Two kinds of role play

A standard role play is exemplified by article 13, *Traffic Accident: a role play*, page 48. This involves the provision of both a context and detailed role-information by the teacher. If role plays are to be invented, substantial preparation will be involved which often cannot be undertaken by busy teachers. There is, however, a short cut to devising role plays, which is no less effective, whereby the teacher provides context and minimal role information and the students then pad out this information through pre-role play discussion. This method is exemplified as follows.

— Teacher input: an English couple are approaching retirement and trying to decide where to live after retirement. The man wants to stay in Bristol (a large industrial city in the southwest of England) where they have always lived. The woman wants to move to Bournemouth (a seaside resort 100 km from Bristol) where they have spent two-week summer holidays for the past ten years but where they do not know anyone.
— Aim: to decide which option to follow.
— Discussion phase: the class divides into two equal groups—'men' and 'women'—to decide on the advantages of staying in Bristol in the case of the men, and vice-versa in the case of the women.
— Role play: the class then regroups into pairs—one 'man' to one 'woman'. Each pair argues out the problem to decide whether to live in Bristol or Bournemouth or whether there is any kind of compromise solution.

This method of building up the basis of the role play through student discussion has the added advantage of allowing students more time to think about their role, and thus identify more strongly with it, than if they are presented with all the relevant information and expected to play their part 'cold'.

The language focus for this role play could be either the first conditional, e.g. *If we go to Bournemouth, we'll lose all our friends*, or comparatives, e.g. *Bristol is more interesting than Bournemouth*—both will inevitably be produced in this context. It would, though, be counter-productive to tell students which forms they are expected to produce, as a major aim of such a production stage activity is to see whether the students see the relevance of, and can use, newly learnt language without being prompted.

4 A suggested procedure for role play

A suggested standard procedure for role play is laid out diagrammatically below, followed by notes relating to the diagram.

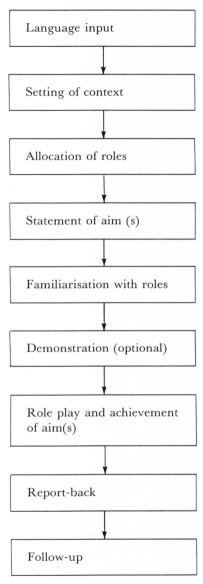

Language input

Setting of context

Allocation of roles

Statement of aim (s)

Familiarisation with roles

Demonstration (optional)

Role play and achievement of aim(s)

Report-back

Follow-up

—*Language input.* This will often mean the presentation and practice stages in the teaching of a language item which is now to be practised within a freer framework. It may also mean the pre-teaching of vocabulary and/or other language considered useful for the context of the role play; this pre-teaching may occur after the context for the role play has been set.
—*Setting of context.* This should be done so as to help the students to appreciate fully the situation in which they will be role playing. Visuals can help to make this more effective; for example the accident plan in Rob Hirons' role play provides vital contextual information.
—*Allocation of roles.* The teacher should decide this, otherwise, if the

choice is thrown open to volunteers, the extrovert students will always get the best roles.

— *Statement of aim(s).* This is vital because it gives the students a concrete result to aim for in the role play and thus provides motivation and prevents the activity fizzling out. It also provides a clear-cut result to discuss in the report-back phase.

— *Familiarisation with roles.* This can take the form of reading role cards or student discussion as in the above example of the retired couple.

— *Demonstration.* This is an optional phase and one which is generally not applicable to a role play. However, if the students are unfamiliar with this form of practice or unsure of what to do, then a demonstration is useful. It is advisable to choose the best students for this, as they can provide a good model.

— *Role play and achievement of aim(s).* One point to note here is that, if some groups finish significantly earlier than others, the teacher should have ready one or two ideas for an activity which can keep them occupied while they wait. This should ideally be in the form of an extension of the role play, e.g. writing up their final decision.

— *Report-back.* This will concern how the different groups reached their aims, i.e. what decisions each group made, etc. This is an important phase because the students are usually interested in comparing their decisions with those of other groups. It also gives the students an opportunity to talk about problems they had and it rounds off the activity. Beware, however, of making this stage unduly long—to listen to fifteen pairs of students reporting back in turn would clearly be tedious.

— *Follow-up.* This can take two forms: firstly, written work based on the role play, perhaps set for homework, and secondly, remedial work based on mistakes noted by the teacher while monitoring student performance.

5   Devising your own role plays

The last section of this article attempts to suggest some broad guidelines to follow when thinking out one's own role plays.

Language and context. The starting point is the language item that needs to be practised. It is necessary to decide in which context(s) this is likely to occur naturally, so that the students will actually need to produce what they have learnt. The students should not need to use the language item too frequently in this context, otherwise the role play becomes more like a controlled practice activity involving repetition of the same form.

Roles. The second step is to decide on the number of roles, which will be dictated by the situation. On the one hand, fewer roles mean more talking time for individuals; on the other hand, more roles, especially at lower levels, mean that the activity is likely to have more momentum as there are more minds on the task in hand. The nature of the roles may also be an inevitable result of the context. Many would say that the students should be able to relate to the role they are playing, yet opinions on this differ. Thus it is argued that teenagers can best play the part of teenagers because they understand how they themselves feel. Yet a lot of credence can also be given to the opinion that students will enjoy taking the part of a character distant from their everyday experience because it appeals to their imagination. Who would not rather play the part of a king than that of an office clerk? It can also be argued that students feel less inhibited when acting roles which are far removed from their true selves.

Essential elements. As has been stressed previously, it is desirable that the role play should have an aim towards which the students are working. Such an aim depends on the role play involving either a conflict which has to be resolved or a task which has to be performed. In other words, the role play should involve decision-making in one form or another, whether it be 'which night the boyfriend's invitation will be accepted' or 'which projects the board of directors will spend the company money on.'

Role information. Do teachers need to provide all role input through role cards or can they provide a brief profile for development by the students? If the decisions on the roles are left to the students, will the role play go as intended? If the teacher is unsure of this, or of the imaginativeness of the class, then it may be safer to produce role cards.

The language of the role cards should be easily within the scope of the students' comprehension. The role cards should also be as brief as possible, whilst at the same time including all necessary information about the circumstances surrounding the intended conversation, the ages and personalities of the characters, their relationship with each other and their attitudes to the subject in hand.

Timing. A role play which has been fastidiously prepared can fall very flat if it takes a disproportionate length of time to set up. It is important to strike a balance here. That is not to say that a lot of useful language practice cannot come out of the preparation stages. Nevertheless, as the role play is the focal point of all the preparation, and if it is to achieve some or all of the aims discussed in the first section of this article, then it is vital that it last for a realistic period of time in teaching terms, in relation to the time spent on setting it up.

Lessons and practical teaching ideas

11

Expressing obligation with 'must': a lesson plan

Eunice Barroso

1	**Level**	Elementary, approximately 90 hours of English.
2	**Aims**	To present, practise and produce some forms of the present tense of *must* for expressing obligation. To develop the skill of listening for specific information. To check or teach certain vocabulary items: *visa / valid / passport / to carry / a gun / an employer / a vaccination.*
3	**Exponents**	*Must I? Yes you must.* *You must/mustn't.* *When/where/what must you ....*
4	**Time**	60 minutes approx.
5	**Aids**	Picture similar to that of *Streamline Departures* (Oxford University Press) Unit 58 (see below). Cassette of *Streamline Departures* Unit 58. 3 sets of handouts, 2 sets of cards, 2 OHP transparencies. OHP, BB, cassette player, Blu-tack.

6 Anticipated problems

Students may spontaneously say *you mustn't* to the question *Must I?*, although this form is not taught. The teacher will not correct this during the lesson, as the contrast between *must* and *need* will be the focus of the next learning point on the syllabus.

7 Procedure

7.1 Warm up

—T puts picture of 006 on BB and elicits from the class his possible name/age/job/nationality, prompting if necessary.
—T writes most suitable suggestions under picture.
—T asks Ss to listen to cassette dialogue and compare their suggestions with the information given on the cassette.
—T plays cassette.
—Report back.

7.2 Presentation

—T elicits from Ss any other information they can remember about cassette content.
—T teaches or checks vocabulary needed for second task (*passport / to carry / a gun*), writes it on BB and does a quick pronunciation/repetition drill on same.
—T distributes handout 1 (see below) and allows Ss one or two minutes to read it through.
—T sets scene for task: Ss must pretend they are 006 and listen to their boss giving them instructions for their next mission.
—T gives instructions for task: Ss must take notes in their diaries (i.e. handout 1) as if they were 006.
—T gives dummy run of activity, if needed, using an identical copy of handout 1 on OHP transparency (or on BB).
—T plays cassette and Ss complete task.
—Ss check answers in pairs.
—Report back: Ss tell T how to complete OHP copy of handout 1 (or BB copy).
—Repetition drill of answers using OHP (or BB) as cue, done in chorus and individually.
—Concept check: (in L₁ if necessary) T asks Ss:
Is 006 going to Moscow by choice or obligation? Who is obliging him? What word shows he is obliged? How do you say *must* in your language? Tell me some of the things you must do even if you don't want to. What is he forbidden to do? What word shows this?

7.3 Practice

—T distributes handout 2 (see below) and Ss read it through.
—T instructs Ss to complete the dialogue in pairs by filling in the blank spaces with the appropriate sentences.
—Ss listen to tape to check their answers.
—Report back: Ss tell T how to complete OHP copy of handout 2.

7.4 Production

Preparation for role play
—T sticks imaginary country cards on BB with Blu-tack and asks Ss to imagine that they want temporary holiday work in one of these countries, but they haven't yet decided which.
—T conducts quick pronunciation/repetition drill on names of countries.
—T distributes handout 3A (see below) and writes on BB contents of

one of 3B cards (see below).
— T elicits suitable dialogue for role play using handout and BB as prompts.
— Repetition drill of dialogue (see below).
— Open pair practice of dialogue.
— Closed pair practice of dialogue.

Role play
— Ss are divided into embassy officials and students wishing to work abroad, one third being embassy officials and the rest students.
— The embassy officials are each given one of the 3B cards and are asked to sit at the desk where the teacher has put the appropriate country name card.
— T does dummy run of activity with two good Ss.
— Students wishing to work abroad visit each embassy and make the necessary enquiries. They may have to wait their turn in the queue, but this is normal at embassies. As they receive the required information, they write it on their memo pad (i.e. handout 3A).
— Each of the prospective visiting students decides which country to go to and why.
— Report-back: Ss say which countries they have decided to visit and why — at this stage, embassy officials can try to get them to change their minds if they wish to for any reason.

7.5   Homework

Ss write a letter to a friend inviting the friend to come on holiday with them and explaining which country they have decided to go to and why.

8   Materials

8.1   Text

M   This is a very important mission, 006.
006   What must I do?
M   You must go to Moscow on tonight's plane.
006   Ah, Moscow! I've got a girlfriend there!
M   We know that . . . but you mustn't visit her!
006   Where must I stay?
M   You must go to the Airport Hotel, stay in your room and wait.
006   Which passport must I use?
M   Your Swiss passport . . . and you must speak Swiss-German all the time. They mustn't know your nationality.
006   What must I take with me?
M   Well, you mustn't carry your gun . . . but take a lot of warm clothes. Good luck, 006!

(From *Streamline — Departures* by B Hartley & P Viney, pub. Oxford University Press, © Oxford University Press 1978.)

8.2 Handout 1:
Diary 006

Must	Mustn't

N.B. Hand-out 1 could easily be written on BB and Ss asked to copy it to save paper on handouts.

8.3 Handout 2:
Jumbled sentences and blank filling

1. Ah! Moscow! I've got a girlfriend there!

2. Which passport must I use?

3. Where must I stay?

4. What must I take with me?

5. What must I do?

Employer: This is a very important mission 006.

006: _____ ?

Employer: You must go to Moscow on tonight's plane.

006: _____ ?

Employer: We know that, but you mustn't visit her.

006: _____ ?

Employer: You must go to the airport hotel, stay in your room and wait.

006: _____ ?

Employer: Your Swiss passport, and you must speak Swiss German all the time. They mustn't know your nationality.

006: _____ ?

Employer: Well, you mustn't carry your gun, but take a lot of warm clothes. Good luck 006.

8.4   Possible dialogue for preparation of role play

A: Good morning.
B: Good morning, can I help you?
A: Er . . . Yes, I'd like to work in Oceania during the summer.
B: Hmm . . . I see . . .
A: Well, er . . . What must I do?
B: Well, first you must find a job.
A: Hmm . . . find a job, before I go?
B: Yes, and you must have a letter from your employer and you mustn't stay more than 30 days.
A: Must I have a passport?
B: Yes, you must have a valid passport.
A: Hmm. Well er . . . thank you.
B: You're welcome. Bye.

8.5   Handout 3A

(✓ or X as appropriate)	Ruritania	Oceania	Orangeland	Spartugal	Tolsity	Zeelack
A job before arrival						
An employer's letter						
A valid passport						
A visa						
Money on arrival						
Vaccinations						
Other						

N.B. Handout 3A could easily be written on BB and Ss asked to copy it to save paper on handouts.

8.6   Cards 3B

Ruritania- regulations for temporary workers.	**Oceania- regulations for temporary workers.**	**Orangeland- regulations for temporary workers.**	**Spartugal- regulations for temporary workers.**	**Tolsity- regulations for temporary workers.**	**Zeelack- regulations for temporary workers.**
Compulsory Cholera vaccination. Valid passport. Employer's letter. Job before arrival.	*Compulsory* Job before arrival. Letter from employer. Valid passport.	*Compulsory* Typhoid vaccination. Identity card. Money on arrival.	*Compulsory* Valid passport. Visa. Cholera vaccination.	*Compulsory* Job before arrival. Employer's letter. Valid passport. Visa.	*Compulsory* Valid passport. Visa. Job before arrival. Employer's letter. Money on arrival.
Forbidden To import food. To stay more than 20 days.	*Forbidden* To stay more than 30 days.	*Forbidden* To have any family in the country.	*Forbidden* To stay more than 15 days. To import drugs or guns.	*Forbidden* To stay more than 3 months.	*Forbidden* To stay more than 6 months.

N.B. These cards need to be cut out.

12

Making and responding to requests: a lesson plan

Sue Gaskin

The lesson below was given to a class of 20 students near the end of their first year of English.

1 Aims

To present, practise and produce polite requests and some appropriate polite responses.
To revise the use of the simple past tense for narrative.
To revise *some / any / a / one.*

2 Exponents

Q. *Could you lend me* | *a* _____, *please?*
                        | *some*

A. *Yes, of course.*
    Yes, certainly.
    I'm afraid I haven't got | *one.*
                               | *any.*

3 Assumed knowledge

The students had already been taught *have got*, countables and uncountables and were familiar with the use of *a / some / one / any*, and with the vocabulary item *broke*.

4 Aids

BB, realia, game for free production stage.

5 Time

55–60 minutes approx.

6 Procedure

6.1 Revision: dialogue about last weekend

(about 10 minutes)
T asks questions and builds up the dialogue with one S.

e.g. *A:* Did you have a good weekend?
      B: Yes, I did.
      A: What did you do?
      B: _____.
      A: | Really? |
            | Did you? |
      B: Yes, I _____.
      A: How nice!

—Tq→Sa. Sq→Sa (open pairs). Sq→Sa (closed pairs).
—Ss report back on what they have found out.
—Ss ask T about T's weekend activities.
Note: the last two steps here should provide T with feedback on
     whether Ss can use the past tense.
—T pretends to be broke, having spent everything last weekend. This
   situation leads naturally into the presentation.

6.2   Presentation of polite requests with affirmative answer

(10 minutes)
—Marker sentence: Tq→Sa. *Could you lend me some money, please?*
—Concept questions on polite forms etc.
  e.g. Which is more polite *Can you* . . . or *Could you* . . .?
—Repetition drill for intonation and pronunciation practice:
  chorus→group→individual.
—T tells S to ask for something politely. Sq→T introducing polite
  responses:

Yes,	*certainly.*	*Here you are.*
	of course.	

—Extend request and affirmative responses to other classroom objects
  trying to include singulars, plurals, countables and uncountables,
  drilling if necessary: Sq→Sa (open→closed pairs).

6.3   Presentation of polite refusals

(10 minutes)
—T introduces polite refusals in answer to Ss' requests.

I'm afraid I haven't got	*one.*
	any.

T gets several Ss to ask for things before going on to drilling the
responses.
—Repetition drill: chorus→group→individual.
  T→Sa. Sq→Sa (open pairs). Sq→Sa (closed pairs).
—Mix positive and negative responses, to check that Ss know which
  response is appropriate to their own situation. Sq→Ta. Sq→Sa (open
  pairs). Sq→Sa (closed pairs).

6.4   Practice: dialogue (planning a party)

(10 minutes)
—Tq: *What do you need for a party?* = vocabulary elicitation. If any
  words are new to Ss, write them on BB after checking that Ss have
  got the pronunciation, including word stress, correct.
    Note: only elicit common, inexpensive objects, i.e. not record-
  players or tape-recorders, as the exponents needed to request such
  objects would be different.
—T reveals dialogue (below) on BB or OHP with polite requests and
  responses blanked out. (N.B. Ideally it should be written on BB or
  OHP transparency before the lesson begins and kept covered until
  this point).

A: I'm having a party on Saturday. Would you like to come?
B: Yes, thanks.
A: But I haven't got any plates, _____ _____ lend me _____ ?
B: Yes, _____ _____ .
A: And I haven't got a cork-screw; could _____ _____ me _____ ?
B: I'm afraid _____ _____ _____ _____ .

Note: there must be a singular and plural in the dialogue and also the affirmative and negative responses.

Tq→Sa. Sq→Sa (open pairs). Sq→Sa (closed pairs).

—Ask Ss to substitute other things needed for the party instead of plates and a cork-screw.

—T gradually rubs off more and more of the 'skeleton' dialogue from BB as Ss become more familiar with it.

6.5	Writing task	Ss complete BB dialogue in writing. T goes round checking written work.

6.6 Production: game

(10 minutes)

—T explains game and rules i.e. Ss are having a party but need to borrow lots of things for it. Each S is given pictures of 4 objects and the aim of the game is to borrow as many things as possible from the others. All the Ss mingle around the classroom and ask if they can borrow things they need for the party (using the polite request form).

S who has a picture of the object requested says: *Yes, certainly, here you are* and hands over the card. S who has not got the object says: *I'm afraid I haven't got* | *one.* | *any.* |

Ss can only ask each other one question and must then move on to somebody else.

Suggested objects:

a/an		some	
transistor		records	
table-cloth		tapes	
jug		plates	
corkscrew		glasses	
bottle-opener		cutlery	
ashtray			

—T demonstrates game with one of the better Ss.

—Ss play the game. T sets a time limit of about 5 minutes.

S who collects the most objects is the winner.

13

Traffic Accident: A role play

Rob Hirons

This role play is intended for use at the production stage of a teaching unit in which the students have previously practised *should(n't)* and *should(n't)'ve* as exponents of the functions of 'criticising' and 'blaming'. Through the role play, the students are provided with opportunities to use these exponents in a realistic way.

1   First stage

The diagram for 'Traffic Accident' is presented on the OHP. The accident is supposed to have happened in the suburbs of a Canadian town.

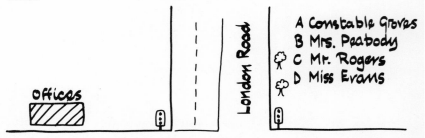

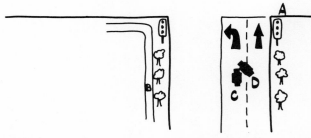

The purposes of the diagram are both linguistic and contextual, providing information and background for the role-play.

1.1   Linguistic aims

— To introduce or check on Ss' knowledge of essential vocabulary, e.g. *inside/outside lane, coming up to (the traffic lights)*.
— To elicit sentences using the vocabulary which they will need later during the role play, e.g. *Mrs Peabody was walking along . . .* and other sentences for the description of the accident.

1.2   Contextual aims

—To introduce to Ss the characters involved.
—To fix the physical setting in the minds and imaginations of Ss, pointing out the row of trees between the road and pavement, and the position of the cars at the moment of the crash, etc.

2   Second stage

This involves a reading comprehension text presented as Constable Groves' subsequent report on the accident. As with the diagram, the purposes of the reading text are both linguistic and contextual.

ACCIDENT REPORT - HALIFAX POLICE

Police Constable - James Groves

Location of Accident - Junction of London Road and Park Avenue.

On April 18th at 09.15 hrs, I was standing on the corner of Park Avenue and London Road. I heard a loud crash and turning round I saw the two cars stopped in the middle of the road. I did not see the crash itself. When I arrived on the scene the two drivers had got out of their vehicles and were arguing noisily.

Mr William Rogers, 56, an engineer had crashed into the side door of the red Toyota belonging to Miss Mavis Evans, 27, a secretary. There was one witness, Mrs Ethel Peabody, 63, who was walking along the opposite side of the road with her dog.

Mr Rogers had rudely accused Miss Evans of being careless and not signalling. Miss Evans said she had signalled but she was very upset and her account of the accident was not clear. She explained that she had been driving to work and was going to turn left at the traffic lights into Park Avenue. I suspected, since it was already 09.15, that Miss Evans was late and in a hurry. When I questioned her she admitted this was true.

Miss Peabody also gave her own account of the accident. She seemed to sympathise with Miss Evans and supported her. Since she was walking along the pavement, her view may have been obscured by the row of trees between the pavement and the road. Mr Rogers tried to get Mrs Peabody to say he was right and it was Miss Evans' fault.

After several minutes when each one had explained what they had seen and there had been much argument and contradiction, I finally calmed everyone down and took their names and addresses. Since nobody was injured they continued on their way.

2.1   Linguistic aims

—The report provides reinforcement of some of the vocabulary and sentences practised with the diagram of the scene of the accident.
—It gives an opportunity for Ss to practise some of the language they would need, e.g. *Mr Rogers had rudely accused Miss Evans of being careless.* Here I ask the class what they thought Mr Rogers had actually said and get as many suggestions as possible.

2.2   Contextual aims

—The report gives extra background to the situation and adds a little 'flesh' to the characters. This can be exploited in the class by asking Ss to imagine what the characters look like and what their personalities are like.
—Looking forwards to the role play, the report gives an outline of the development of the argument in paragraphs 3 & 4. Paragraph 5 shows how Constable Groves finally ends the situation. This clear finishing point helps prevent the role play slowly fizzling out with a resulting anti-climax.

3   Third stage   The final stage of the preparation before the role play begins is provided by the role cards.

Constable Groves

You were standing on the junction of Park Avenue and London Road when you heard a loud crash. You have come to the scene of the crash where Miss Evans and Mr Rogers are arguing noisily.

You try to calm them down, obtain evidence from old Mrs Peabody and get details from them. Nobody is hurt but both cars are damaged.

Use these ideas and think of other things you are going to say.

Mrs Peabody

You are an old lady. You were walking along the pavement on the left-hand side of the road. You noticed both cars passing you and saw the red car turn suddenly in front of the blue one.

You say Miss Evans is right because Mr Rogers is rude to her. Really you are very shocked, confused and not sure.

Use these ideas and think of other things you are going to say.

Miss Evans

You were driving your red Toyota. You were going to your job as a secretary in the offices in Park Avenue. You were late and anxious to get to work. You wanted to turn left into Park Avenue. You did not signal until you started turning and did not look to see if there was anything behind you.

You are shocked and angry with Mr Rogers, who is rude.

Use these ideas and think of other things you are going to say.

Mr Rogers

You are a middle-aged man. You have been driving for 25 years and have never had an accident. You do not like women drivers.

You are rude to Miss Evans. You say she was driving too fast and did not signal to turn. You try to get Mrs Peabody to support you.

Use these ideas and think of other things you are going to say.

The role cards provide the final details and point to ideas which the students can develop while trying to think themselves into their roles. Mr Rogers will have to think about the things he will say to try to get Mrs Peabody's support. Mrs Peabody will have to think about her description of what she saw, and Constable Groves will have to work out things to say to calm the others down. During the role play they will all have to respond to unpredictable twists and turns in the argument. The attempts of Mr Rogers and Miss Evans to sway Mrs Peabody will probably recur throughout the role play. When the students have been given sufficient time to prepare, they can be put into groups of four and the role play can begin.

4 Conclusions

I have used this role play successfully on several occasions, with the argument raging for between 5 and 10 minutes before being ended by P.C. Groves. The class always found themselves bringing in *should* and *should've* quite unconsciously and appropriately in such utterances as *You should've signalled first, You shouldn't be so rude, You shouldn't have been going so fast*, etc. I think that many of the elements of this role play can serve as a model and be adapted in order to devise others. It is important to realize that 'input' is as important at the production stage as it is at the presentation stage of the lesson. Students will not suddenly start interacting at their first sight of a cue card. To recapitulate, the teacher must:
—present and practise essential vocabulary in the context of the role play;
—elicit some of the language which will be used in the role play;
—make the setting and topic of the role play clear;
—present the characters of the role play in sufficient detail, but leaving the students to add their own ideas;
—provide a clear finishing point for the role play.
The preparation needs to be carefully staged but, if done well, will feed the students' imaginations and encourage the 'willing suspension of disbelief' essential for this kind of activity.

14

A revision lesson plan using information transfer, a discourse chain and role play

David Palmer

1 Objectives

The students will be able to book a hotel room and confirm it by letter.

2 Language generated

—Giving and asking for personal details:
My name is 'X'.
May I have your name, please?

Do you want me to spell that?
Could you spell that, please?
D-A-V-I-D.

—Indicating the purpose of a communication:

I'd like to | *book* | *a room, please.*
| *reserve* |

—Signalling or asking about plans and intentions:

I'll be | *arriving . . .* |
| *staying . . .* |

When will you be arriving?
How long will you be staying?

—Dates and times:

From June 6th till 15th.
For | *the weekend.* |
| *three days.* |
Till the | *morning* | *of Monday the 10th.*
| *evening* |
| *afternoon* |
Next Friday evening.

—Numbers:

29, 29th, 2, 2nd, 3, 3rd etc.

—Types of hotel room:

Double/single
Overlooking the | *sea.* |
| *park.* |

Quiet, light, big.
With | *bath.* |
| *shower.* |
| *toilet.* |

Note: This task-centred lesson focuses on difficulties as and when they arise. In effect, the syllabus is generated *a posteriori*. Our role here as teachers is to help students develop the communicative strategies necessary to complete the task. If their strategies involve language exponents which are different from those we have predicted, but still appropriate to the task, all the better—we can help them refine and develop these strategies.

3   Materials

—A cassette or tape-recording of three different guests reserving rooms at a hotel. (See **6** below for tapescript). A cassette-player or tape-recorder.
—Copies of a handwritten letter of reservation for each student or pair of students.
—Copies of hotel register (blank).
—BB. Cards for the game.

4   Time

About 2 hours. Could be broken into two periods: stages 5.1–5.3 and stages 5.4–5.5.

5 Procedure

5.1 Warm-up
           (approx. 10 minutes)
           —Pre-questions on BB.

Name of Hotel	
Name of Guest	
Type of Room	
Arrival Date	
Departure Date	

—Reading for information. T distributes copies of the letter.

> 42 Braemar Road
> Gosport
> Hampshire
>
> 21st April 19..
>
>
> Cumberland Hotel
> 23 Lascelles Terrace
> Blackpool
> Lancashire
>
> Dear Sir,
> I am writing to confirm the reservation I made by phone this morning.
> I should like a double room with bath overlooking the sea.
> I shall be arriving in the evening of Friday 27th May and leaving the morning of Monday 30th.
>
> Yours faithfully
> George Jerrold

—Feedback: Ss compare their answers in pairs. Ss give T information
  to complete BB table.

5.2   Revision/oral practice

(approx. 30 minutes)

—T sets scene:

'We are going to try to reconstruct the original phone call. I will play the part of the hotel receptionist. The phone rings . . . I pick it up and I say, *Hello*. How do you find out if it's the right hotel?' T elicits suggestions from class: *Hello, is that the Cumberland Hotel?*

—Repetition drill for pronunciation and intonation: chorus → group → individual.

—Paired practice of the two line dialogue:

A: Hello.
B: Hello, is that the Cumberland Hotel?

Tq→Sa. Sq→Sa (open pairs). Sq→Sa (closed pairs).
Note: when eliciting from the class, T should accept and, if appropriate, note or focus on other acceptable alternatives. T elicits and drills in the same way the following two-line dialogues:

A: May I have your name, please?
B: Yes, Jerrold, George Jerrold.

A: Could you spell that, please?
B: Yes, Jerrold. J-E-double R-O-L-D.

A: Do you want a double or a single, Mr Jerrold?
B: A double, with bath, please; and overlooking the sea if possible.

T discusses other types of room at this point—overlooking the park, quiet, light etc.

A: When will you be arriving?
B: Friday 27th May, in the evening.

T draws attention to the difference between the written form of dates and the spoken form, *Friday the twenty-seventh of May*.

A: How long will you be staying, Mr Jerrold?
B: Till the Monday—that's the 30th—in the morning.

5.3   Listening practice and information transfer

(approx. 20 minutes)

—T sets scene: Ss to imagine they are the hotel receptionist. They are going to hear three guests phoning to reserve rooms. They should note down the details in the register.

—T distributes copies of blank register.

CUMBERLAND HOTEL									
23 LASCELLES TERRACE									
BLACKPOOL, LANCASHIRE									
NAME	ROOM PREFERRED					SEA VIEW	PARK VIEW	No. OF ROOM	ARRIVAL DATE	DEPARTURE DATE
	DOUBLE	SINGLE	BATH	SHOWER	WC					

—Ss listen to the recording and do the information transfer.
—Ss check in pairs.
—Confirmatory listening.

5.4 Discourse chain
for further practice

(approx. 25 minutes)
—T explains that Ss are now going to practise the conversations they heard. It is not necessary for them to remember exactly what was said. The discourse chain on the OHP or BB will help them. Any appropriate exponent is acceptable, and indeed this is a chance to try out alternatives.
—Dialogue with first guest: T↔S demonstration, S↔S open pair demonstration, S↔S closed pairs with student chairs placed back to back to simulate a telephone conversation.

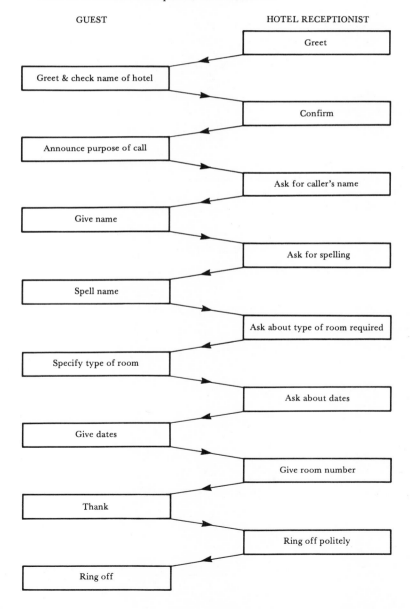

GUEST   HOTEL RECEPTIONIST

Greet

Greet & check name of hotel

Confirm

Announce purpose of call

Ask for caller's name

Give name

Ask for spelling

Spell name

Ask about type of room required

Specify type of room

Ask about dates

Give dates

Give room number

Thank

Ring off politely

Ring off

—Ss now reverse roles and go on to practise the second call, using their completed hotel register as a guide. During this activity T may progressively erase the discourse chain prompts from BB or OHP.

—Ss practise the third call using only their completed hotel registers.

—Writing phase: T shows Ss how to confirm the booking by using the model letter. (approx. 10 minutes)
Note: depending on the level of the students, it might be advisable to talk through, or even write up on BB, a version of the letter for the first caller, before asking Ss to do this alone.

—Each S chooses one of the calls heard and writes a letter confirming the booking.

—Ss exchange letters and check the details against what they have written in their hotel registers.

5.5 Role play for production

—T divides class into two equal groups of hotels and holiday makers.

—T gives preparation instructions.

a) Hotels in Blackpool: each S receives a booking plan and a blank hotel register form as used for the listening activity. The hotel receptionists must:
   —give their hotels names and write these on the hotel documents.
   —for each room in each hotel, blank out 20 days on the booking plan, which are previous bookings.
   —make clear name cards on pieces of paper and place them where they can be seen by all.

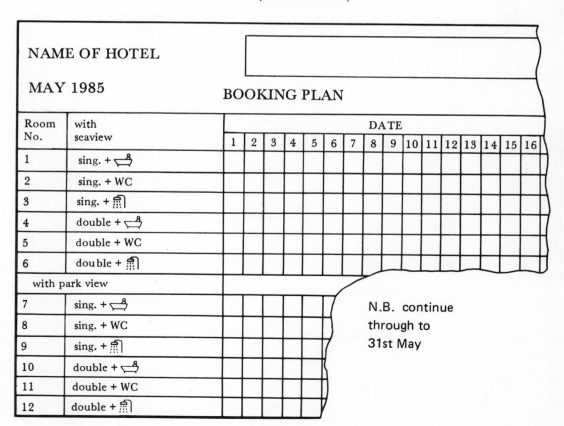

Room No.	with seaview	DATE															
		1	2	3	4	5	6	7	8	9	10	11	12	13	14	15	16
1	sing. + 🛁																
2	sing. + WC																
3	sing. + 🚿																
4	double + 🛁																
5	double + WC																
6	double + 🚿																
with park view																	
7	sing. + 🛁																
8	sing. + WC																
9	sing. + 🚿																
10	double + 🛁																
11	double + WC																
12	double + 🚿																

NAME OF HOTEL

MAY 1985   BOOKING PLAN

N.B. continue through to 31st May

b) Holidaymakers: the Ss play themselves. They each have five days' holiday to take in the month of May, which they will take in Blackpool. The Ss must:
— choose the five days they wish to take their holiday.
— decide exactly what kind of rooms they want—single/double, with or without bath, sea view etc.
— be prepared to spell their names in English.
— note down all these decisions, which must not be modified during the course of the role play.

—T gives instructions for the role play.
The names of the available hotels in Blackpool are written on BB. May is a very busy period in Blackpool and the hotels are pretty full. There will be a rush for rooms. Each hotel is to set up its name in a visible position and sit back to back with an empty chair.

Holiday makers now choose a hotel and try to make their bookings. If there is no room at the required time they must 'phone' another hotel until they get their booking. The telephone lines of hotels are 'engaged' if someone is already 'phoning'.

The object for holiday makers is to get their booking as quickly as possible and note down the hotel and room number. For hotels, it is to fit as many extra guests in as possible, but all these new bookings must be properly recorded in the register.

Note: it would be useful to reverse roles and have another round to give everyone a chance to practise booking.

—Writing phase—possibly as a homework assignment. Confirm the bookings in writing.

6 Tapescript for listening activity

Note: The following is a transcript of the tape made for this lesson. You will notice that the dialogue contains all the hesitations, repetitions and imperfections of natural speech. This was because, instead of reading from a script, we simulated as closely as possible the conditions of a real telephone call of this kind—the caller spoke from some dates he had scribbled on a piece of paper, and the receptionist actually wrote down the details as he was given them.
Receptionist = R. Caller = C.

6.1 First caller

R: Good morning.
C: Hello, is that the Cumberland Hotel?
R: Speaking.
C: Er, I was wondering if I could reserve a room, please?
R: Yes, how many people?
C: Erm, a double room, please, with shower if possible.
R: Uha, and . . when will you be arriving?
C: On Tuesday, next Tuesday the 27th.
R: OK, I'll . . . just have a look in the register, sir, one moment please. Mm. . Uha, yes, yes we have one double room with shower, very nice room overlooking the park. That's number 25.
C: That sounds nice.
R: OK, and how many days will you be staying, sir?
C: Er, um, well, we'll be leaving on the Friday, that'll be the 30th May.
R: OK. So, that's from Tuesday till Friday. That's fine. And your name, sir?

C: Er, the name's Whitfield.

R: Uha. Whitfield. Mr. Whitfield. W.H.I.T.F.I.E.L.D, right?

C: That's right, yeah.

R: OK, look forward to seeing you, sir. Bye bye.

C: Thank you very much. Bye bye.

6.2   Second caller

R: G'morning, Cumberland Hotel.

C: Oh, good morning, erm, I'd like to book a . . . a single room please.

R: Would that be with bath, sir?

C: No, erm, no, just with, just with erm a erm toilet, if erm if possible.

R: Uha. Er, ah, when will, when will you be staying, sir?

C: Well, erm, I'm going to arrive on, erm, Friday the 23rd, the 23rd of May. . .

R: OK, sir I'll just look in (*C:* erm, some time in the afternoon) the register.

C: Aha.

R: Yes. That seems to be OK. Friday the 23rd of May, you said?

C: Aha.

R: OK. We've got a single room (*C:* Oh, that's good) and your name, sir?

C: Erm, my name's Walters. D'you, d'you want me to spell that?

R: No, No. OK, Mr Walters, and how long will you be staying?

C: Well, erm, till the erm, Sunday—just . . . just the weekend. That's erm, Sunday the erm, 25th.

R: I see. OK. Fine. Look forward to seeing you, sir. Right, bye.

C: Thank you very much, thank you. Bye bye.

R: Bye bye.

6.3   Third caller

R: Good morning, Cumberland Hotel.

C: Oh, good morning; I would like to book a room, please.

R: Fine, ah just one moment, I'll get the register. OK, then, when do you . . .? What date is it?

C: From the 6th of June till Sunday—the 8th.

R: Uha.

C: And, erm, erm, it's, oh well, preferably I would like a room overlooking the sea.

R: OK. Is that a single or a double room, madam?

C: A double . . . with bath.

R: Double room with bath overlooking the sea, madam. Number 33's free. Yes—OK.

C: Uha.

R: And your name, madam?

C: Teresa Silva.

R: Erm, Teresa?

C: Silva.

R: Could you, could you spell that?

C: S.I.L.V.A.

R: S.I.L, OK, fine. OK then, see you on the 6th.

C: Yes, exactly, OK.

R: Right.

C: Thank you very much.

R: Bye bye

C: Bye.

Section B
The Listening, Reading and Writing Skills

Background

15

Listening skills

Alan Matthews

1   The need for training

Should valuable classroom time be spent on training our students to understand spoken English? Definitely yes! I suspect that in many schools, listening practice is hardly touched on—or if it is, it will be incidental or even accidental! If one of our main aims is to teach our students oral communication, then we have no option but to give prominence to the development of listening skills as well. Communication cannot successfully take place unless what is spoken is also understood. Indeed in my experience, students often seem to have greater difficulty in following what is said to them than in making themselves understood.

Broadly speaking, I think we should aim to provide our students with sufficient listening practice to enable them to understand with reasonable ease both native and non-native speakers of English when they speak at normal speed in unstructured situations.

Fortunately there is usually no shortage of authentic listening material available. Even when students have little or no chance to visit an English-speaking country, they are able to listen to English by tuning in to the BBC World Service and other broadcasts in English such as Voice of America, by listening to the multitude of pop songs in English, by watching British, American, Australian etc. films on the television and at the cinema. (Unfortunately for our purposes, some countries have foreign films dubbed rather than sub-titled).

2   Type of material

Listening practice is very often catered for with less than ideal materials: texts which are fully scripted tend to be overused and, although such texts can and should feature in the overall listening programme, they do not go far enough on their own. Many of the commercial materials available are of the fully-scripted type.

To establish what sort of material is most suitable to use, perhaps the best starting point is to ask yourself what you listen to in your everyday life in your native language. Probably a mixture of:

—conversations and discussions (between two or more people) at home, in school, over the telephone etc., both with you as an active participant and also overhearing.

—monologues: people telling you stories, anecdotes, jokes etc.; talks and lectures, sermons, contributions at meetings, songs etc.

—TV and radio programmes of all different sorts, including weather bulletins and news broadcasts.

Characteristic of almost all of the above—except a few TV and radio programmes (such as news broadcasts), sermons, songs etc.—is that they are unscripted, i.e. not written down in advance and read aloud, not rehearsed beforehand but spontaneous and natural. This is the sort of English most frequently heard and therefore what our students should above all be exposed to for listening practice.

Natural, spontaneous speech differs in many important respects from written prose. Below is an extract from an unscripted monologue (from *Themes* by Alan Matthews and Carol Read, Collins, 1982) with many of the features of natural speech labelled.

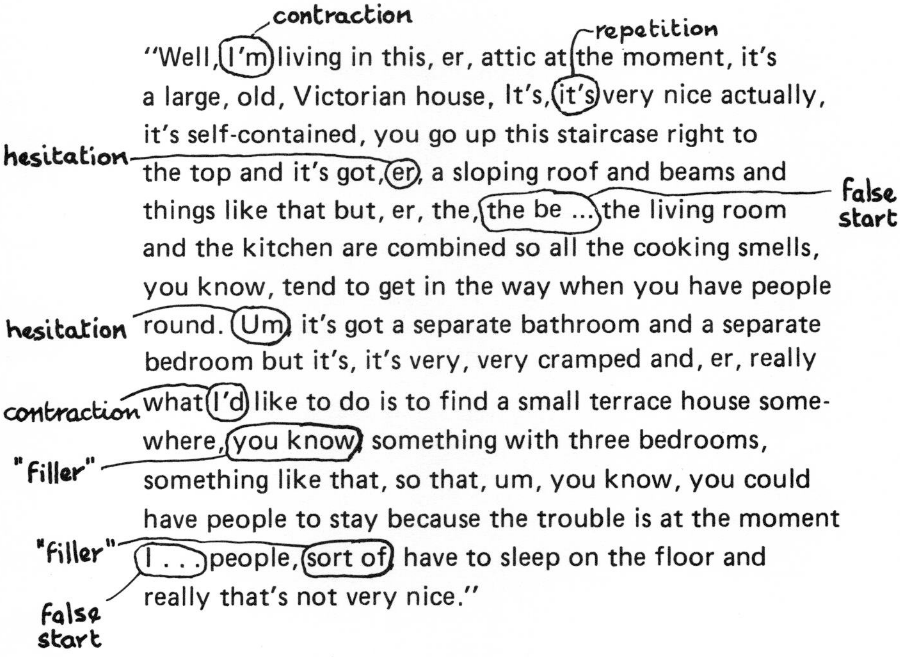

"Well, I'm living in this, er, attic at the moment, it's a large, old, Victorian house, It's, it's very nice actually, it's self-contained, you go up this staircase right to the top and it's got, er, a sloping roof and beams and things like that but, er, the, the be ... the living room and the kitchen are combined so all the cooking smells, you know, tend to get in the way when you have people round. Um, it's got a separate bathroom and a separate bedroom but it's, it's very, very cramped and, er, really what I'd like to do is to find a small terrace house somewhere, you know, something with three bedrooms, something like that, so that, um, you know, you could have people to stay because the trouble is at the moment I ... people, sort of, have to sleep on the floor and really that's not very nice."

[Annotations: contraction (I'm), repetition (it's), hesitation (er), false start (the be ...), hesitation (Um), contraction (I'd), "filler" (you know), "filler" (I ...), false start]

These features are a natural and inevitable part of spontaneous speech. If the same information were written rather than spoken, it would be considerably more fluent, more polished, more concentrated, with a tighter overall organisation—not better or superior in any way, but different.

The best type of material, then, for listening practice will be conversations, monologues etc. of a type that students are most likely to hear 'in real life' outside the classroom—unscripted for the most part, although fully scripted news broadcasts, songs and the like should also play a part. It is also important to ensure that the students are exposed to as wide a range of accents as possible, both native (and not just R.P.)

and non-native. In this way, we will be equipping our students reasonably well to tackle the real thing. It is of course impossible to lay down precisely what the content of such listening texts should be, but they should concentrate on topics of relevance and interest to the students and be appropriate to their age.

3 Using material in class

Orientation

Whatever the level of the students, it is generally advisable to orient them to what they are about to hear. Briefly introduce the topic of the text by asking the students a few simple general questions, by eliciting their own opinions etc. If need be, pre-teach a few key words and phrases. Also, tell the students what sort of passage they are going to hear, whether a discussion, a dialogue or a monologue.

Always set the students their task before they listen to the passage. If they are not given a precise purpose prior to listening, they will not know why they are to listen, what they have to listen out for or what sort of listening to do. The task, largely dependent on the type of passage and its content, may include listening for the gist (cp. skimming); for specific details (cp. scanning); for intensive, detailed comprehension; responding emotionally (*I like it because . . .*); giving an opinion about the passage (*I think it's one-sided because . . .*) etc. Often more than one sort of listening can be practised with the same text.

Tasks

For a first listening the students may be given a few fairly straightforward pre-questions to help them establish some very basic facts (the number of speakers, where they are, whether they are in a good or bad mood etc.). This breaks the ice and gives practice in listening for gist or for specific information. For a second—and maybe third—listening the students may be asked to extract much more detailed information.

The types of task available are numerous and, for the most part, well-known. However it would seem sensible to give the students tasks which involve as little writing as possible, so that their attention can remain on the text (unless, of course, the point of the listening is to provide note-taking practice). Tasks such as information-transfer, true/false questions, picture-sequencing, sentence-sequencing etc. are examples of largely non-writing tasks. It is also worth remembering that the same listening passage can be used at a range of levels as long as the tasks are made correspondingly easier or more challenging.

Follow-up work

Of course it would be a waste to discard the listening passage at this point. A lot of useful extension work is possible: focusing on recurrent structures or functions for remedial practice, listening for features of textual organisation (for instance, logical connectors), doing an oral and/or written reconstruction of part of the passage. Getting production mileage from a text is a good thing—as long as the text is not flogged to death and the students bored as a result.

4 Is the tape recorder necessary?

It would be foolish to suggest that a tape-recorder does not come in handy! But, thinking realistically, a tape-recorder is an expensive item for a school or for an individual to buy and in many cases is simply not available. So is all lost? No, far from it.

The teacher can be a perfectly adequate source of listening practice. (Many non-native speakers of English often seem reluctant to take on this teaching resonsibility, yet are happy enough to be models of acceptable English at all other times). In fact, live listening practice has its advantages—gestures, facial expressions, eye contact etc. are all present, and this is more realistic than a disembodied voice from a tape-recorder.

Bearing in mind what was just said, it is important not simply to read aloud a fully scripted text to the students, as this would result in unnatural English. To produce a monologue from notes guarantees the inclusion of natural features of spoken English and is therefore far preferable. (You could take both parts in a dialogue, with different voices, but this is unsatisfactory for obvious reasons).

5 A simple text and task

Finally, here is an example of a very simple listening text for elementary students which was recorded from notes.

Notes

> Friends of mine—Jones (Jim & Anne)—live in a flat (3rd floor)—don't know why—very noisy—centre of London—silly because: 3 children David (10), John (8) and Sue (2)—David has 2 dogs—Sue, a kitten.

'Spontaneous' monologue

I want to tell you, er, about some friends of mine, um, the Jones family, that's Jim and, er, Anne Jones. Now they, they live in a flat, on the third floor. Well, you know, I think they're crazy. I don't know why they live in a third floor flat because it's very, very noisy and it's right in the, er, in the centre of London. It's really rather silly, because, well, they've got three children, there's David, he's ten; John, he's eight and Sue, she's only two. And, well, David, he's got two dogs and Sue's got a kitten.

Student's task sheet

	Jones family
Where live?	
Kind of home?	
Children's names and ages?	
Pets?	

16

Reading skills

Mary Spratt

1 Why do students need to read in English?

The answer often given to this question is that, particularly at the elementary and intermediate levels, they need to read to consolidate their spoken language. So, for example, they first practise a new structure orally and then read a short text which has been specially written to include many examples of this same structure. However, short texts of this kind very often do not contain the same kind of language as 'real' reading texts, which typically feature a wide range of structures and vocabulary, appropriate styles and registers, sentence-joining devices, varying formats and specific kinds of textual organisation. The type of reading we carry out on such 'real' reading texts is also very different from the traditional classroom approach to a specially written text, i.e. comprehension questions focusing on a particular structure. 'Real' reading texts demand one or more of a number of different reading skills, such as skimming for gist, scanning for specific information, reading for inference, reading for detail.

It therefore seems that, if we wish to give students real practice in reading rather than use reading to consolidate their oral work, the type of text and reading activities we employ in the classroom must be appropriate. Of course, one could ask why reading deserves teaching as a skill in its own right. My answer to this would be that if students use English at all after they leave school, it may well be in reading, as they study textbooks written in English in their further education programme, or read newspapers, magazines and periodicals, for example, to keep themselves up to date in their job fields, current affairs, social issues, entertainment etc. Also, if students never look at, say or hear another word of English after they leave school, learning to read in English will nevertheless equip them with reading skills which they can transfer to their own language. Furthermore, students who learn to enjoy reading in English may become more motivated to learn English in general—a boost for any teacher.

If we accept that we should teach reading as a skill in its own right, what texts and activities are suitable?

2 Text selection

Outside the classroom, we mostly read things that, for one reason or another, we are interested in. Why not, then, apply the same principle to our choice of reading matter for students, selecting topics, styles of writing, lay-outs and formats that will appeal to them and have some relevance? One criterion for text choice, therefore, is interest.

A second criterion is authenticity of language. Authentic language is language from which the features of real language have not been filtered out for language-teaching purposes. To learn to read properly, students must, early on, learn to deal with all those features of written English already described. Authentic language is not necessarily difficult. Many newspaper articles, brochures, leaflets, passages from magazines or books etc. are written in simple (not simplified) language, and many of those texts which do contain more complex language can be made accessible to elementary students by being accompanied by easy tasks.

A third criterion for text selection is variety of format, register and textual organization. Outside the EFL classroom we may read letters, articles, instructions, cookery books, detective stories, cartoons etc. Students should be exposed to this full range. Texts suitable for teaching reading in its own right are increasingly to be found within EFL textbooks and magazines. Some other sources are tourist brochures and pamphlets, timetables, menus, instruction leaflets, newspapers, magazines, comic strips, novels and poems.

3   Reading skills

It was stated above that the teacher should select activities suitable for promoting reading as a skill in its own right, but that reading in fact involves various different skills. We need to isolate and understand each one. The following are some of the main reading skills required by the general EFL student:
— recognising the letters of the alphabet
— reading groups of letters as words
— understanding the meaning of punctuation
— understanding the meaning of vocabulary items
— understanding the grammar of a sentence
— understanding the relationship between sentences and clauses in a text
— recognising the effects of style
— recognising the organisation of a text
— making inferences
— reading longer texts (extensive reading)
— skimming for gist
— scanning for specific information
— reading for detail
N.B. This list does not include those reading skills required for more specific purposes e.g. speed reading and reference skills, as they are not usually part of the general EFL student's more identifiable needs.

I would like to elaborate on three of the skills in the above list as, unlike the others, what they involve is not evident from the label given to them.

Understanding the relationship between sentences and clauses

The relationship between sentences and clauses in a text may be expressed through two kinds of sentence-joining device. These are logical connectors and reference devices. Logical connectors are the conjunctions and adverbs placed between sentences and clauses to show their relationship. The following represent the main categories:

Relationship	Examples of logical connectors
Cause and effect	thus, therefore, so, consequently, as a result
Contrast and concession	but, yet, however, although, whereas
Time	then, while, after, when
Addition	what's more, besides (that), in addition to this
Exemplification	for example, for instance, such as
Conclusion	to conclude, in brief, in short
Rephrasing	in other words, that is to say

If readers do not recognise the force and meaning of these connectors, they will lose the thread of what they are reading. Yet often these words are not taught systematically.

Reference devices are words which refer to words in the following or previous sentences. In the following examples, the ringed words are reference words, the boxed words are those they refer to and the words in brackets indicate by what means the reference words perform their referring function.

—When I saw my friend last night, he gave me a present. (*pronoun*)

—Jim used to work in Milan but he left there last year. (*pronoun; adverb of place*)

—I like icecream and so does my brother. (*auxiliary verb*)

—They met in 1973 and have been friends since then. (*adverb of time*)

—He acted very rashly. I don't approve of that type of behaviour. (*demonstrative adjective and word from the same word field*)

—I don't like cities, let alone Paris. (*word from the same word field*)

If readers do not realise that these words have a reference, or what that reference is, misunderstandings will result.

Skimming for gist

This skill involves skimming over the 'surface' of a piece of writing to understand its general content or gist. It is the kind of reading we do when, for example, we glance over a page of a newspaper to see if there is anything worth reading in greater detail, or when we leaf through a book to find out its subject matter.

Scanning for specific information

This involves darting over much of a text to find the specific item of information that we wish to discover. This skill therefore also involves the ability to reject or pass over irrelevant information. It is the kind of reading we do when, for example, we read through someone's biography to find out the date of their marriage or the name of their spouse, or when we glance through a telephone directory looking for a particular person's telephone number.

4 Classroom activities

We can now turn to the classroom activities that are appropriate for developing the different reading skills. These are very many so I will select only some of the main ones and, amongst these, only those which develop the last eight skills on the above list, as these areas are less charted than the others. Examples of some of these techniques can be found in other parts of this book, as will be indicated below.

Skill	Activities
Understanding the relationship between sentences and clauses	1. Jumbled sentences or paragraphs. 2. T circles the reference devices in a text and Ss work out what they refer to. 3. T gives Ss a passage in which the logical connectors are blanked out. Ss have to read the passage and work out what the connectors must be. 4. Prediction exercises, e.g. on an OHP. Ss read the first part of a text up to and including a logical connector. They then predict the next line, which is masked, etc. throughout the text.
Recognising the effects of style	1. Multiple choice or true/false questions on style. 2. Discussions on the style of the passage. 3. Parallel passages in different styles.
Recognising the organisation of a text	1. Jumbled paragraphs. 2. Discussing the function of particular paragraphs.
Making inferences	1. True/false or discussion questions on possible interpretations of the text.
Extensive reading	1. Ss read in their free time. 2. Ss read on a self-access basis from a class reading bank. No tasks need be set on this reading.
Skimming for gist	1. The text is used simply as a spring-board for discussion on a particular topic. 2. Ss read through a passage and then suggest a title for it. 3. Ss match different text titles to series of short texts within a given time limit.

Scanning for specific information	1. Underlining or circling the required information in a given time limit.
	2. Pre-questions focusing on specific information.
	3. Team games, e.g. the first team to reply to T's question on a specific item of information gets a point.
Reading for detail	1. Information-transfer exercises.
	2. Note-taking on the order of events or emotions in a text.
	3. True/false questions.
	4. Jigsaw reading.

Examples of some of these activities can be found in the following articles.

Activities	*Article*
Information transfer	*Information-transfer for listening and reading* (page 79).
Exercises on skimming, scanning and reading for detail.	*Reading in a foreign language at an elementary level* (page 84).
Note-taking on order of events.	*Reading, writing and communication* (page 94).
Exercises on skimming, reference devices and textual organisation.	*An elementary reading and writing lesson* (page 118).
Skimming, scanning and inference work.	*A reading skills lesson* (page 123).

Of course, not all texts will lend themselves to practising all the reading skills; some texts clearly lend themselves to certain skills rather than others and a teacher must look out for this. Nor does any one reading lesson have to cover all the skills. The guidelines indicated by learning-load, saturation and interest apply to a reading lesson as they do to any other. What is important is that, over the term and the year, the teacher ensures that the students have access to an appropriate range of text and activity types, and thus provides the students with practice in those skills which seem appropriate to their needs.

17

Writing skills

David Palmer

1 Features of written English

Written English is probably more familiar to most teachers as a subject of analysis than is spoken English. English in the written mode has several characteristics which are best highlighted by comparing it with spoken English.

The passage below is a transcript of a stretch of spontaneous spoken English taken from Crystal & Davy's *Advanced Conversational English* (published by Longman). It is followed by my 'translation' of it into a certain style of written English. I have used a 'translation' to highlight points of contrast, but in composing written English, of course, it is not normal to translate in this way. Moreover, you will notice that in adopting a specific style, I have had to assume a certain kind of reader, whereas in composing a piece of writing we are normally conscious from the start of the reader or type of reader we are writing for.

from 'Advanced Conversational English'	*'translation'*
B: I'm very suspicious of the press generally and I can tell you because not only, I mean, that's that's one case that you've given (yes) but also in, in their reporting, of, erm, affairs, foreign affairs.	I am generally very suspicious of the press, not only in their coverage of cases like the one referred to in your article, but also in their reporting of foreign affairs.
A: Yes.	
B: Because living in Cyprus I've seen quite a number of historical events, you know, (mm) I was, I was there when they tried to assassinate Makarios for example.	Living in Cyprus, I have witnessed quite a number of 'historical events', for example the assassination attempt on Makarios, which have been inflated by the press. I consider this dangerous partly for the reason given, i.e. that people can be made to believe a situation to be very serious if they read about it in print.
A: Yes, yes of course.	
B: And, erm, so much of this is blown up out of all proportion in the press, and I think it's dangerous partly for the reason that you've said that, erm, in a way it makes people believe that a situation is very serious if they read it in, er, in print, you know in black and white. (Yeah).	

In comparing these two stretches of English language, it may be useful to group features under four headings.

Grammatical and syntactic features

Here it is easier to list all the things that writing does not do and spontaneous speech does. For example, writing has no false starts, interruptions, hesitations and 'non-standard' syntax. (But of course non-standard syntax may be 'standard' for spontaneous spoken language.) What exactly do we mean by the grammatical and syntactic features of writing?

Note the position of the sentence adverbial *generally* in the two versions and the position of the signal phrase *for example.* In the written version these are placed where they will help the reader to follow the writer's argument rather than serving partially as 'fillers', as they appear to do in the spoken version.

Compare *when they tried to assassinate Makarios*, of which the basic SVO (subject-verb-object) syntax is transformed in the written version into a nominal group. These extended nominal groups are more typical of written English, and in certain styles even longer nominal groups like 'The Makarios assassination attempt' are appropriate.

Notice also a tendency away from more active and personal forms in the spoken version—*that's one case that you've given, the reason that you've said* and *it makes people believe*—towards more passive, impersonal forms, like subjectless non-finites, together with the use of modals that tend to tone down the force of the spoken version—*the one referred to in your article, the reason given* and *people can be made to believe.*

In addition there is a more confident and precise use of grammatical cohesion devices in written English because the reader is able to refer back with ease. For example, we have *I consider this dangerous* instead of the less specific reference of *I think it's dangerous.*

Lexical features

The written version uses a more precise vocabulary covering a smaller semantic field, because the writer has more time to encode than the speaker. e.g. *witnessed* for *seen.* There is also a tendency to use Latinisms in place of words of Anglo-Saxon/Germanic origin—possibly because the first languages to be extensively written in Britain were Latin and French, and English was somewhat disdained, being associated with the vulgar masses; thus *inflated* is used for *blown up*, and *consider* for *think.*

Organisational features

As the written passage is a translation of a stretch of spoken English, it does not exemplify the organisational features of a planned piece of writing very well. However, composed writing is usually clearly planned, its topic sentence leading into supporting sentences, logical connections clearly signalling points and links in the argument, and each paragraph being restricted to a single main topic. Because it is planned, it normally requires fewer repetitive exemplifications of points in the manner of *if they read it in print, you know in black and white.*

In addition, the use in speech of *you know* and similar phrases, which are intended to establish contact with the listener, are absent from written discourse, though in certain sorts of prose, other kinds of contact phrases such as 'firstly I shall discuss' and 'as is commonly known' may be appropriate.

Graphic or visual features

The visual features of spoken language are facial expressions, gestures, body movements and proximity. In addition there are other suprasegmental features such as voice quality, intonation, stress, pause and so on which writing somewhat inadequately tries to indicate with graphic features such as paragraphing, punctuation, underlining, quotation marks, italics etc. In the written version I have tried, for example, to render the self-mocking tone of *historical events* by putting it in quotation marks, but the effect can at best be an approximation. Note also that writing uses abbreviations that speech normally does not, such as e.g., i.e., etc.

2   Writing skills

If we look at our students' written work, we will normally find that it is inadequate for a number of reasons. Some of the errors may point to unfamiliarity with the language itself—especially lexical and grammatical errors—but others will be attributable to the medium rather than the language—for example problems of organising information, punctuation and spelling. Some of these problems may well also occur when students write in their first language, reminding us that writing is a special skill that does not spring naturally from an ability to speak a language.

We can analyse the specific skills attached to writing under five headings.

Graphical or visual skills

Writing graphemes (letters of the alphabet), in upper or lower case as appropriate, joined in the conventional way. This is likely to pose a difficulty only to students whose first language is written in a different 'alphabet'.

Spelling. Here the first language interferes, as well as previous knowledge of the second language. Students may often apply the phonetic conventions of their native language to spelling English words.

Punctuation and capitalization. Here students' attention needs to be drawn to the fact that conventions differ from language to language. Awareness is the first step towards remedy.

Format, such as the layout of a letter, or a memo, or a shopping list. Again these differ from one language to another.

Grammatical skills

This refers to the students' ability to use successfully a variety of sentence patterns and constructions. Their facility in this will very much depend on their oral proficiency, but may well be slightly ahead of it.

Expressive or stylistic skills

This refers to the students' ability to express precise meanings in a variety of styles or registers. In order to do this, they will not only have to be able to select appropriate vocabulary, but also appropriate sentence patterns and structures for the written medium. The students' reading experience will probably have a strong influence on their success with this skill.

Rhetorical skills

This is the students' ability to use linguistic cohesion devices—connectives, reference words, elipsis, and so on—in order to link parts of a text into logically related sequences.

Organisational skills

These are similar to those involved in *Rhetorical skills* above, but here we are concerned with the organisation of pieces of information into paragraphs and texts. This involves the sequencing of ideas as well as the ability to reject irrelevant information and summarize relevant points. This is a skill that many students find difficult in their first language, but which affects their performance in many academic disciplines.

In developing the writing skill, we need to devise activities that cover all the sub-skills described above, both separately as practice activities and together as written production tasks, rather than expecting students automatically to transfer their oral ability onto paper.

18

Integrating the skills

Carol Read

The purpose of this article is two-fold: to describe what is meant by 'integrating the skills' and to discuss the advantages that this can have for both the teacher and the learner.

1   What are integrated skills?

The integration of skills in the language classroom can be defined quite simply as a series of activities or tasks which use any combination of the four skills — Listening (L), Speaking (S), Reading (R), Writing (W) — in a continuous and related sequence. For example:

Activity	*Skills practised*
1. T introduces topic — 'Animals'. T asks Ss prepared questions to elicit what they know about lions e.g. *Where do lions live?, What do they eat?, How long do they live?* ↓	**S, L**
2. Ss read short descriptive passage on lions to check/find out the answers to questions in 1. ↓	**R**
3. Ss compare how many answers they got right in 1, and how much information was new to them. ↓	**S, L**
4. Ss work in pairs and choose another animal. They discuss and make notes in answer to a set of questions e.g. *Where does it live?, What does it eat?* ↓	**S, W**
5. Ss write short descriptive passage on animal they have chosen based on the information in their notes and using the original passage on lions as a model.	**W**

The activities in the sequence may be related through the topic or through the language or, as in the case of the example, through both of these. An important feature of the sequence is the interlocking nature of the activities; to a large extent each task develops from those that have come before and prepares for those that are to follow. The skills are thus not practised in isolation but in a closely interwoven series of tasks which mutually reinforce and build on each other.

2 Why integrate the skills?

There are two main reasons for devising activity sequences which integrate the skills. The first is to practise and extend the students' use of a particular language structure or function and the second is to develop the students' ability in two or more of the four skills within a constant context. In the case of the former, the combination of skills used clearly depends on the item of language being taught and the mode—spoken or written—to which it is most appropriate. In the case of the latter, it depends on which skills are to be the principal focus of the teaching sequence. The main aim of the activity sequence outlined above, for example, is to develop Reading and Writing skills, with a particular focus, in this case, on the language of description. Schematically, we might view in the following way some more potential combinations of activities which integrate the skills

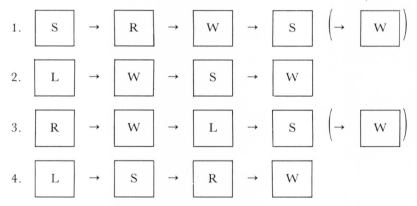

1. S → R → W → S (→ W)

2. L → W → S → W

3. R → W → L → S (→ W)

4. L → S → R → W

There are two points to note in relation to the above. Firstly, it is likely, although not necessary, that listening will precede speaking and reading will precede writing. This means that students receive an input in a complementary receptive skill before they are expected to produce their own output. (See activities 2 and 5 in the example above). Secondly, a writing task usually comes at the end of a sequence. Writing is often a good way of concluding and giving final reinforcement to the activities that have gone before. It is also frequently suitable to set such a task for the students to do at home.

There are a number of important advantages in providing students with the kind of integrated skills practice I have described.

Continuity

It allows for continuity in the teaching/learning programme. Tasks and activities are not performed in isolation but are closely related and dependent on each other. In the sequence outlined opposite, for example, the students can only successfully do the final writing task (5) as a result of the preparation in earlier activities (particularly 2 and 4).

Similarly, this activity (5) serves in itself as consolidation and reinforcement of language that has been practised earlier in the sequence.

Input before output

It helps to ensure that there is input before output. We cannot expect learners to perform a task without orienting and motivating them to what they will be expected to do and providing them with the linguistic means that will enable them to be successful. In an integrated skills approach, learners can be provided with a suitable input which may be in the form of a direct model, as in the example above, or a much freer stimulus. This input will then form the basis for the learners' own output—or productive use of the language—in a subsequent task. In this sense, an integrated skills approach capitalises on the complementary relationship between Listening/Speaking and Reading/Writing and, by so doing, helps to enhance the teaching/learning of each individual skill.

Realism

It allows for the development of all four skills within a realistic, communicative framework. The use of such a framework helps to promote awareness not only of how the different skills relate to particular communicative needs, but also of how they lead naturally into each other as in real life. For example:

A telephones the station to enquire about train times.   **S, L**
↓
A takes down information in note form.   **W**
↓
A tells *B* the information. *A* and *B* decide which train to take.   **S**
↓
A writes card to *C* confirming travel plans and time of   **W**
arrival.

Appropriateness

It gives learners opportunities to recognise and redeploy the language they are learning in different contexts and modes. This helps the learners to recognise the appropriateness of a particular language form and mode in different contexts and with different participants. It is crucially important that an integrated skills sequence does not blur important differences that exist between spoken and written language. At an elementary level, for example, there might be differences between the appropriateness of contracted forms for speech and non-contracted forms for writing. Such differences should be brought out by the activities in the sequence and practised by the students.

Variety

Activities involving all four skills provide variety and can be invaluable in maintaining motivation. This is especially true in the case of large classes such as in primary and secondary schools, where interest in any one activity is likely to be short-lived.

Recycling

It allows naturally for the recycling and revision of language which has already been taught and is therefore often helpful for remedial teaching. It allows for language which is already familiar to the learners to be presented in a variety of new and different ways.

Confidence

It may be helpful for the learner who is weaker or less confident in one particular skill. For example, a learner who is better at reading than listening may be able to use the ability to understand a written text as support to performance in a subsequent listening task which is based around the same topic or theme.

19

Notes, summaries and compositions — Part I

David Cranmer

1 Introduction

Among the many tasks we set our students are note-taking and the writing of summaries and compositions. Note-taking and summary-writing are regarded as ways of checking comprehension of a text, and composition as a way of seeing whether the student can write continuous prose rather than just isolated sentences. In so far as these tasks fulfil their objective, they are valid in their own right, nor is it the purpose of this article to argue otherwise. Increasingly, however, they are seen as a means of training organisational and study skills in preparation for higher education. With that in mind, the purpose of this article is to take a look at current practices in the teaching of note-taking, summary and composition, to point out their weaknesses and to suggest a coherent alternative, to enable students to function adequately not just in terms of pure language (vocabulary and structures, which in any case are better dealt with at and below the sentence level) but also in terms of how that language is organised.

2 A false separation

The single greatest problem, I believe, is that although note-taking and summary are seen as related to each other, composition tends to be considered in isolation from the other two. I wish to suggest otherwise. Many teachers tell their students to prepare their compositions in note form before writing the composition itself. That being so, composition as well as summary should have a preparatory note stage, and the only difference between them is that, whereas the notes for a summary are derived from a pre-existing text, those for a composition are normally derived from thoughts. Each process may be regarded as the same but with a different mode of input and output.

Input		*Output*
text	→ notes	→ summary
thoughts	→ notes	→ composition

Another great problem is that students are often simply told, when being asked to take notes or write a composition: 'Oh, and don't forget to make a plan first' or when writing a summary: 'And remember to leave out the unimportant bits'. But they are given little or no guidance as to *how* to take notes, *how* to plan or *which* are the 'unimportant bits'. This is not to say that there are not recognised ways of going about such things, but these are too seldom actually taught and in any case can have serious weaknesses.

3   Weaknesses in current approaches

To take a look at summary, the most usual type is what is known as *précis*. This requires the student to reduce a text to about half its length, say a 400-word text to 200 words. What I wonder is just how useful such an exercise really is. In real life a 400-word text is scarcely so forbidding that the greater ease of reading a mere 200 words warrants the effort of reducing it. But if we could reduce a 10-page article to 200 words or a 200 page book to 10 pages that really would be useful.

A similar weakness exists in the usual type of composition plan, namely that it is too detailed, consisting of strings of single words and phrases, all of which will appear in the final version. Although it may be argued that this ensures that students have the vocabulary they need before embarking on the composition itself, it fails to look at the overall shape and coherence of the composition—you can't see the wood for the trees. In my experience, the greatest problem is not so much the vocabulary but the coherence from sentence to sentence. It is in the *organisation* of the composition that students need to be trained.

The greatest weakness, however, shows itself most clearly in note-taking (though related weaknesses apply also to summary and composition). This is the assumption that notes should always be taken in much the same way, traditionally in linear form. In other words, each note you take is written on the line after the previous note, gradually filling the page from top to bottom. This form of note-taking has only seriously been challenged by Tony Buzan in his book *Use Your Head* (BBC Publications, 1974). He argues that we do not *think* linearly but constantly refer back to the central topic, and back and forth between various aspects of the topic. Notes should do likewise—draw out the central topic, relate all its aspects to it and to each other. In terms of their layout, the notes should look something like this:

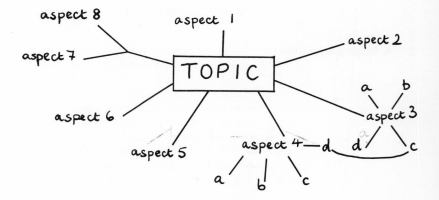

The various aspects radiate from the central topic, but can also act as sub-topics (aspects 3 and 4) from which further aspects (a,b,c and d) radiate. The close relationship between aspects 7 and 8 is shown by having them as two branches of the same radial; the link between aspects 4d and 3c is shown by a line joining them. By having the topic prominent and central in this 'brain pattern' (Buzan sees this type of diagram as reflecting the way the brain stores information), everything is kept in proportion, and the way in which the various aspects relate to the topic and to each other can be shown quite clearly.

The advantage of this type of note-taking to an organisation-centred approach is obvious, since it is the very organisation of the text that determines the precise shape of the brain-pattern. There is one problem, however. Buzan would claim that notes can and should always be in the form of a brain pattern, i.e. he wholly rejects the use of linear notes. But some texts are, in fact, linear in their organisation, and brain-pattern notes are no less inappropriate for these than linear notes are for other texts. The point is this: notes must reflect the organisation of the text from which they are taken.

4   Text-types

A number of text-types are commonly recognised among language teachers—narrative, description, instruction, argument, process, biography, comparing and contrasting, and so on. These kinds of distinction are clearly useful to an approach aimed at training organisational skills, since implicit in the label applied to each type is a different type of organisation. Unfortunately, how exactly the different text-types relate to each other is confused and the labels given to them not necessarily clear. Some teachers talk about 'narrative-description' (but which is it?); some regard 'process' as a type of general 'description' since it describes something that is generally true. Because of this confusion, I would like to suggest interpretations for the text-type labels which will both make their structure (organisation) apparent and show the relation between them.

For this clarification, it is necessary to divide text-types into two fundamental categories—those that include a time sequence and those that do not. I shall call the former *chronologically sequenced* and the latter *non-chronologically sequenced*. This division is crucial, for while chronologically sequenced texts follow a linear structure (because man perceives time as linear), non-chronologically sequenced texts follow other, more complex structures.

Of the text types mentioned above, narrative, biography, instruction and process are chronologically sequenced. Of these, narrative and biography are closely related because they both contain a sequence of events. In fact, for the purposes of this article, I shall regard narrative as a generic term, biography thus being a variety of narrative along with stories, accounts of historical events, 'What I did last holiday/weekend'—indeed any text that contains an event sequence. Instruction and process are also closely related, though on an equal level. They share the common use of connectors that indicate stages—*First, Next, Then, After that, Finally, When*, etc. Both lack a clearly defined grammatical agent: in instruction, the chief verb form is the imperative, which lacks an overt subject; in process, the most common verb form is the present simple passive without a 'by . . . . .' phrase.

The relations between the remaining three (non-chronologically sequenced) text types—description, comparing and contrasting, and argument—are much less close. Nevertheless, comparing and contrasting may be regarded as a double/triple/quadruple, or whatever, description, according to how many items are being compared/contrasted. Argument is often similar (comparing and contrasting points of view) but, unlike the other non-chronologically sequenced types, it is concerned with thoughts, not concrete objects. Nor does it necessarily have to involve opposing ideas. Argument is, for the purposes of this article, any non-chronologically sequenced text that deals with thoughts, and its structure can vary widely. This article is an example of argument.

5 Note-taking and note-making

In section 3, I complained that neither linear nor brain-pattern notes alone will necessarily follow the structure of the text from which they have been derived. In section 4, I suggested a way of looking at the different structures inherent in various text-types. Before we come to a conclusion, a further distinction relating to those points needs to be made.

There are two types of notes—those drawn from a text, and those in preparation for a text. The process of drawing notes from a text I shall call *note-taking*; the process of preparing notes to be expanded into a text I shall call *note-making*. This is an important distinction because, while note-taking will follow the structure of the text being noted, note-making follows, or in many cases determines, the structure of the text to be written.

6 Conclusion—a proposed approach

Firstly, the close relationship between the three types of task (note-taking/making, summary and composition) should be recognised in terms of an input-output system. Our teaching material should not only reflect *our* recognition of this, but make our *students* aware of it too.

Secondly, we should teach our students to function in a variety of ways, not just one. We need to teach them ways of dealing with the varieties of chronologically sequenced texts, and other ways of dealing with non-chronologically sequenced texts. For example, linear note-taking should be taught when working from chronologically sequenced texts, and brain-patterns (and variants) for non-chronologically sequenced texts.

Lastly we need to teach both how to *take* notes from a text and how to *make* notes in preparation for a new text, and, in the case of summary, how to *take* notes from one text and convert them into notes *made* in preparation for the summary.

See also *Notes, summaries and compositions Part II* on page 98 and *Part III* on page 106.

Techniques

20

Information transfer for listening and reading

David Palmer

1 What is information transfer?

We are all constantly exposed to information in various forms. It is probably true to say that concentrated 'institutional' information is presented to us more frequently in a visual symbolic form and less frequently in a purely linguistic form than ever before. Sometimes a schematic or symbolic presentation may be almost universally intelligible; sometimes the information is only partially visual, being supplemented by condensed linguistic information and therefore less widely communicative.

Both kinds of presentation can provide the language teacher with a useful source of material for information-transfer activities, by which I mean an activity involving the reproduction of information either from a diagrammatic or semi-diagrammatic form into a fully linguistic form, or vice-versa.

2 Advantages of information transfer

Authenticity

Information-transfer activities can use realia from the English speaking environment.

Real tasks

The transfer activity itself is an authentic task in that native speakers commonly do it in the normal course of their everyday lives. For example, the railway clerk at the station Enquiries Office constantly transfers his own semi-diagrammatic timetables into linguistic information for members of the public who telephone about train times. They too, in their turn, probably note down that information in a semi-schematic way rather than in its fully linguistic form.

Communicative
tasks

Because information-transfer activities are real tasks, they are also communicative—otherwise people would not be wasting their time doing them. When you book your flight at the travel agent you rely on the clerk to interpret the information on the computer screen and communicate it to you.

Repetitive tasks

Information presented in a diagrammatic form is frequently, by nature, a concentrated collection of similar items of information—for example, our train timetable tells us repeatedly when a train will depart from, stop at, and arrive at a limited number of places. This means that the linguistic equivalent may well be expressed by repetition of a certain structure. In this way, information-transfer activities can be very appropriate to the controlled practice stage of a lesson.

Productive tasks

An information-transfer exercise usually provides students only with the bare bones of information—they must supply the linguistic flesh with which the information will be expressed. Thus, if it is appropriately staged, an information transfer can fit into the free production stage of a lesson.

Development of all skills

Ideally an information-transfer activity forms a kind of pivot around which any of the language skills may revolve.

Figure 1

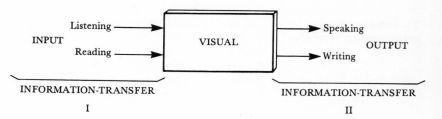

Figure 1 shows how a diagram or 'visual' may be built up from information read or heard by the student. The visual then becomes the basis of a second information-transfer in which the student reproduces the information linguistically in either a spoken or written mode. This article is concerned chiefly with the input end of this process, the first information-transfer.

Self-access

Information-transfer can provide useful self-access activities for developing listening and reading skills since students can check their performance against the 'correct' visual. This non-linguistic correction key minimizes the proof-reading errors that are inherent in linguistic answer keys.

3 Basic information-transfer strategies

Information-transfer tasks fall into a number of basic categories which can be realized through a number of scenarios often at several language levels.

Maps and plans

In this type of task, the student has to label, mark positions or plot routes on a map or a plan.

Selected scenarios   L = listening, R = reading

— *Classroom*
    Input: Description of students' seating in a class (L R).
    Task: Label desks with names of appropriate students.

— *Holiday tour*
    Input: Overheard dialogue, recounting or planning a holiday (L).
                Travel agent's itinerary (R).
                Postcard from family on holiday (R).
    Task: Plot route on map labelling places of interest and dates.

— *Weather forecast*
    Input: Weather forecast (L).
    Task: Enter weather symbols on a map.

— *Flight routes*
    Input: Newspaper report (R) or, interview (L) with Director
                General of an airline, giving details of new routes,
                closures, etc.
    Task: Plot routes on world map.

— *Seating plan*
    Input: Description (L R) of guests seated at a dinner party.
    Task: Label guests on diagram of table.

Other possibilities include: plan of a street; architect's plans; underground (tube) map; theatre seating plan; plans of traffic accidents.

It is quite often possible to provide the same basic information input at a number of different language levels. For example, the description of the seating plan above can be quite elementary, as in: *Mr Brown is sitting at the head of the table. On his left is Mrs Smith and on his right is Mr White. Mr Green is sitting on Mrs Smith's left.*, or it can employ more complex discourse, in which case the difficulty of the task is increased as the student has to filter out redundant information as well as recognise the functions of complex cohesive devices, as in: *Mrs Jones, a bit of a gossip, is sitting opposite Mr Green talking to her old friend Mrs Smith, who's sitting on her right. Mrs Smith, however, is talking right across the table to Mr White, the tall white-haired gentleman on the other side of Mrs Jones.* This becomes a sort of puzzle and indeed might be set as a problem-solving task in which the student has to seat the guests amicably according to their likes and dislikes. For example: *Lady Grey is quite a snob and insists on sitting in the place of honour at the head of the table. She is very jealous of Miss Sidebotham because they both like Mr Gable, a bachelor*, etc.

Grids and tables

These are better described as semi-diagrammatic information and include railway timetables, car-hire price lists or any kind of information analysed into tabular form.

Selected scenarios

— *Passport details*
    Input: Interview at passport office (L).
                Literary or police description of person (R).
    Task: Fill in 'personal details' page of passport.

— Train or bus timetables
Input: Telephone enquiries answered by railway/bus enquiry office (L).
Task: Complete a semi-complete timetable with destinations or times given in the dialogue.

— Football results and pools
Input: Authentic radio reports of the football results, or, at a more advanced level, randomly organised recordings of outside broadcast commentators giving the results of their particular matches (L).
           Newspaper report of the day's football (R).
Task: Complete a newspaper list of results or a pools coupon.

— Pop group
Input: Magazine article on pop group (R).
           Any other kind of personal information survey taken of a group of people (R).
Task: Tabulate information in simplified form.

Other possibilities include: flight announcements board; surveys and polls; class timetables; class attendance register.

Diagrams and charts

This kind of material, already extensively used in ESP (English for Specific Purposes) courses, can, with careful selection, be equally effective in general English classes.

Selected scenarios

— Family tree
Input: Prose description of family relations, e.g. history text (R) or clues given in conversation (L).
Task: Plot names on family tree, or draw tree itself.

— Flow charts
Input: Tour of factory showing how, for example, cars are made (L).
           Recipe instructions (R).
           Lecture on process, such as education system (L).
           Semi-technical texts on processes, e.g. photography, houseplant care, operating a washing machine, applying for a tax rebate (R).
           Bank clerk telling customer how to get traveller's cheques changed (L).
Task: Label and possibly complete diagram illustrating the process.

Other possibilities include: temperature and climate graphs/histograms; sociograms; pie graphs.

Diaries and calendars

Transfers involving plans, dates and times often give useful practice in discriminating numbers at less advanced levels.

Selected scenarios

— Office holidays
Input: Employees ask boss for permission to take their holidays at certain times (L).
           Employees write letter to boss on same subject (R).
Task: Plot holidays on Year Planner.

— *Personal engagements*

Input: Secretary tells boss his programme for the week (L). Some of this information may come in the form of letters or memos to be processed by the students (R).

Task: Enter details in authentic diary.

Other possibilities include: doctor's and dentist's appointment book; hotel register.

Note: Remember that some of these tasks can be very much simplified by giving some of the linguistic information to the students before asking them to do the listening task. For example in the second scenario, the engagements that are given orally by the secretary can also be given in jumbled order on the students' worksheet. Their task is then to recognise them and copy them into the right days of the week as they listen.

Miscellaneous lists, forms, coupons, etc.

The basic strategies used in the above scenarios can be extended and combined to suit a wide range of situations and visual formats.

Selected scenarios

— *Programme design*

Input: Conversation at theatre booking agency (L).
Radio ad. for play or film (L).

Task: Design a programme or poster giving full details about the play or film.

— *Menu prices*

Input: Dialogue between couple dining and waiter (L).
Gastronomic newspaper article (R).

Task: Write or complete details on menu.

— *Shopping list*

Input: Wife sending husband on errand (L).
Recipe instructions (R).

Task: Write shopping list.

Other possibilities include: car rental forms; list of dietary requirements.

4 Devising information-transfer tasks

It is probably easier to start with the authentic visual rather than with the input material and to construct the task around the visual. Suitable visual material can be found in encyclopaedias, publicity brochures, transport timetables, atlases, sociology or general science textbooks, *Time* and similar newspapers and magazines, as well as many EFL textbooks. Select a visual that will clearly provide material for the structure or language function you wish to teach or to practise in the follow-up to the initial reading or listening task. It may be necessary to adapt or rework the visual to suit the task, or simply to allow students enough space to write in the information, but an authentic diagram or table with information erased will probably provide greater motivation.

The input material should also be as realistic as possible. A passage of prose read aloud is unlikely to be suitable for a listening task, and a dialogue is equally inappropriate to a reading task. Ask students to listen for information they would reasonably expect to listen for in the real world, e.g. the facts in an argument about a car accident or a sociological lecture, the scores in a football results broadcast, the times, airlines, flight numbers and gatenumbers in an airport announcement. Apply the same kind of criteria to reading tasks and, in both cases, try to avoid artificial language or language situations. The railway enquiry clerk, for example, is most unlikely to give an enquirer the times of all the trains between London and Doncaster, or the times of their arrival at every intervening station, but in the course of several enquiries he or she might reasonably give out a fair amount of the information.

Finally, remember to test the material on yourself or your colleagues before letting your students loose on it. You are almost certain to find inaccuracies and ambiguities, as well as ways of improving or extending the task.

21

Reading in a foreign language at an elementary level

Mike Beaumont

Much has been written recently outlining the different types of reading activity a skilled reader engages in and the various cognitive skills involved in the reading process. But practical applications in the form of teaching materials have principally been directed at the more advanced levels of language learning. In the very early stages, teachers are concerned, necessarily, to develop the mechanical reading skills. As soon as students have these, however, the teacher can, and indeed should, move on as quickly as possible to practising the different types of reading activity and to developing the associated cognitive skills. Beginning this kind of work at the elementary level, students are more likely to become efficient readers than if such training is left until the more advanced stages.

1   Efficient reading

What, first of all, is the nature of efficient reading?
—It is purposeful. In general terms, we read either for information or for pleasure. First-language teachers recognise the latter. We second-language teachers often forget it.
—The type of reading varies according to the purpose. Crudely, we scan for specific information, rejecting the majority of what appears on the page because it is irrelevant to our needs; we skim, attempting

to extract the gist of a text; or we read intensively with the aim of decoding the whole of the writer's message.
—It progresses as quickly as the purpose requires. Efficient readers utilise the minimum number of semantic and syntactic clues to achieve their purpose.
—It is silent. Reading aloud is a specialised skill used, for example, by actors and newsreaders but seldom by the general reader. If it is used, its purpose is to communicate to another person a written message to which that person does not have access.
—It is text-based. Reading seldom involves the decoding of individual sentences isolated from context.
—It involves complex cognitive skills. Readers do not merely decode the message. They make predictions and inferences based on what they read; they may impose their own organisation on the information they extract. At a more sophisticated level, they react to what they read, assessing the accuracy of its facts, the value of its opinions, or the quality and appropriatness of its style.

For the purposes of illustration, consider children reading a poem in their native language, in this case English.

> The common cormorant or shag
> Lays eggs inside a paper bag
> The reason you will see no doubt
> It is to keep the lightning out.
> But what these unobservant birds
> Have never noticed is that herds
> Of wandering bears may come with buns
> And steal the bags to hold the crumbs.
> *Anon.*

Analysing the activity in terms of our six characteristics we find:
—The purpose is pleasure (presumably).
—The reading is intensive.
—The reading will proceed quite slowly bearing in mind the two preceding points.
—The initial reading will be silent though, if the children like the poem, they may wish to read it to somebody else and/or eventually learn to recite all or part of it.
—The poem constitutes a text, i.e. a coherent string of connected sentences.
—An example of the kind of prediction readers are likely to make as they go along is that the final word of the second line will be *bag*. This is done on the basis of what the reader knows about the conventions of rhyming and because of the limited number of nouns that, in this context, are likely to follow *paper*. Inferential skills may be called upon if, for example, the reader does not know what a *cormorant* or *shag* is. The fact that they lay eggs should lead to the inference that these are alternative names for a type of bird.

In terms of the readers' reaction to the text, they may object, for example, to the way in which the writer reinterprets the laws of nature, taking *paper* to be impervious to *lightning*. Of course, if they do object, then they are unlikely to find the poem very amusing. Alternatively, they may regard the rhyming of *crumbs* with *buns* as a flaw in the poet's style. And so on.

2 Techniques

Keeping these features of the reading process in mind can provide us with a range of techniques for developing the reading skills of a foreign-language learner at the elementary level. Consider the following matrix of information:

	windows	chimneys	trees	roof	door	gate
Sue	2	1	1	red	green	green
Linda	2	2	1	red	red	green
Mary	2	2	2	red	red	red
Jean	1	2	2	green	red	red
Teresa	1	1	2	green	green	red
Carol	1	1	1	green	green	green

From this, we can derive six paragraphs, each of which contains slightly different information:

Sue's house has two windows and one chimney. It has a red roof and a green door. It has one tree in the garden and a green garden gate.

Linda's house has two windows and two chimneys. It has a red roof and a red door. It has one tree in the garden and a green garden gate.

Mary's house has two windows and two chimneys. It has a red roof and a red door. It has two trees in the garden and a red garden gate.

Jean's house has one window and two chimneys. It has a green roof and a red door. It has two trees in the garden and a red garden gate.

Teresa's house has one window and one chimney. It has a green roof and a green door. It has two trees in the garden and a red garden gate.

Carol's house has one window and one chimney. It has a green roof and a green door. It has one tree in the garden and a green garden gate.

In the exercises that follow, I shall try to show how even material at this very simple level can be used to train different reading skills. In each case, the overall purpose of the reading is to extract information.

Skimming

Exercise 1
Read the paragraphs and write one word in each box.

There are ☐ paragraphs. How many?

Each paragraph is about a girl's ☐

Find two numbers. What are they? ☐ ☐

Find two colours. What are they? ☐ ☐

The completion of this task should provide the students with a good general idea of the content of the six paragraphs.

Scanning

Exercise 2
Write a girl's name in each box. Do it as quickly as possible.

Her house has two chimneys and a green gate. ▭

Her house has one chimney and a red roof. ▭
etc.

Write a colour in each box. Do it as quickly as possible.

Mary's house has a ▭ door.

Carol's house has a ▭ roof.
etc.

Intensive reading

Exercise 3
Write a girl's name in each box and colour the pictures.

N.B. Pictures used by the teacher would need to be coloured where appropriate.

Predictive and organisational skills

For each of these exercises (1–3), the development of the predictive skills will be assisted if the information is presented in the same order in each paragraph. This consistency of organisation will enable the readers to locate the information they require with increasing speed as they work their way through. If, however, we remove this consistency, for example

> Linda's house has a tree in the garden and a green garden gate. The door of her house is red. The roof is also red. Her house has two chimneys and two windows.

> Teresa's house has a green roof with one chimney. It has one window and a green door. The garden gate is red and her garden has two trees in it.   *etc.*

then not only will the student have to read more intensively, but reorganisational skills will also be required.

Inference

Exercise 4
Write a girl's name in each box.

Her favourite colour is green. ☐

Her house is very warm. ☐

Her favourite colour is red. ☐

Her house is very cold. ☐

Her chimneys are green. ☐

Her chimney is red. ☐

Clearly, the answers to this exercise are not so straightforward, and the teacher will want the students to justify the responses they make. They can do this quite satisfactorily, I would argue, using language similar to that of the text. In support of the answer *Carol*, for example, for the first sentence, a student can simply say *Her roof is green, her door is green, and her gate is green*. Another student may argue that the answer is *Teresa* because *Her roof is green, her door is green, and she has two trees in her garden*. There is no single right answer. It is the thought that counts, and the fact the students have to find, from their current language competence, the words to express it.

3 Conclusion

I am sure that there are other ways of exploiting this material for reading practice. The important thing is that every reading exercise we set our students, whatever their level, should have the clear aim of developing one or more of the specific subskills of reading and not just leave their development to chance.

22

Writing in class

Donn Byrne

1 Should students write in class?

Should we ask students to write in class? With a few exceptions, such as activities closely linked to some form of oral work (e.g. making notes during a listening exercise), most teachers will probably feel that class time should be almost entirely devoted to developing oral skills, for which their guidance or mediation is essential. Besides, time is short—and students can never get enough oral practice. Writing, on the other hand, can be conveniently given to the students as an out-of-class activity, to be done in their own time and at their own pace as homework, thus serving to increase the amount of language contact time.

On the whole, this point of view is sensible and it is not the purpose of this article to question the basic premise: that oral skills should get preference in the classroom. However if, in the long term, we want our students to learn to write acceptably, we need to consider whether there are some advantages in getting them to do a certain amount of writing in class and, if so, what kind of activities are appropriate.

Disadvantages of writing out of class

First, let us look at some of the *disadvantages* of treating writing mainly as an out-of-class activity:

—Students tend to see it as an institutional task imposed on them by the teacher. If they are at school, it is 'just another homework'; if they are mature students, it has all the overtones of 'school'. It has to be done whether they like it or not, and whether or not they have enough time to do it. In these circumstances, students rarely see writing as something which can be enjoyable.

—There are problems in identifying suitable tasks for homework. We can of course ask students to write 'exercises' (although not all modern coursebooks provide suitable ones for this purpose). We can attempt to devise something more ambitious—a piece of guided writing of some kind. But then, we are often up against the problem of length: a piece of homework has to be more or less substantial to make it worth setting, but it is not always easy to devise something relevant and interesting, especially in the early stages.

—It is difficult to devise activities which bring out the communicative value of writing. Even when students are asked to write something in the form of a letter, which has all the trappings of communication in that it is addressed *to* someone, in the eyes of the students it is still something *for* the teacher to look at and correct.

—There is no immediate 'feedback': the students carry out the task and hand it over to the teacher. By the time they get it back, even one lesson later, they have probably lost all interest in it, together with any suggestions the teacher may have for improving their writing.

I do not think it is possible to solve all these problems. Students *do* need homework, as an extension of the lesson, and some form of writing practice is one of the ways of meeting that need. Probably exercises of some kind, which reinforce what has been learnt orally and which do not *pretend* to be communicative, are best suited to that purpose in the early stages. At least, since they are exercises, it is appropriate for the teacher to *correct* them.

Advantages of writing in class

However, it is important for the students to begin to appreciate early on in a language course that writing is a form of communication and to learn how this is done through the written medium. This has to be done in the classroom because this is the only place we can provide them with someone to communicate with: that is, with one another.

In this respect, teaching writing is very similar to teaching oral skills. For oral work, we try to develop as much learner interaction as we can, not just a one-way flow between teacher and student. We get students to talk to *one another*: across the class, in pairs or in small groups. Although we may monitor these activities to a greater or lesser degree, since this is one of the roles of the teacher, gradually the students come to appreciate in this way that they can use the language to communicate for various purposes. The same can be true for writing; the students can be shown how it is used to obtain or exchange information, for example, or to get something done, if they use this medium to communicate with one another in the classroom.

2 Simple writing activities

Let us look at a very simple activity of this kind before analysing the advantages further. Let us imagine that the students have just been learning how to talk about their likes and dislikes with reference to a range of activities such as swimming, playing football, dancing, watching TV. They have practised this orally across the class and in pairs. It is at this point that a quick writing activity can be introduced: the students are asked to write notes to find out more about one another's likes and dislikes. Their notes can be based on a model like the one below:

```
                                        May 1, 19 . .
        Dear . . . . . ,

                Do you like . . . . . . . . . . ?

                                Yours,

                                . . . . . . . . . . . . .
```

The students can write half a dozen notes of this kind to one another in 3 or 4 minutes. By way of reply, they simply write *Yes* or *No* on the note and send it back. But they can also be asked to answer notes as well, thus setting up a flow of correspondence. For example:

```
Dear . . . . . ,                    May 1, 19 . .

        What do you like doing in your spare time?

                        Yours,

                        . . . . . . . . . . . .  .
```

The student who gets this note then answers:

```
Dear . . . . . ,                    May 1, 19 . .

        Thank you for your note. I like . . . . . . .
and . . . . . . . . . I don't like . . . . . . . . . .! What
about you?

                        Yours,

                        . . . . . . . . . . . .
```

The advantages of organizing a writing activity in this way should be apparent. The learners feel that they are communicating because they are in contact with someone through the written medium and because, in this case, they have used writing to find something out. And unlike many written tasks, they enjoy doing it!

Pedagogically, even through a simple activity of this kind, they are practising many of the essential features of a letter (which students often fail to learn even at more advanced stages of a language programme). It is possible, too, for them to ask you for advice or for you to check there and then what they have written. One of the best ways of checking is in fact to join in the activity yourself!

In terms of lesson organization, this short written phase can then be followed up with related oral practice. All the students have certain information about other students in the class which they can exchange—across the class, in pairs or in groups. The writing activity has also provided a welcome break from intensive oral work. It is perhaps sometimes forgotten how much of a strain it is for students to listen and talk all the time: a short break relieves the tension, and they can return to their oral activities refreshed and, one hopes, able to learn more effectively.

A variety of language items, structures or functions, can be practised through the exchange of short notes as illustrated above, ranging from simple enquiries such as:

Have you got a (pet/car)? (What is it like?)
Which month is your birthday in? / When exactly is your birthday?
What is your favourite (sport/TV programme/subject)?
Who is your favourite (actor/singer)?
What did you do (last night/over the weekend)?
I like your (sweater). Where did you buy it?

to requests and invitations:

Would you like to (play tennis) with me (on Saturday)?
Would you mind lending me (name of record/book) if you've got it?
Why don't we (go to the cinema together) (tonight)? If you're free,
please meet me at/in/on (name of place).

The students can also be asked to write short letters to one another. You
can give them an outline, like the one below:

May 1, 19 . .

Dear . . . . . ,

     Would you like to . . . . . *(+ activity)* on . . . . . *(+ day)*? If
you can come, please meet me . . . . . *(+ place & time)*. You can't
miss it, by the way: . . . . . *(+ exact location)*.

     Looking forward to seeing you!

                Yours,

                     . . . .

PS. Don't be late!

Or you can give them instructions such as: *Invite someone to do something
with you (such as going for a walk). Say exactly when and where you will meet.*

The person who receives the letter must write back accepting or
refusing the invitation—or perhaps making a counter-proposal.

So far I have described activities which involve students writing *to* one
another: they do not involve the exercise of any great writing skill, but
they are valuable because they demonstrate that writing is a way of
communicating and not just another tedious task. Children, by the way,
enjoy this form of writing activity just as much as adults.

3 Extensive writing activities

However, I should also like to give some examples of activities which
involve more extensive writing and for which the students have to
collaborate (at least at a certain stage of the activity). Once again, there
is a close parallel with oral work (the use of pairs and groups) and again
oral work and written work are interlinked, this time through a
discussion stage. These activities, taken from Donn Byrne: Teaching
Writing Skills (Longman 1979), are suitable for use at a post-elementary
level.

—Select from magazines a variety of ads for well-known products and
paste them on to cards. Ask each student in the class to choose one of
these ads and to write a short letter of complaint either about the
product or the ad.

Divide the class into groups, each representing a big firm
responsible for advertising a number of these products. Then
distribute the letters to the appropriate 'firms' and ask them to
discuss and write their replies. These should then be given to the
person who wrote the letter of complaint.

Note that the first stage of the activity can be done as homework.
However, the letters are not written *for* (or corrected by) the

teacher—they are *used* for a class activity. At the second stage, after the 'firms' have discussed their replies, the students may work in pairs on the actual letter. You must, by the way, organize the work in class so that students do not deal with their own letters of complaint!

—Divide the class into groups. Ask each group to draw up a notice on a given topic: for example, starting a pop group or a club; starting a protest against . . .; raising money for . . . At least two groups should work on the same task, so that they can compare their notices. They might then be asked to write a final notice, combining the best ideas from each.

—Divide the class into groups. Give each group the job of describing one feature of their town, such as:
—places of interest
—good places to eat at
—entertainment facilities
—sports facilities
—local industries.

Each group should then write their description in such a way that the feature described sounds attractive to someone visiting the town. Each student should also make a copy of the description. Then form new groups, making sure that they contain at least one representative from each of the original groups, and ask them to write a full report on their town based on these descriptions. The report may be accompanied by a map showing the location of the various places of interest (etc).

—Divide the class into groups and ask each group to decide on some action they would take to improve their town—for example, pulling down a certain building, providing a facility of some kind (such as a new swimming pool), widening a street. Each group should then announce, in the form of a press report, what they propose to do.

Each student in the class is then invited to respond to one or more of these proposals: for example, by writing a letter to the press; by writing, in collaboration with one or more other students, a public protest or a notice calling for a meeting to protest against the proposal; or by writing an anonymous letter to one of the people concerned with a certain proposal. Writing anonymous letters is an activity which students really enjoy! Note that for this second stage, the students can select the kind of activity which most appeals to them. They can also do it as a homework, although not one to be 'corrected' by the teacher but to be read by their fellow students.

4 Conclusion

Should we ask students to write in class? I think the answer to this question should be a qualified *yes*. There is room in most lessons for short writing activities of the kind I described in the first part of this article, which not only provide a welcome alternative to intensive oral work (at the same time offering opportunities for using what has been learnt in this way) but also show the learners that they can communicate through the medium of writing. And there is room, although less often perhaps, because these activities take up time, for writing activities that form a natural part of a role play activity or small scale simulation. An important feature of both these types of activity is that they involve learner interaction. For it would certainly be a waste of valuable class time if we asked students to do on their own in the classroom the kind of written work which they can do on their own out of class.

23

Reading, writing and communication

Ron White

It is very difficult to learn to write without reading examples of written communications which provide a model or guide. It is also difficult for students of EFL to produce some kinds of composition—such as expository writing—which differ from the types of writing they are familiar with in their own language. There is, however, one type of writing which is a more universal type of discourse, and that is narrative. As Dubin and Olshtain (1980) point out, 'the sequence of elements is the most apparent in the narrative' because, of course, 'the basic organizational structure of a narrative is chronological' (Howe 1972, cited by Dubin and Olshtain).

It is to the teaching of narrative writing that I will now turn. There are two main aspects of narrative which I suggest focusing on: firstly, chronological sequence, and secondly, the past tense. We are able, in the teaching of narrative, to combine three fundamental elements: *function* (reporting), *form* (the past tense or preterite) and *notion* (sequence). In addition to these elements, we can also introduce the exploitation of authentic texts, that is of language written originally for communication in a non-pedagogical context.

The text I will take by way of illustration is a newspaper report of a court case (see the end of this article for the complete text). The headline is as follows:

CONTEH, THE DRIVER, BANNED FOR A YEAR

We begin by asking students who they think Conteh is. Naturally, most of them say he is a driver. We then tell them to read on.

Boxer John Conteh was banned from driving for a year yesterday after a court heard how his Rolls Royce collided with six cars in London's West End.

The students now learn that Conteh is a boxer and so some discussion follows as to why the newspaper referred to him as *the driver*. We also note that six cars were collided with, so the accident must have been rather spectacular (not to mention that Conteh's own car was a Rolls Royce!).

We continue with the second paragraph of the report, and the students are told to underline three things: (a) the names of the places where the accident occurred, (b) the speed of Conteh's car and (c) the time of the accident.

> The collisions in <u>Piccadilly</u> and nearby
> <u>Duke Street</u>, <u>St James</u>, were described by
> Mr Kenneth Dow, prosecuting. He said one
> witness estimated the speed of Mr Conteh's
> Rolls Royce as about <u>80 mph</u> as he drove
> along <u>Piccadilly</u> at <u>3 am</u> on November 23rd
> last year.

Having established the location and time of events, we now go on to the action in detail. As will be clear from the extracts, the range of vocabulary and structures is outside that of most pre-intermediate students. This, however, is of little importance if we concentrate on features of the text which the students can easily recognise. In the present case, the names of the cars are the easily recognised element in the text, so we focus the students' attention on these by telling them to ring and number the names of the cars in sequence.

> The first collision was with a silver
> (BMW.)¹ It was dented and scratched along
> its offside. Then he hit (a Mercedes,)²
> damaging its rear bumper and denting and
> scratching it.
>
> The driver of (the next car)³ Mr Conteh
> hit was thrown on to his passenger as
> his seat collapsed. Mr Conteh then
> pulled across the road and hit (a Ford Escort)⁴
> and swung back and struck (a Hillman)⁵ parked
> on the foot-path. Mr Dow said the
> Rolls Royce then veered across Piccadilly into
> Duke Street, St James , where it hit (a Lancia.)⁶

We can list the names of the cars on the blackboard, like this:

—a BMW	—a Ford Escort
—a Mercedes	—a Hillman
—the next car	—a Lancia

Then we can ask the students to find all the words (i.e. verbs) which tell (a) what Mr Conteh and his car did, and (b) what happened to the other cars. We can then build up the information on the blackboard like this:

	A BMW was hit and scratched.
He hit	a Mercedes. It was dented and scratched.
He hit	the next car. The driver was thrown on to his passenger.
He hit	a Ford Escort.
He struck	a Hillman.
He hit	a Lancia.

Some attention can be given to the different verbs of movement used in the report: *pulled across, swang back, veered across.* The next step is to find out why Conteh crashed into the cars (even though we already know that he was going very fast for a street in the middle of London). The students are told to read the next paragraph and to underline all the verbs.

> Mr Anthony Edwards, for Mr Conteh, said
>
> the boxer <u>had hit</u> some of the vehicles
>
> when he <u>swerved to avoid</u> another car
>
> <u>pulling</u> in front of him. He <u>had</u> then
>
> <u>had</u> difficulty controlling the Rolls.

In the construction *swerved to avoid*, the *to* + verb structure indicates reasons or cause.

Having picked out the main sequence of events in the report, we now transfer this information to a plan. The students' task is to plot the path of Conteh's Rolls Royce on a plan of Piccadilly, numbering in sequence and naming the vehicles with which he collided. Next, the students use this plan to reconstruct the story of events. At this point the text is removed, although the verbs—or synonyms suggested by the students—could be left on the blackboard as a further cue.

We have now reached the writing phase of the lesson. This form of writing is essentially a reconstruction of the original report, in a simplified or modified form, though preserving the sequence of events and content.

The next step is to move on to parallel writing in which new information is provided. Even more important, though, is to give the students a writing task in which (a) they have a reader other than the teacher in mind, and (b) there is a chance for them to convey or exchange information with a partner. This can be done by dividing the class into A and B groups or pairs. Group A is given one plan on which is displayed information about an accident, while group B is given a plan showing a different accident. The students' first task is to report on the accident depicted in their own plan. The reports are then exchanged with a partner. Next, the students use their partner's report to draw a plan of their partner's accident.

We can summarise this as follows:

Student/Group A
—Writes report of the accident shown in Plan 1.
—Gives the report to B.
—Reads B's report.
—Draws a plan based on B's report.
—Compares the plan with B's original map.

Student/Group B
—Writes report of the accident shown in Plan 2.
—Gives the report to A.
—Reads A's report.
—Draws a plan based on A's report.
—Compares the plan with A's original map.

—Discusses inconsistencies, difficulties with B.

—Discusses inconsistencies, difficulties with A.

This procedure has a number of important features. Firstly, the students have a 'real' reader for whom they are writing. (Teachers are not 'real' readers.) Secondly, the writer is accountable to the reader. In other words, if an inadequate report is written, the reader will not be able to draw a complete plan and can then come back to the writer and criticize the inadequacy of the report and ask for more information and clarification. The inadequacy of the report may stem from inaccurate language (e.g. the incorrect use of prepositions indicating spatial relationships) or confusion over sequence (e.g. reporting events in a sequence which is inconsistent with the items located on the original plan).

So, then, the sequence of steps I have described link reading and writing, and lead from controlled reconstruction to controlled communication. Another important feature of the example just described is the use of an authentic text. Even though some of the language is well beyond the level of many students, the activities which they are asked to perform are within the range even of a beginner. This may help to illustrate that difficulty is not in the language but in the tasks that students are asked to perform. The principle to keep in mind here is a simple one: if the language is easy, give the students a difficult task; if the language is difficult, give them an easy task. (I am indebted to Evelyn Davies and Norman Whitney for formulating this distinction so succinctly.)

Conteh, the driver, banned for a year

Boxer John Conteh was banned from driving for a year yesterday after a court heard how his Rolls Royce collided with six cars in London's West End.

It was a "very bad case" of reckless driving, chief metropolitan magistrate Evelyn Russell told the former world light heavyweight champion.

At Bow Street Magistrates' Court, Mr Conteh (27), pleaded guilty to reckless driving and failing to stop after an accident. He was also fined a total of £850 and ordered to pay £40 costs.

Two other charges of careless driving and failing to report an accident were not proceeded with.

The collisions in Piccadilly and nearby Duke Street, St James, were described by Mr Kenneth Dow, prosecuting. He said one witness estimated the speed of Mr Conteh's Rolls Royce at about 80 mph as he drove along Piccadilly at 3 a.m. on November 23 last year.

The first collision was with a Silver BMW. It was dented and scratched along its offside. Then he hit a Mercedes, damaging its rear bumper and denting and scratching it.

The driver of the next car Mr Conteh hit was thrown on to his passenger as his seat collapsed. Mr Conteh then pulled across the road and hit a Ford Escort and swung back and struck a Hillman parked on the footpath. Mr Dow said the Rolls Royce then veered across Piccadilly into Duke Street, St James, where it hit a Lancia.

Mr Anthony Edwards, for Mr Conteh, said the boxer had hit some of the vehicles when he swerved to avoid another car pulling in front of him. He had then had difficulty controlling the Rolls.

Mr Edwards said that Mr Conteh "very much regretted" the inconvenience caused to the owners of the cars.

Mr Conteh, who fights Matt Franklin for the world light heavyweight title on August 18 said after the hearing that his wrist, which he injured in the collisions, was now better.

References

Howe, James, *The Making of Style*. Philadelphia: Chilton Book Co. (1972)

Dubin, Fraida & Olshtain, Elite, 'The Interface of Writing and Reading', *TESOL Quarterly*, Vol XIV, No. 3 (September, 1980).

24

Notes, summaries and compositions — Part II

David Cranmer

1   Introduction

In my article on page 75 I suggested that notes, summaries and compositions should be considered not in isolation but as part of an input-output system, with either texts or thoughts as *input* going through a note stage prior to *output* either as a summary or composition. In addition I drew two distinctions: between *note-taking* (the taking of notes from a text) and *note-making* (the making of notes in preparation for writing a text), and between *chronologically sequenced* texts (those that contain a time sequence) and *non-chronologically sequenced* texts (those that do not). The latter distinction was shown to be crucial to the teaching of extended writing because the different types of text would require different treatment.

This article sets out to give an idea of some teaching techniques for chronologically sequenced texts and simple non-chronologically sequenced texts.

2   A simple non-chronologically sequenced text

I choose to begin with *Describing People* because it is simple both in language content (which means you can teach it at very low levels) and in organisation (which means I can show you, and you can show your students, the most basic properties and uses of brain-patterns). Look at this simple description of someone:

Bill is in his early thirties. He's tall, slim and good-looking. He has brown hair, blue eyes and a moustache.

This will serve us as a model for analysis and later for production.

Analysis

In terms of language content, the description consists of three sentences, which involve the use of adjectives, nouns, the subject pronoun *he* and the two verbs *be* and *have*. The only slightly complicated expression is *in his early thirties*. In terms of organisation, it is also straightforward. The overall topic may be identified as *Bill*. Various aspects of him are mentioned: his age, height, build, looks, hair, eyes and distinctive features. So let us now proceed to making the brain-pattern.

Making a brain-pattern

Bill, as the topic, must go in the centre of the brain-pattern and the various aspects should radiate from that centre. The brain-pattern could look like this:

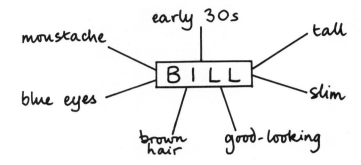

(*Note:* There is no rigid format for brain-patterns; they can, and indeed should, be modified to serve our purposes, as servant not master.)

This pattern contains all the information we are given about Bill, and for a native speaker would be quite adequate. As a tool for language teaching, however, there are many things we can do to improve it.

How many times have your students written *He has 30 years*, using the wrong verb, or *He is in early 30s* and many other variants with the wrong preposition or without the possessive (mistakes a native-speaker would not make)? The correct forms can be put into the brain-pattern too. Furthermore, you can indicate what information belongs in which sentence, and the order within each sentence, simply by numbering/lettering the items accordingly:

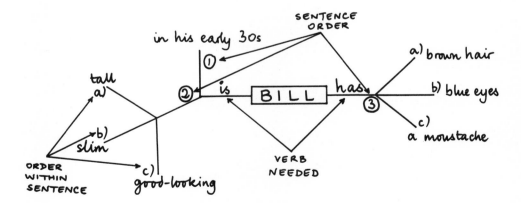

So far so good, but where does it get us, apart from teaching students to analyse? Well, this in itself is no bad thing, for it has enabled us to draw their attention to the use of *be* and *have* in describing people and to the idea that the aspects of the description are not in purely random order. Next, however, I would want to revise and add 'describing people' vocabulary as a preliminary to letting the students make their own descriptions. Traditionally, at this point, lists of 'describing people' words would be elicited and added to, written on the board and copied into the students' notebooks. But instead of just a series of lists, why not store the information in a brain-pattern, a master brain-pattern derived from the 'Bill' brain-pattern? It would look something like this:

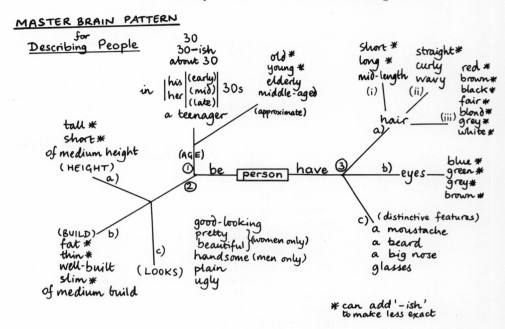

The advantages of displaying the information like this are manifold. Here are some of them:

(a) How all these vocabulary items relate to the original description of Bill is clear, because the Bill brain-pattern is constantly there in the background as a reminder.

(b) Because of point (a), we never lose sight of which items follow *be* and which follow *have*.

(c) New organisational information can also be added, simply by extending the brain-pattern. Notice how the order of adjectives before *hair* has been indicated, using the same type of number system as elsewhere in the diagram (*long, straight, brown hair* not *straight, brown, long hair*).

(d) Most importantly, the information can be retrieved and put into a new description easily, because the vocabulary, the grammar and the organisation are all displayed in one place, instead of grammar rules being in one place, vocabulary lists in another and very likely no organisation existing at all.

Production

I would now get the students to choose items from the master brain-pattern and display them in a Bill-type brain-pattern. Then I would draw their attention to the original prose description of Bill, reminding them to use a subject pronoun (instead of *Bill*) in sentences 2 and 3, and to use commas and *and* correctly. They would now be ready to write their own descriptions.

You may feel that this is a very long-winded method of producing 'parallel writing'. The students could surely produce the same new descriptions without all this brain-pattern business. To a certain extent this may be true. I would argue, however, that the extra time spent on producing the brain-patterns is small and well worth it. This is not only in terms of the four advantages I cited above. Because the lay-out of a brain-pattern is visual, and visual memory is better than verbal, retention of the information (lexical, grammatical and organisational) is better. Most important of all, the mental discipline involved in producing and working from this simple brain-pattern is the ideal training for the organisation of the much more complex types of texts the students will be required to write in years to come (free compositions, etc.), where they will have no parallel text to guide them. (*Note:* Similar brain-patterns can be made for describing things and places.)

3 Note-taking/making & summary of a chronologically sequenced text

Unlike the use of brain-patterns for simple description, which can be taught at a very low level, note-taking and summary need to wait until students have an adequate basic grasp of the language, i.e. they should be working on material the grammar and vocabulary of which do not in themselves present an obstacle. Because the progression of time is conceptually simpler than other types of logical progression, it is best to begin with chronologically sequenced texts. Of these, only narrative is suitable for note-taking and summary, since instructions and accounts of processes normally contain little information that can be left out, while narrative typically includes not only a central event sequence, but a substantial amount of description.

The key to reducing a chronologically sequenced text is to find the sequence and discard the rest. (A narrative lacking descriptive detail remains a narrative, but take away some of the events and you are left with nonsense.) Biography (a variety of narrative) is the ideal text-type with which to introduce students to summarising techniques because the principal events can be located simply by pinpointing the dates. I would suggest that mid-intermediate students could usefully tackle the note-taking/making and summary of biography.

Choosing a text

To teach the techniques initially, the ideal text is one with about half a dozen dates (preferably giving the date of birth, death and other central events). From my own experience, suitable texts are not difficult to find, so do not force a text that does not really work—look for another. Below is an example of a typical text which I shall use to demonstrate my note-taking/making and summary techniques.

William Shakespeare

When William Shakespeare was baptised on 26th April 1564 at Holy Trinity Church, Stratford-upon-Avon, no-one could have guessed that he would become the most famous writer of all time—that his works would be translated into dozens of language, performed in virtually every country of the world, and for hundreds of years. And yet, in spite of his fame, our knowledge of much of his life remains extremely limited.

To begin with, although by tradition Shakespeare's birthday is celebrated on 23rd April, the exact date is in fact unknown. Nor, indeed, do we know any more about his childhood. We can only presume that he lived with his family in Stratford and attended the local grammar school. At the age of 18 he married Anne Hathaway, a farmer's daughter eight years older than he was, and they had three children during the next three years.

From then on there is another gap, of around seven years, about which nothing is known for certain. According to some sources he went to sea, and this would explain how he was able to write so imaginatively about storms and shipwrecks. Others say that he used to poach deer from the Lucy Estate at Charlecote, a village near Stratford, and that he left for London to escape prosecution. Whatever is the case, by 1592 he was already a well-established actor and playwright in London.

In 1594 he joined the newly-formed Lord Chamberlain's Company, which performed plays at the Globe Theatre. This theatre, like most others of its time, was a tall, round building, consisting of a stage surrounded on three sides by the audience, who either stood immediately in front of the stage or sat in the balconies which lined the walls. The theatre was open-air, which meant that the theatre-season was determined by the weather and, as there was no lighting, all performances took place in the afternoons.

Of all his plays, *The Tempest* is generally considered to be the greatest. It was finished in 1612 and is the last play which he completed. It combines a strong plot, a varied group of characters and a balance of comedy and seriousness. It covers a whole range of emotions and raises questions about revenge and freedom.

The last years of his life were spent in retirement at Stratford-upon-Avon, where he had bought considerable amounts of land through the wealth his fame had brought him. He died in 1616 on 23rd April, the same date as his traditional birthday.

Note-taking

So that the students get a general idea of the text they are working on, give them five minutes to read it. Give them no longer, otherwise they will look at detail instead of gist. Also give then a quick task that either tests global understanding or requires them to get to the end quickly; e.g. in this case ask 'Which is considered to be Shakespeare's greatest play?'

After the first reading, get the students to draw up four columns in their notebooks and head them *Date—Subject—Event—Completion* (the first three taking up the left-hand half of the page, the Completion taking up the right). Give them the first note but in the wrong order, e.g. *was baptised 26 April 1564 Stratford-upon-Avon William Shakespeare*. The students must decide which parts of the note are which and put them in the right column:

Date	*Subject*	*Event*	*Completion*
26 April 1564	William Shakespeare	was baptised	Stratford-upon-Avon

Now get the students to pick out and write down the remaining dates. As we are dealing with a chronologically sequenced text, these should be written linearly, one below the other, thus reflecting the innately linear nature of the progression of time. (I suggest that, to avoid problems with vocabulary such as *poach, deer, escape* and *prosecution*, it is best, with this particular text, to include only the information about Shakespeare that is known for certain.) This will give you, in addition to '26 April 1564', *1582, 1592, 1594, 1612* and *23 April 1616*. Suggest that the students use WS as an abbreviation for William Shakespeare, and point out the verb form used for an event in the past (past simple). N.B. Warn the students that *was born*, unlike most of the other 'event' verbs of the text, is passive. The students now add the subject and event to the dates they already have—insist on just the verb for the event, nothing more. This will give you, in addition to 'WS was baptised', *WS married, WS was, WS joined, 'The Tempest' was finished* and *WS died.*

Whereas the Date, Subject, and Event are very straightforward, the Completion requires some skill, and what should or should not be included is to a large extent subjective. Generally only up to about four words are necessary—just enough to complete the sentence grammatically—articles and possessive adjectives normally being omitted. The notes with Completions should look something like this:

Date	Subject	Event	Completion
26 April 1564	WS	was baptised	Stratford-upon-Avon
1582	WS	married	Anne Hathaway
1592	WS	was	already actor/ playwright in London
1594	WS	joined	Lord Chamberlain's Company
1612	The Tempest	was finished	(greatest play)
23 April 1616	WS	died	Stratford-upon-Avon

(My inclusion of 'greatest play' in the 1612 Completion is to explain why *The Tempest* rather than any other play is mentioned.)

Note-making

Unlike notes taken from a text, which look backwards at that text and reflect its structure, notes made in preparation for a new text look forwards and determine or, as in this case, are determined by the structure of the new text. With chronologically sequenced texts, this presents no great problem because the time sequence must always remain the same.

One change, however, often needs to be made: an *active→passive, passive→active, passive→passive* transformation. The reason for this is that, in a good paragraph, the topic should remain the same throughout and if possible should be the subject of each sentence in the paragraph. In this respect, there is often a conflict between the original text, which, since it consists of several paragraphs, deals with several (albeit related) topics, and the summary, which, since it will be of only one paragraph, should have only one topic, in this case 'William Shakespeare'. With our Shakespeare text the problem arises only once, with the penultimate paragraph and the note it has generated:

1612 'The Tempest'   was finished   (greatest play)

Unlike the other notes, the subject is *The Tempest*, not WS. A passive→active transformation solves the problem very simply, producing instead:

1612 WS   finished   'The Tempest' (greatest play)

Now the topic 'William Shakespeare' is the subject of this and the other notes, and so will become the subject of every sentence in the summary.

Here are some similar transformations which have been found necessary in other texts I have worked on:

(a) In a text about Marco Polo:

Kublai Khan	*sent*	*Marco Polo*	*as envoy to various countries.*
MP	*was sent*	*by KK*	*as envoy to various countries.*

(active→passive, to make Marco Polo the subject).

(b) In a text about Alexander Fleming:
1945   Nobel Prize   was given   to AF.
1945   AF   was given   Nobel Prize.
(passive→passive, to make Alexander Fleming the subject).

Making the summary

To write a good summarising paragraph about Shakespeare, it is not enough simply to make notes into sentences, for this will only produce a sequence of sentences, not a paragraph. A paragraph must contain variety and yet form a unified whole. The simplest way to produce variety is to vary the position of the time phrase: elicit from the students where else it could go. (Answer: at the end of the sentence.) Also elicit whether it makes a difference. (Answer: generally no, but for the first sentence the time phrase is best last so that William Shakespeare, the topic, can open the paragraph.)

To create unity, it is necessary to use various cohesive devices. The first and most obvious is to use *he* instead of *William Shakespeare* in the second and succeeding sentences. Another simple way is the judicious joining of closely related sentences with *and*. A useful way of varying and unifying at the same time is to replace the date by *after N years* or *N years later* where the two events have a clear relationship. The 1594 sentence lends itself well to this treatment.

The final summary would look something like this:

A summary of William Shakespeare's life.

William Shakespeare was baptised in Stratford-upon-Avon on 26th April 1564. In 1582 he married Anne Hathaway. He was already an actor and playwright in London by 1592 and two years later he joined the Lord Chamberlain's Company. In 1612 he finished *The Tempest*, his greatest play. He died in Stratford-upon-Avon on 23rd April 1616.

What have we achieved?

First, and most obviously, we have produced a summary. Additionally, however, we have achieved many other things, enough to make the exercise worthwhile even for those who do not consider note-taking and summary worth doing in their own right.

Structures
—We have revised the use of the past simple for past events in a more advanced task than when we initially taught it, thereby not insulting our students' knowledge.
—We have revised active↔passive transformations, actually giving a reason for the transformation, not just as a manipulative exercise.
—We have revised the position of adverbs of time, again giving reasons why they might be better in the one position rather than the other.

Skills
—We have practised the two types of speed-reading: skimming for gist (the first reading of the text) and scanning for particular information (locating the dates in the second reading).
—We have practised structuring a paragraph in such a way that the information is clear, with the topic made plain at the beginning of the first sentence and with succeeding sentences adding supporting information.
—We have given practice in using some of the cohesive features of a well-written paragraph.

4 Planning a narrative composition

Many people (including a lot of my students) feel that there is no point in making a plan for a composition. All sorts of arguments are put forward to avoid writing one. Some say that the time and effort required are too great; others say that it constricts their spontaneity or that they can in any case plan perfectly adequately in their heads. It is my belief that these are just excuses hiding a number of problems and misconceptions. The two obvious problems are ignorance and laziness. I say that without intending any insult or value judgment; it is simply that many students have never been taught how to plan and human beings innately try to get out of anything that requires time and effort. The misconceptions concern the amount of time and effort needed (which, as well shall see, are slight) the type of plan (which need not constrict spontaneity) and total inexperience of planning on paper, thus making a virtue of the necessity of planning in the head.

Narrative composition, unlike non-chronologically sequenced composition, is not so complex in organisation that the content in itself requires a plan. (The sequence of events ensures a basic logic.) I believe that a plan is still useful, however, in that it focuses the mind on the task in hand. Let me briefly illustrate the kind of plan I have in mind by discussing two very different actual plans which students of mine have written, and which could act as models.

A highly structured plan

Written by a girl in preparation for a composition entitled 'A funny thing happened to me last week . . .'

—*got up late*
—*didn't have time to have breakfast*
—*went to a café*
—*bought a cake*
—*the dog ate the cake*

(Notice that these notes are also linear, reflecting the structure of the composition to be written.) Here she has very quickly (this plan might take 2 minutes to write) recorded the principal events (simple past verb plus a brief completion), while allowing plenty of scope to add descriptive detail later (about the café, cake, dog, her mood etc.). This type of plan is ideal for the weaker or less imaginative student (though this girl was neither) because of two features. First, by getting the plot written down at the planning stage, the student's mind is left freer to concentrate on correct *language* at the composition stage instead of having to worry about what comes next in the story. Second, because these notes include the event verbs, this crucial element of the story can be checked: Are they the right tense? Is the form of the irregular verbs right? Here is an excellent opportunity to exploit self-correction, by reminding the students about the verbs at this stage, before they embark on the composition proper.

A free plan

Written by a boy in the same class in preparation for a composition entitled 'A mysterious tale'.

Introduction: (*How I got there and why the house is haunted*)
Body: *What happened (I don't know yet)*
Conclusion: (*The end of the story and how I got away*)

Like the highly structured plan, this one was written very quickly and focused the writer's mind on the basic plot. It differs, however, in that, by not recording every event, it allows for much greater spontaneity and imagination. (No-one could reasonably describe this plan as constricting.) For the bright, imaginative student who has little difficulty in the control of language (as in the case of the boy who wrote this plan), this type of plan is clearly preferable.

But does a plan really result in a better composition? All I can say is that when I have asked students in class to write a composition, advising them to make a plan (which I want to see), those who have done so, however brief the plan, almost without exception write better compositions than those who have not. (There are always bright but lazy students who refuse to write a plan but write well nevertheless.) From my own experience—I never wrote plans till three years ago—writing from a plan is so much easier than trying to fill a blank page from a blank mind.

25

Notes, summaries and compositions — Part III

David Cranmer

In this third article I shall be looking at more complex non-chronologically sequenced texts, of the kind that students of intermediate level upwards are required to handle.

1 Traditional approaches

There are two approaches to summary currently in practice. The first, and very much the more common, I shall call the text-reduction approach. This consists of underlining the 'important' parts and crossing out the 'unimportant' ones (without a clear definition of which are which), so that you are left simply with a cut version of the original text. Its principal features are that it involves a process of contraction, necessarily following the structure and wording of the original text (and thus uncreative) and that it reduces the text only to a rather limited degree (to about half the original length).

The second approach I shall call the paragraph approach. This consists of identifying the topic of each paragraph and writing a single sentence about it, drawing in the main points of that paragraph. Although it is more creative than the text-reduction approach, since you are not required to use the exact wording of the original text, it still follows the structure of the original text rigidly, the order of the sentences in the summary religiously following the order of the paragraphs in the original text. It does, of course, allow for a much shorter summary than the text-reduction approach but, in doing so, gives all paragraphs equal weight. This means that a paragraph with many important points is treated in the same way as one that merely illustrates something trivial.

I would like to propose a third approach, which will enable us to produce summaries of varying lengths, flexible in structure, creative in wording, with the ideas given the right weight and properly related to each other.

2   The brain-pattern approach

Unlike the text-reduction and paragraph approaches which move more or less directly from text to summary, the brain-pattern approach, in line with the input-output system I described on page 75, has a crucial note stage—notes taken from the text are displayed in a brain-pattern and then made suitable for the summary to follow. Let me demonstrate and explain the procedure with an example text.

First the student must read the text through quickly (skimming) to establish two things: the topic of the text and its overall structure (how many principal sections there are and how they are related).

Nothing Succeeds Like Excess

by Roy Blake

When we read about the great days of Hollywood in the 1930s, it seems incredible that the studios could have spent so much money and employed so many stars. But when we realise what the people in charge of the studios were like, it is surprising that they made any good films at all.

Almost all the owners of the big film companies had come to America as salesmen and suddenly realised that they could make a lot of money from films. They owned the production companies and the cinemas as well as the studios, so they were so powerful that no one could make a successful film without them. In private life, they were such ignorant, unattractive people that their employees thought they were monsters. There are so many amusing stories about them that we sometimes forget that they had such a dangerous influence on the cinema for such a long time.

Carl Laemmle of Universal was a family man. He employed so many of his relations that when he died, seventy of them were working for the company. Samuel Goldwyn never learnt to speak English properly. 'I can answer you in two words,' he said once: 'im possible'. Harry Cohn of Columbia had a nasty sense of humour; he gave his visitors electric shocks by pressing a button connected to their chairs. Everyone hated Louis B. Mayer so much that when someone asked Goldwyn why so many people had come to his funeral, he said, 'They want to make sure he's dead.'

'Gone with the Wind' is probably the most famous Hollywood film of this period. The story of how Vivien Leigh was chosen for the star role of Scarlett O'Hara illustrates the title of this article. The studio interviewed 1,400 girls for the part. They made so many screen tests that the test film was almost as long as 'Gone with the Wind' itself. But when the producer, David O. Selznick, began shooting the picture, he still had not found the right actress. He was going to start by filming the burning of Atlanta. He waited for an hour because his brother Myron was late. Finally everyone got so impatient that he had to start without him. The enormous imitation city was set on fire. Then Myron arrived and introduced him to Vivien Leigh. 'I want you to meet Scarlett O'Hara,' he said.

'Gone with the Wind' was so successful that it ran for three years in London. You can still see it in cinemas today. Vivien Leigh won an Oscar. She gave such an outstanding performance that she was more famous than her husband, Sir Laurence Olivier, for a long time. But all the previous screen tests must have seemed a terrible waste of money.

It was not quite as simple for Vivien Leigh as it sounds. She had to do a test with three other actresses before she got the part. But she had two great advantages. She was a very beautiful, talented young woman. And Myron Selznick was her agent!

The topic is 'The great days of Hollywood' (not 'Owners of film companies', nor 'Gone with the Wind' etc.). After a brief introduction, there are two principal sections. They both relate to the central topic but do not otherwise relate to each other.

We are now ready to begin a brain-pattern. The topic goes in the centre. A line extends out on either side, one for each principal section. The sub-topics of the two sections, having been identified (as 'Owners of the film companies' and 'Most famous film—*Gone with the Wind*'), are written at the end of each line. We must now find something to say about the central topic and sub-topics. When were the great days? Who were the owners? Who starred in *Gone with the Wind*? The answers are added to the brain-pattern at the end of another line. The brain-pattern would look like this:

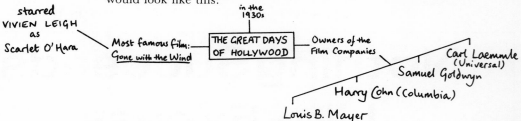

Precisely where the lines are to be placed and which items should be written at the end of which lines depends on a combination of the structure of the text and individual discretion. In the absence of a text requiring some other pattern, I prefer to start at the top and work clockwise round, but one could equally begin at the bottom or one of the sides and/or work round anti-clockwise. The above diagram already provides us with a minimal summary, consisting of a topic sentence (central topic + comment) and two secondary sentences (main sub-topics + comments):

The great days of Hollywood were in the 1930s. Among the owners of the film companies were Carl Laemmle (Universal), Samuel Goldwyn, Harry Cohn (Columbia) and Louis B. Mayer. The most famous film of the period was *Gone with the Wind*, which starred Vivien Leigh as Scarlet O'Hara.

In this summary, we may be certain we have included central elements precisely because we have started at the centre. However, the summary is only 48 words long and, while it is adequate for a very general outline or to fulfil the instructions 'Write a summary of not more than 50 words', plenty has been omitted. No problem. All we have to do is add another layer of information to the brain-pattern and thence to the summary.

What else do we know about the film owners in general? And the individual owners? What about the popularity of *Gone with the Wind*? What else are we told about Vivien Leigh? We can add these pieces of information to the brain-pattern at the end of further lines, so that we can easily see that they form an additional layer.

Since we have now more than doubled the information we have drawn from the text, to write a summary straight away is not so easy. We need to think about paragraphing. We also, I believe, need to think about the order of the sentences, for what may have been the best order in the original text will not necessarily be the best order in the summary. The summary, while obviously reflecting the original text, is not the original text but a separate text in its own right, organically generating its own logic and therefore structure. This being so, the notes we have taken will now have to be made suitable for a summary.

Firstly, then, let us decide about paragraphs. The natural division is into two, the first containing the topic sentence and the information about the owners, the second containing information about the famous film. Secondly, we must order the sentences (by numbering them) and decide what pieces of information should go in the same sentence, also deciding, and if necessary indicating, how to join these pieces of information (with 'and', 'who', 'which' etc.).

That done, just as with chronologically sequenced summaries, we have to perform active → passive transformations wherever to do so will enable us to maintain the topic as the grammatical subject (see page 103 for an explanation of this). In our Hollywood text two cases clearly call for this information: *Everyone hated Louis B. Mayer* → *Louis B. Mayer was hated by everyone* and *You can still see it (Gone with the Wind)* → *It can still be seen* (because we are interested in Louis B. Mayer and *Gone with the Wind* not 'everyone' and 'you'). For similar reasons, a change from *Myron Selznick was her agent* to *Her agent was Myron Selznick* is desirable (to link the grammatical subject 'Her agent' to the topic). With all these note-making decisions indicated on the brain-pattern, it will ultimately look like this:

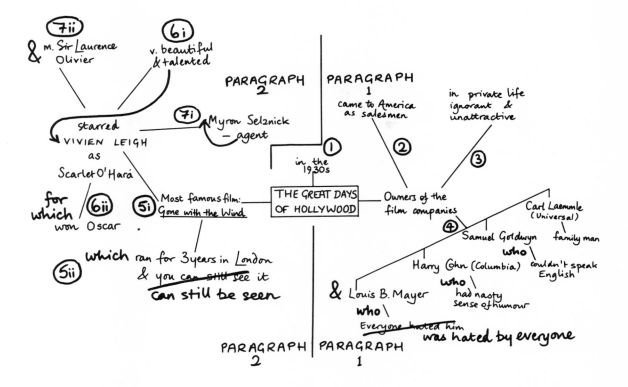

and this will be the summary:

The great days of Hollywood were in the 1930s. The owners of the film companies came to America as salesmen. In private life they were ignorant and unattractive. Among them were Carl Laemmle (Universal), a family man, Samuel Goldwyn, who could not speak English properly, Harry Cohn (Columbia), who had a nasty sense of humour, and Louis B. Mayer, who was hated by everyone.

The most famous film of this period was *Gone with the Wind*, which ran for three years in London and can still be seen. It starred the very beautiful and talented Vivien Leigh as Scarlet O'Hara, for which she won an Oscar. Her agent was Myron Selznick and she married Sir Laurence Olivier.

It seems to me that with this summary nothing of importance has been omitted but, if necessary, it would be possible to add yet a further layer giving more details of some of the anecdotal information (about the casting of Scarlet O'Hara, Harry Cohn's nasty sense of humour etc.).

Both the three-sentence and two-paragraph summaries above are what I would call general summaries, in other words they summarise the whole text. But outside the language classroom how often do we really need to summarise a whole text? Surely we equally often approach a text with a view to obtaining much more specific information, of which the text contains only a small amount. To take as an example the Shakespeare text on page 101, we summarised what was actually only one element (albeit the principal one), that is to say the biographical. We could equally have gone to that text to find out about the Globe Theatre or *The Tempest*. Then again, what would we do if we wanted to take notes from a text simply to keep them in storage without knowing whether ultimately we would need all the information or only part? The brain-pattern approach serves both of these purposes too. In the former case, you would draw a smaller brain-pattern, with your particular focus of interest as the topic in the centre, and the information the text gives you radiating from it. In the latter case, if you later found you needed only part, you could draw out just that section from the brain-pattern immediately surrounding your focus, adapt it to that focus, and write a summary from that. Let me exemplify briefly what I mean.

Supposing in the Hollywood text your only interest was, or ultimately proved to be, Vivien Leigh. This would be your brain-pattern:

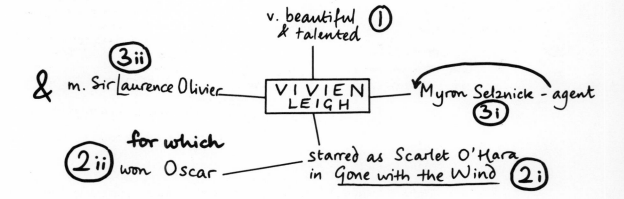

The summary would reflect your focus by having its own topic sentence (a general statement about Vivien Leigh) and by ordering the sentences according to your particular priority.

Vivien Leigh was very beautiful and talented. She starred as Scarlet O'Hara in the famous Hollywood film *Gone with the Wind*, for which she won an Oscar. Her agent was Myron Selznick and she married Sir Laurence Olivier.

Advantages of the brain-pattern approach

By now you will be aware of the manifold advantages of the brain-pattern approach. Firstly, it is flexible—it allows for summaries with varying amounts of detail, of all or part of the text, for immediate use or for storage as a brain-pattern till later. Secondly, a summary produced in this way is a genuinely creative piece of writing, akin to composition, and not just a shadow of a pre-existing text; it can therefore be used to train and/or reinforce composition skills. Above all, because the brain-pattern requires the student consciously to identify the topic and to relate everything to it and its sub-topics, it does, I believe, result in a much greater depth of comprehension than traditional approaches—and comprehension is normally the stated aim of summary.

3 The 'pro-con' composition

The final hurdle of most writing courses in the 'pro-con' composition, the composition that compares two sides of an argument. It is appropriate, therefore, that I should finish by tackling it. Unlike summary, which has a crucial note-taking stage, requiring only relatively small changes to make the notes suitable for the summary, composition requires pure note-making in the form of a plan.

The importance of a plan for non-chronologically sequenced compositions cannot be overstated. This is for two reasons. In the first place, the ideas for the composition enter the mind in no particular order. They need ordering and relating to one another, otherwise the composition will wander aimlessly and illogically. Secondly, and arising from the first point, because of the relative complexity of the content of such a composition, it is impossible to concentrate simultaneously on the correctness and appropriateness of the language. This is true for native speakers and all the more so for the foreign learner. So it is essential to begin with a plan to get the content sorted out before embarking on the composition itself, where it is the language that must be controlled.

To demonstrate the procedure which I use, I will take you through the preparation stages of a composition entitled 'The Advantages and Disadvantages of Television'. I have chosen it purely at random, for no better reason than that it is the most recent composition I have planned with a class.

Getting the ideas down

The first thing is simply to get all the ideas down. In class, I usually put the students into pairs and get them to write their ideas and then report back. Alternatively, the ideas can be elicited from the class as a whole and written directly onto the board. I lay out the ideas in a modified brain-pattern with two sub-centres, corresponding to the two sides of the argument. Below are the ideas my class had, laid out in this way. I have omitted the 'silly' ideas but otherwise left them as they were given to me in class. For ease of reference, I have labelled the the points with letters.

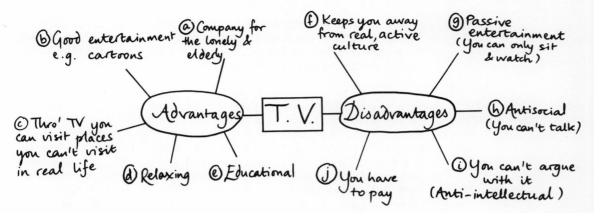

In some pro-con compositions the arguments have parallel points on both sides. When this is so it is better to lay them out in two columns, point against point. You don't, of course, have to use brain-patterns just because they are new!

Relating and ordering

The next stage is to see whether any of the points are closely related. Of the advantages, (c) and (e) are clearly related, and possibly (b) and (d), since bad entertainment is not likely to be relaxing. Of the disadvantages, (g) and (i) are related. The links should be shown on the plan.

Now we can decide on the order in which we wish to present the arguments. There is often more than one possible order, but as a general rule, the more important points should be first or last, where they can be given most prominence, and the less important points in between. The order decided on should be indicated with a number, just as in the preparation for the second Hollywood summary above.

Logical connectors

The final preparation stage involves adding connectors to the notes to indicate the logical relationship between the various ideas. The closely related ideas need to be joined with *for instance, for example* or *such as* if one is an example of the other, or with *in other words, that is to say* or *to put it another way* if one is rephrasing the other, and so on. If they are simply additional points, you can use 'list' connectors: *Firstly, Secondly, Finally/Lastly* (not 'At last'), *In the first place, In the second place*, etc. or connectors of addition: *In addition, Not only that but, Furthermore, Besides that, also* (but be careful about the position of *also* in the sentence). To give an idea final prominence, you can use: *Above all, Most important of all, Best/Worst of all*, or *Last but not least*.

The final plan would look like this:

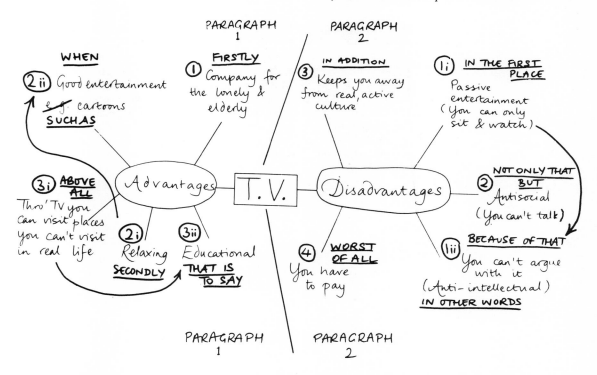

The final stage

All that remains is for the student to prepare a topic sentence for each of what in this case will be two paragraphs—a 'pro' paragraph and a 'con' paragraph—and then rewrite the plan in sentences. The topic sentences introduce the topic and, in this instance, simply need to establish the existence of the advantages and disadvantages of TV using 'Television has . . .' and 'There are . . .' That the disadvantages are in addition to and in conflict with the advantages can be indicated by the use of the connectors *also* and *however*. The student is now ready to write the composition and to concentrate on using correct language. Here is a suggested version.

The advantages and disadvantages of television

Television has a number of advantages *(Topic Sentence)*. Firstly, it provides company for the lonely and elderly. Secondly, it is relaxing when there is good entertainment such as cartoons. Above all, through television you can visit places you cannot visit in real life—that is to say, it is educational.

There are also a number of disadvantages, however (*2nd Topic Sentence*). In the first place it is passive entertainment—you can only sit and watch. Because of that, you cannot argue with it; in other words, it is anti-intellectual. Not only that, but it is anti-social—you cannot talk when it is on. In addition, it keeps you away from real, active culture. Worst of all, you have got to pay for it.

4   Conclusion

It would be possible to give still more examples of different types of writing tasks and how to set about them. By now, however, the principles and procedures I use should be clear enough for you to extend them without great difficulty for use with other tasks. The key points to remember are: first, a note stage is essential for all tasks whether the input is in the form of thoughts or texts and whether the output is a summary or a composition; second, notes taken from a text differ from those made in preparation for a text, and it is often necessary consciously to convert the former into the latter; most important of all, the procedures used must vary according to the structure of the text you are dealing with, according to whether the text is chronologically-sequenced or not, and must be adaptable within that primary division.

Lessons and practical teaching ideas

26

A listening lesson

Ian Forth

Level: *elementary to lower intermediate*
Time: *approx. 60 minutes*
Aim: *intensive listening practice*
Aids: *2 cassette players, BB and task sheets (see below)*
N.B. either the teacher or a student could read one of the listening passages if a second cassette player is not available.

1 Warm up

1.1 Word association. Teacher writes up on BB the headings *Italy* and *Cuba*. Ask students to write down the first 3 things that come into their heads when they think of these two countries e.g. *Fidel Castro, sugar, spaghetti*.

1.2 Feedback. Students 'shout out' their lists and the teacher writes them up on BB. Do not 'edit' or exclude any suggestions—however subjective. (Note: this not only orientates the students towards the task but also elicits many of the vocabulary items that will occur in the listening task.)

2 Generating an opinion gap and the desire to listen

2.1 Put the following terms and statistics in a 'pool' on BB or OHP. Explain any unfamiliar items and give some pronunciation practice. Then ask the students to allocate these items under the appropriate country depending on their opinion.

Wine
income over $10,000 p.a.
more than 300,000 sq. kms
under 120,000 sq. kms
average temp 28°C
15 million people
income about $5,000 p.a.
just under average temp 35°C
about 100 million people
10 million people
income under $3,000 p.a.
Fishing
about 150,000 sq. kms
Tobacco

2.2   Students compare and discuss their lists in pairs. Do not correct or arbitrate on any differences of opinion at this stage. These differences create a personal involvement and will be solved when listening.

3 Information transfer

3.1   Divide the class into two groups (A and B) and organise one group around each cassette player in two parts of the room, group A to listen to 'Italy' and group B to 'Cuba'.

3.2   Hand out the appropriate task sheets to each group and check that students understand the items on the form. Explain that each group is going to listen to some recorded information about their respective country and that they must transfer the relevant facts to their forms. For added realism, the students should imagine that they have just telephoned the Embassy of the country in question and they are listening to a pre-recorded information service. During this stage, students will naturally form sub-groups to compare and exchange answers and this should be encouraged.

Blank forms:

A. Italy	**B. Cuba**
Location:	*Location:*
Area:	*Area:*
Population:	*Population:*
Average Annual Income:	*Average Annual Income:*
Average Temp C°:	*Average Temp C°:*
Main Industries:	*Main Industries:*

Answers:

A. Italy	**B. Cuba**
Location: Southern Europe/ Mediterranean Sea	*Location:* Central America/ Caribbean Sea
Area: 301,000 sq. km.	*Area:* 112,000 sq. km.
Population: 53,000,000	*Population:* 8,500,000
Average Annual Income: $11,000	*Average Annual Income:* $2,000
Average Temp C°: 18°C	*Average Temp C°:* 30°C
Main Industries: car manufacture, wine, tourism, fishing	*Main Industries:* sugar, tobacco, rum

Notes: A context involving giving information by phone has the advantage of being more realistic than a face-to-face dialogue on audio cassette because the speaker is unseen during a telephone call. The pre-recorded information service allows for realistic repetition of the same information until it has been understood. It is helpful, in this case, if the students can operate the cassette players themselves.

As a pre-recorded message, this information should be fully scripted, not semi-scripted. No transcript of the information has been provided, as the fully scripted version could have different wording according to the teacher's choice. What is important is that it should be written in a style appropriate to a pre-recorded information service.

4 Information sharing

4.1 Pair off students from groups A and B and give each pair the following True or False statements.
—Italy is a little bit bigger than Cuba.
—It's much wetter in Cuba.
—Both countries depend heavily on tourism.
—Cuba is much larger than I imagined.
—People earn about the same amount of money in both countries.
—The climate in both countries is very similar.
—The population of Cuba is about half that of Italy.
Note: In order to decide whether these statements are True or False, students must share and combine their information. Thus, full understanding is shown by their ability to convey to someone else what they have heard and to use and interpret this information in a larger context.

4.2 **Reporting back**. The entire class discuss their findings and the T/F statements are checked on the BB or on an OHP.

5 Extension—listening for pleasure

Record the following 'spoof'. The facts acquired from the previous section will allow students to pin-point the mis-matches:

A Report on Cuba and Italy
In Cuba there are many more people than in Italy. Many Cubans work either on the spaghetti plantations or in Fiat car factories. At weekends, they go swimming in the clear blue waters of the Mediterranean or drink Chianti at home. On the other hand, Italians prefer drinking rum. If you visit Cuba you can visit Rome, listen to opera or relax in the hot European sun. If you go to Italy, don't forget to bring back some of their excellent cigars.

Students can either sit back, listen and enjoy the passage or, if you wish to check comprehension formally, you can ask them to shout out *Stop!* when they hear a mistake or absurdity and to supply the correct version.

6 Further activities

Ask the students to choose one or more activities from the following list:
—Discuss parallel information about your own country;
—Write a report on either Cuba or Italy or both;
—Discuss where you would prefer to live and why;
—Write or role play an interview with someone who has visited one of the countries;
—Prepare questions for a general knowledge quiz on the two countries and your own.

27

An elementary reading and writing lesson

Carmelita Caruana

Elementary level students are not often asked to do very much more than write individual sentences; teachers seem to believe that the writing of anything more should be left to intermediate and advanced students. Yet even when students know only one or two tenses and have a fairly narrow vocabulary, it is still possible to get them to write good continuous prose following the model provided by a simple reading text. In this lesson for elementary students, reading comprehension is followed by text analysis; this analysis helps students to understand how to write connected prose rather than a collection of sentences.

1 Aims

To develop reading and writing skills via:
— reading tasks involving understanding the use of reference words and connectors, and analysis of the organisation of information within paragraphs. The reference words focused on are: *the, it, its, these, them.* The connectors studied are: *and, but, another.*
— a parallel writing task based on the text used above.

2 Aids

Text and Yes/No comprehension questions, reference exercise, jumbled sentences exercise.
(See also **Materials** on page 120.)

3 Time

80/90 minutes

4 Procedure

4.1   Warm up

(10 minutes)
— T asks Ss about capital cities they have visited and want to visit, leading on to a discussion about Argentina and Buenos Aires.
— T asks students what facts they know about Buenos Aires.
— T revises or teaches: *I think it's . . .*; *I'm not sure about . . .*; *I don't know.*
— T asks Ss about population, location, climate and problems of Buenos Aires. Ss respond using above language and other exponents if known.
— T asks Ss to read the text, which contains all this information and against which they can check their guesses. (See 5.2)

4.2   Comprehension work

(approx. 10 minutes)
— T distributes Yes/No questions (see 5.1) and the text (see 5.2).

— Ss read text.
— T checks answers orally.

4.3   Study of reference words

(15–20 minutes)
— T explains to Ss that they are now going to do some preparation for writing a text similar to the one they have just read.
— T writes on BB: *John is a doctor. He is 34 years old.*
— T asks Ss: There are two different words in these sentences which both talk about the same thing. Which are they?
— T continues with same procedure on this sentence: *Arthur has many problems. One of them is money.*
— T asks Ss why we use *he* and *them* in these sentences, and asks Ss to give other examples of similar words.
— T points out the importance of connecting sentences well.
— T explains, in L₁ if necessary, the next task: Ss have to look at the underlined words in the reference exercise (see 5.3), decide what the underlined words refer to and write their reference by the underlined word, as in the two examples.
— T divides the Ss into groups and distributes the reference exercise.
— T checks task with class as whole.

4.4   Study of connectors

(15–20 minutes)
— T tells Ss that besides connecting sentences in this way, we also need to organize our information into a logical order in paragraphs.
— T asks Ss, in L₁ if necessary: 'Why are there three paragraphs in the text? What is each about? How are the first and second paragraphs connected? How do the words *another* and *but* in paragraph 2 help the reader?'
— T asks Ss to put their text away and then explains that they will have to re-order their jumbled sentences (see 5.4) using the reference words and the connecting words as clues.
— T divides class into pairs or groups and gives each pair or group a jumbled-sentences exercise to work on.
— T checks with the class, insisting that they not only give the right order of the sentences but also explain which words 'told' them the right order. The class discuss whether or not they agree with what the other Ss say.

4.5   Composition writing

(30 minutes)
— T asks Ss for similar facts about their own town or capital city, i.e. location, population of city, proportion of country's population living in city, problems, climate.
— T asks Ss: 'How shall we organise this information? What shall we put in each paragraph?'
— T reminds Ss about reference, connecting words, logical organisation, logical development and punctuation.
— T asks Ss to collaborate in pairs to write their own parallel text.
— T checks Ss' work as Ss write.
— Ss get into groups and compare their work and choose the best composition in their group.

5 Materials   (adapted from *Contemporary English*, Book 1, by R. Rossner et al, Macmillan)

5.1   Yes/No questions   (a) Is the capital of Argentina on the Atlantic Ocean?
(b) Is the present population of Buenos Aires six million?
(c) Do most of the population of Argentina live in the capital?
(d) Is the city government trying to stop the traffic problem?
(e) Are thousands of families building new blocks of flats to live in?
(f) Is it very hot in July in Buenos Aires?
(g) Do the cars and buses always move slowly in Buenos Aires?

5.2   Text   Buenos Aires is on the River Plate, 150 miles from the Atlantic Ocean. It is the capital of Argentina. The population of the city and its suburbs is increasing rapidly (it was about 6,000,000 in 1974, and experts predict a population of about 10.5 million by 1984). Approximately 30% of the total population of Argentina live in Buenos Aires. Many parts of the city are very beautiful, but, like New York, Caracas, Mexico City and other large cities, Buenos Aires has many problems.

Traffic is one of these problems. The main streets are crowded with cars, buses and trucks and the traffic often moves very slowly or not at all. Another problem is housing: thousands of families cannot find a suitable house or flat, and they are living in difficult conditions. But the city government is building many new blocks.

The weather in Buenos Aires is generally good. In summer (January and February) the average temperature is 23° Centigrade (73° Fahrenheit); in winter, it is 11° Centigrade (52° Fahrenheit). The parks in the city are very beautiful and people can walk, play games or have picnics in them.

5.3   Reference exercise

Buenos Aires is on the River Plate, 150 miles from the Atlantic Ocean. __It__ (*Buenos Aires*) is the capital of Argentina. The population of __the city__ and __its__ (*Buenos Aires*) suburbs is increasing rapidly (__it__ was about 6,000,000 in 1974, and experts predict a population of about 10.5 million by 1984). Approximately 30% of the total population of Argentina live in Buenos Aires. Many parts of __the city__ are very beautiful, but like New York, Caracas, Mexico City and other large cities, Buenos Aires has many problems. Traffic is one of these problems. (etc.)

5.4   Jumbled sentences

(a) Approximately 30% of the total population of Argentina live in Buenos Aires.
(b) It is the capital of Argentina.
(c) Many parts of the city are very beautiful, but, like New York, Caracas, Mexico City and other large cities, Buenos Aires has many problems.
(d) Buenos Aires is on the River Plate, 150 miles from the Atlantic Ocean.
(e) The population of the city and its suburbs is increasing rapidly (it was about 6,000,000 in 1974, and experts predict a population of about 10.5 million by 1984).

6   Examples of students' written work

Lisbon is on the Tagus and the Atlantic Ocean. It is the capital of Portugal. The population of the city and its suburbs is about 2,000,000. Approximately 20% of the total population of Portugal live in Lisbon. Many parts of the city are very beautiful, e.g. Belém, Rossio, Estufa Fria, Castelo de S. Jorge, Alfama, but, like Paris, Madrid, Barcelona, Lisbon has many problems.

Traffic is one of these problems. The main streets are crowded with cars, buses and trucks and the traffic usually moves very slowly in the rush-hour or not at all. Another problem is housing: thousands of families cannot find a suitable house or flat, and they are living in difficult conditions. But we hope that the city government take a resolution as soon as possible.

The weather in Lisbon is generally good. In Summer (July, August, September) the average temperature is 25° centigrade; in winter, it is 10° centigrade. The parks in the city are very beautiful (Eduardo VII Park, Monsanto Park, the Zoo) and people can walk, play games or have picnics in them.

LISBON IS ON THE RIVER TAGUS ; AND ON ATLANTIC OCEAN. IT IS THE CAPITAL OF PORTUGAL. THE POPULATION OF THE CITY AND ITS SUBURBS IS ABOUT TWO MILLION. APPROXIMATELY 20 % OF THE TOTAL POPULATION OF PORTUGAL LIVE IN LISBON.

MANY PARTS OF THE CITY ARE VERY BEAUTIFUL, BUT, LIKE NEW YORK, CARACAS ; MEXICO CITY AND OTHER LARGE CITIES , LISBON HAS MANY PROBLEMS.

TRAFFIC IS ONE OF THEM. THE MAIN STREETS ARE CROWDED WITH CARS, BUSES AND TRUCKS, AND THE TRAFFIC OFTEN MOVES VERY SLOWLY OR NOT AT ALL. ANOTHER PROBLEM IS HOUSING : THOUSANDS OF FAMILIES CANNOT FIND A SUITABLE HOUSE OR FLAT, AND THEY ARE LIVING IN DIFFICULT CONDITIONS. THE CITY GOVERNMENT IS NOT BUILDING NEW BLOCKS.

28

A reading skills lesson

Mary Spratt

WHY HAWAII IS THE WORLD'S TEST-BED FOR THE DAY THE OIL DRIES UP

1 Pele is the ancient and malevolent Hawaiian goddess of volcanoes. Her traditional home is Mount Kilauea, youngest and most active of the volcanic peaks crowning this most improbable of American states. Now the US wants to put Madam Pele to work, and John Shupe is the man giving her the news.

2 Dr Shupe, a tall, silver-haired engineer of military bearing, believes that by tapping the raw heat of the volcanoes that form the backbone of this balmy island chain set in the vast void of the Pacific, he can help America kick its $90 billion-a-year imported oil habit.

3 Shupe has a dream. Besides drilling into volcanoes, he wants to dot the Hawaiian archipelago with windmills tall as Big Ben, harness the surfer-infested waves, trap the power of the Pacific sun, turn man's garbage into gas and produce many other energy goodies. He wants to make the 50th state wholly self-reliant in energy, renewable energy, by 1999. And if it can be done in one state, why not the other 49 . . . the world?

4 Dr Shupe, Hawaii's pioneering Energy Research Co-ordinator, doesn't see his scheme to turn the islands into a national energy laboratory as at all quixotic. 'The technology is *there*,' he says, seated in his map-covered office in the University of Hawaii. 'We know it works. It isn't a question of if, but when.'

5 The 50th State's political bosses are gung-ho about the idea: Governor George Ariyoshi says it is ludicrous that islands so rich in renewable energy sources should rely on imported oil for more than 90 per cent of their energy needs. His ally, Hawaii's Senator Spark Matsunaga, wants the state to become 'energy pathfinder for the globe'.

6 Recently, with the political establishment's blessing, Shupe and his Hawaii Natural Energy Institute (HNEI) put together the world's first conference on renewable energy. Some 600 scientists and engineers gathered on the university campus in Honolulu to work out a ground plan for keeping the world running when the oil runs out.

7 It isn't a scheme that warms every Hawaiian heart. Some environmentalists mutter darkly that paradise will be turned into 'the Pittsburgh of the Pacific'. Native Hawaiians – at the bottom of the economic heap in a multi-racial society afflicted with all the mainland ills of inflation, pollution and crime – fear a new wave of exploitation and uglification.

8 Yet there's no doubt that Hawaii offers the perfect setting for Dr Shupe's experiments. It is the southernmost state, on the same latitude as Bombay and the Saudi deserts, but its shores are cooled by the California current that sweeps down from the Arctic. Balmy trade winds blow with unflagging constancy. The sun shines virtually 365 days a year, giving an average temperature of 75°C, varying with the seasons by only six degrees. In the primordial Hawaiian tongue there is no word for weather.

9 'We have no oil, gas, coal, and of the 50 states, we're the most vulnerable to upsets in the global market – being 2,500 miles from the west coast,' says Shupe. 'But we're blessed with every imaginable renewable energy source, including the world's friskiest set of volcanoes.'

10 Each island consists of one or more volcanic peaks, rising directly from the deep ocean floor. Kilauea's elder sister, Mauna Kea, measures 30,000ft from base to tip – more than Everest – and it's on the slopes of the volcanoes on Big Island (Hawaii) that HNEI hopes for a major geothermal strike. 'We've already bored the world's hottest geothermal well,' says Shupe. 'Signs are that the whole area may be underlain by an immense geothermal reservoir that could provide more than 1,000 megawatts for 100 years.'

11 Geothermal energy, with its already tried and tested technology, promises the quickest pay-off. But isn't it a shade risky to build plant on a volcano?

12 Not really, says Shupe's number two, Professor Paul Yuen, director of HNEI. Power plants could be set far from eruption sites, or on old cinder cones unlikely to erupt again, then linked to the heat source by piping. If that was carried away in a blast, it's easily replaceable. Besides, eruptions here are less than apocalyptic, he adds. 'You have time to get out of the way. Volcano watching is a local sport. Hawaii is the only place where people run to an eruption rather than away from it.'

1 Pre-questions

1.1 What do you know about Hawaii?

1.2 Note down all the vocabulary you can think of connected with energy and its sources. Then compare your list with your partner's.

2 First reading

'Hawaii: an .... place to test alternative energy theories'

Skim the passage and then fill in the missing word in the above sentence.

3 Second reading

3.1 Below are 12 points each summarizing a paragraph in the passage. Read the passage again and match the points with the paragraphs.

	Paragraph Number
Local climatic conditions	
The first world conference on renewable energy	
Shupe's reason for wanting to exploit volcanoes	
Is geothermal energy safe to use in Hawaii?	
Politicians' reactions to Shupe's plans	
Local reactions to Shupe's plans	
Shupe's dream	
Introducing Hawaii and Mr Shupe	
Shupe's belief that this scheme is practical and realistic	
Yes, geothermal energy is safe to use in Hawaii.	
Hawaii's present energy situation	
Hawaii's geothermal potential	

3.2 Check your answers with your partner. Iron out any disagreements.

3.3 Complete, in note form only, the following table about Hawaii's energy potential.

Kind of energy	Where this energy can be found in Hawaii	How much of this energy there is in Hawaii
Solar		
Wind		
Bio-mass		
Wave		
Geo-thermal		

4   Memory check

Without looking at the passage again, go back to the twelve points and, in groups or pairs, see what you can remember about each of them.

5   Inference questions

What is meant by the following?

— The US wants to put Madame Pele to work (para 1).
— surfer-infested waves (para 3).
— the other 49 . . . the world? (para 3).
— the 50th state's political bosses are gung-ho about the idea (para 5).
— paradise will be turned into 'the Pittsburgh of the Pacific' (para 7).
— in the primordial Hawaiian tongue there is no word for weather (para 8).
— Volcano watching is a local sport. Hawaii is the only place where people run to an eruption rather than away from it (para 12).

6   Vocabulary questions

What is the meaning of the following words? Try to work out their meaning from the text.

Para 1:   a peak; to crown
Para 2:   to tap; balmy
Para 3:   to drill; to dot; to harness
Para 7:   to warm the heart; to mutter darkly; uglification
Para 9:   frisky
Para 10:   a strike; to bore

How do you pronounce them?

7   Role play

7.1   Preparation
A journalist is going to interview Mr Shupe about Hawaii's energy situation, its energy potential and methods of exploitation. Divide into pairs. One person takes on the role of journalist and notes down all the questions he wants to ask Mr Shupe. N.B. Journalist—remember that

not all of your readers are happy about Mr Shupe's plans. The other person takes the role of Mr Shupe and prepares to answer all likely questions. N.B. Mr Shupe—don't miss this opportunity to publicize your scheme and convince Hawaii's inhabitants of its usefulness.

Use the passage to help you in your preparation.

7.2   Act out the interview.

8   Written work

Imagine you are Mr Shupe—you have received a letter from a native Hawaiian saying he fears you will ruin the island completely. Write a reply in which you explain why yours is the only solution to Hawaii's energy problems. Use the passage to help you.

29

Island: an integrated skills activity

Les Dangerfield

This activity can be used at any level and can be limited to one lesson or developed over several. It involves the students in the creation and development of an imaginary island.

'Island' needs no preparation of visual materials and only a minimum of artistic skill during the lesson. More importantly, it provides an interesting and motivating context for language practice.

The initial stages require the class to work as one unit to establish the basic features of the island. However, later developments provide ample opportunity for extension work in small groups.

1   Orientation

Warm the class up to the lesson by discussing islands in general, e.g. how many they can name, how life is different for people on an island from that on the mainland.

You will usually find that the students want to create their own paradise; this is important for motivation and the generation of language, particularly, in the development stages, in that points of conflicting opinion occur simply because people have differing ideals.

2 Pre-teaching

Depending on the level of the class, you may need to pre-teach or revise vocabulary for geographical features and other aspects of the island that you intend the students to talk about. However, quite a lot of vocabulary will have to be taught as and when the need arises.

3 Establishing the island's basic features

—Draw an irregular shape, filling most of BB (see below for an example).
—Elicit 3 or 4 suggestions for names of the island, and take a quick vote to decide on the final name.
—The students then invent and describe different aspects of the island while the teacher adds representational drawings and labels to the island map as directed, e.g. *The north coast of the island is very rocky* and *There's a mountain in the north-west of the island.* Where drawing a feature is difficult, then labels can be used, such as for the cliffs in the example island. You may find areas of dispute, leading to discussion, at this stage. These should be encouraged. Decisions can be made by a quick show of hands wherever it seems impossible to reach an agreement by other means. The teacher's role here is that of chairperson and, where necessary, provider and corrector of language.

   Students should keep their own copies of the map.

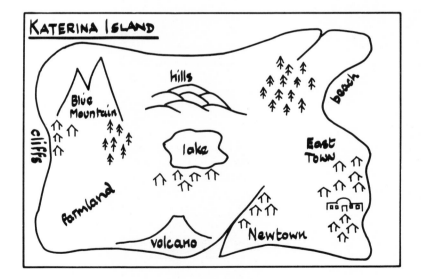

Suggested aspects of the island to be developed:
—overall size (brief)
—climate (brief)
—geography—see the example map; do not crowd the map with too many physical features
—man-made items: main roads and railways (if any), towns and villages with basic details of the towns—names, populations, main sources of work, etc. (include farming areas and products)
—a basic outline of the island's system of government

4 Group work on more detailed aspects

The earliest point at which group work can be introduced is after the establishment of the basic features of the island's towns.

Groups representing each town, village and rural area, could go into further details on such topics as employment, places of interest etc., and then report back to the class. Conflicting information, such as two towns having parliament buildings, may need to be sorted out—though there may be a historical or political reason for this!

When the basic details of the island have been established, the students' own 'characters' on the island can be developed. Again, they can do this in small groups or pairs to maximise their talking time and involvement. The teacher need only outline areas for consideration e.g. age, where they live and work on the island. The students then report back to the whole class, though with large groups it would be inadvisable to have all students doing this.

5 Written homework

Do not simply ask students to write a description of the island or of their life there. Make sure that they have a context in which to do so, such as a letter to a pen-friend in England. According to the level of the class, students may need some kind of framework, such as a list of points to be mentioned.

6 Further activities

The development of the island will have taken a minimum of 1½ hours. It will therefore be necessary for the teacher to take a copy of the map so that it can be quickly redrawn at the beginning of subsequent 'Island' lessons. Ideally, it should be clearly drawn on a large sheet of paper which can easily be removed, stored and re-used. Although students should have their own copies of the map, a large copy is necessary as a central focus for discussion.

The following are examples of what can be done to exploit the island for further oral and written practice. The activities are suitable for upper intermediate and advanced classes, but could be adapted for lower levels.

6.1 Oral practice—a role play

—Depending on the level of the class, you may need to teach or revise exponents of certain functions, such as giving opinions.
—Present the situation to the class:

> An important foreign power has offered to provide financial aid to build an airport on the island, provided that it can use the airport for refuelling its military aircraft. The government has called a meeting of representatives of the island's various interests to discuss the matter and to decide whether or not to accept the offer.

—Discuss the pros and cons of airports in general and of possible airport sites on the island, using this discussion to teach any anticipated vocabulary needs.
—Elicit from the class what the major interest groups on the island could be and then divide the class equally between them. There are two possibilities here. You can allow the groups to decide on their own attitude towards the airport scheme, preparing their arguments in groups before the actual meeting. This has the advantage of allowing students to express their own feelings more freely, but may

lead to a serious imbalance of opinion for or against the airport. Alternatively, you can hand out role cards, prepared in such a way as to represent a broad spectrum of opinion. This ensures that there are conflicting opinions at the meeting, leading to argument and maximizing discussion.

I have provided sample role cards (see below) which apply to the example island. They divide the class into six groups as follows:
The holiday trade/the unemployed: in favour of the airport
The urban residents/ the government: undecided.
The conservationists/ the farmers: opposed to the airport

Notice that if the airport is accepted by the meeting, the class then has to decide where it should be built, and on this subject the role cards divide the interest groups into different factions from those mentioned above.

Suggested management of the role-play:
—Divide the class into six groups, each representing a different interest. Where the class does not divide exactly into six, the extra members can be allotted to the 'government' group, as the government representation will also chair the meeting(s).
—Each interest group meets to read its role card and to develop further arguments to support its opinion.
—The class then regroups for the main meeting so that there is one person representing each interest group at each meeting. For instance, with a class of 30 students, you would have five people representing each interest group and thus five separate meetings attended by one member of each interest group. The government representative should be the chairperson at each meeting, calling on other representatives to speak in turn.
—All representatives at each simultaneous meeting should present their arguments and be given the opportunity to criticize other representatives' opinions.
—Each group should then vote on whether to accept the airport plan or not. Votes should be counted for the entire class to come to a final decision—in my experience the airport plan is usually accepted.
—The groups should then meet to discuss and decide where the airport should be located—a decision again being reacted by class vote.
Throughout this procedure, the teacher should act as organizer and provider of language when needed.

6.2 Written practice

A written follow-up to the role-play could be to write the front pages of island newspapers, with a report on the airport meeting as a central feature. I would suggest that the class be divided into three groups according to their attitude to the airport (for, undecided and against) so that, when completed, the front pages can be exchanged between groups to be read with a critical eye for biased reporting!

Once again, this is an activity for fairly advanced students and a certain amount of pre-task teaching may be needed on headline-writing and organizational skills applicable to writing newspaper articles.

Other articles and even advertisements can be written by the students and the tasks divided, e.g. in a group of ten students, three could write the main article, two pairs could write a further two articles and the remaining three write advertisements. Each group would need a large sheet of paper on which to lay out the completed front pages, which could be put on display in the classroom.

This task would, however, need a considerable amount of time to complete. Shorter alternatives would be to write reports on the meeting or letters to an island newspaper expressing opinions on the airport. These tasks could be done either individually or in pairs.

A more elementary written follow-up could be the writing of a 'parallel' description of the island in the context of a letter to a penfriend from an inhabitant of the island. You would need to provide a parallel text in fairly simple language, describing another island, perhaps first used as a reading comprehension. The class could then write a letter with their own description of their island, simply substituting different facts and figures for those in the original text and copying it out in the format of a letter.

7   Island role cards (based on Katerina Island)

The holiday trade

You own hotels, gift shops & restaurants on the island, especially in the area along the west coast north of East Town. You strongly support the airport plan because it would bring a lot of tourists to the island.

You do not want the airport in the area to the east of the lake because it would cause problems of noise and air pollution near the beach.

The unemployed

You want the airport because it would provide jobs.

Most of the unemployed live in East Town and you want the airport in the area to the east of the lake because elsewhere it would either be too far away for work or too near your homes.

The urban residents

You are undecided about the airport. On the one hand, it would bring money and work to the island but on the other it would bring a lot of people who might destroy the island's way of life.

The government

You are undecided about the airport. A powerful foreign government has offered you money to build the airport but wants to use it for its military aircraft when necessary. You are afraid of becoming involved in world politics. On the other hand the airport would bring money and work to the island.

You do not want the airport to be near East Town or Newtown because this would be unpopular with your voters.

The conservationists

You do not want the airport because of the damage it would do to the countryside and wildlife of the island.

> *The farmers*
>
> You do not want the airport because of the foreign imports of farm produce it would bring.
>
> If the island must have an airport, then you think it should be in the eastern part so that it does not pollute your fields.

30

Graphs and charts for integrated skills practice

Les Dangerfield

Graphs and charts have become an increasingly common means of presenting information of all kinds in newspapers, magazines and books. They can also provide a very useful basis for language practice for a number of reasons:
—The same graph can be used to practise all four skills.
—The same graph can be used at different levels, the language used to describe or talk about them being made simple or more complex as necessary.
—Authentic graphs representing information about the real world can be used, providing increased interest value.
—They can be used as a guideline for unscripted listening comprehension, i.e. the teacher gives a commentary based on the graph.
—They can provide guidance for written work.
The following three lesson plans are all based on graphs or charts and illustrate most of the above points.

1 An elementary lesson plan based on pie charts

A pie chart is a diagram in the form of a circle divided into segments representing, for example, proportions of world car output produced by different countries or, as in the example below, proportions of someone's day spent on different activities.

1.1 Aims

—to give oral/aural practice, in pairs and as a class, of the past simple tense, affirmative and interrogative.

—to provide guided practice of the use of time adverbials and sequencing connectives (gap-filling exercise).

—to give guided writing practice, focusing on the use of the past simple with time adverbials and sequencing connectives to narrate a day's activities.

1.2   Aids

—one completed pie chart representing one of Tim's workdays (see below) for alternate students and another different completed pie chart, perhaps representing one of Tim's Saturdays, for their partners.

—one blank pie chart (see below) for each student with a list of activities in jumbled order.

—one blank-filling reading passage for each student.

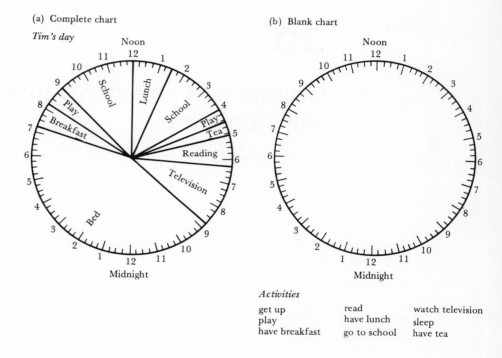

(a) Complete chart

Tim's day

(b) Blank chart

Activities

get up	read	watch television
play	have lunch	sleep
have breakfast	go to school	have tea

1.3   Assumed knowledge

—past simple tense
—clock times

1.4   Procedure

1.4.1   Warm-up

Ask Ss about their activities the previous day and get them to ask each other questions in open pairs, eliciting a variety of possible questions, such as: *When/at what time did you start school? How long did you spend at school? What did you do after that?*

1.4.2   Oral practice (questions and answer)

—Divide the class into pairs, handing out a completed pie chart to one S in each pair and a blank chart with word prompts to the other.

—Draw a blank chart on BB (or use a prepared OHP transparency) and ask Ss the first one or two questions as examples, filling in the chart accordingly.

For example: *Q: When did Tim get up?   A: At a quarter past seven.*
(Draw a line on the blank chart between the centre and the 7.15
mark.)

> *Q: What did he do next?   A: He had breakfast.*
> *Q: When did he finish breakfast?   A: At a quarter past*
> *eight.*

(Draw a second line on the chart and write the word *breakfast* between
the two lines.)

— Ss then ask and answer questions in pairs until the charts are
complete. Ss asking the questions use the word prompts given with
their blank chart as a guide.
— On completion of the blank charts, Ss should check the completed
blanks with their partners' originals to make sure that they accurately
correspond.
— Hand out a second and different chart to those Ss who had previously
had the blank charts, and a blank chart to their partners. Ss then
repeat the above steps so that all Ss have had practice at both
questioning and answering.

1.4.3 Reading

Hand out the following text with the words and phrases in italics
missing. These should be written above the passage in jumbled order.
All spaces in the passage should be of equal length.

Tim's day

Tim got up at a quarter past seven *and then* had breakfast. *After*
breakfast he played for three quarters of an hour *before* going to
school at nine o'clock. He spent three hours at school learning
History, English and Maths. *Next/After that* he had lunch *for an*
hour. He doesn't like school meals very much, but that day it was
steak and kidney pudding which he likes. He started classes again
at half past one and finished school *two and a half hours later.*
After that/Next he played with his school friends for *half an hour*
and then went home for tea. *Between* five o'clock and half past
six he read an adventure story. *Finally*, he watched television
before going to bed very tired at *a quarter to nine.*

— Ss complete the blanks, using the given words and phrases and
compare the completed exercise as a class or in pairs.

1.4.4 Oral practice (narrating)

— Collect in the gap-filling exercise so that Ss cannot refer to the written
text.
— Ask Ss to look at one of the original pie charts.
— Elicit the story of Tim's day from Ss, choosing one S for each
sentence and recapping occasionally for reinforcement. For example:

Teacher: Marianella, what did Tim do first?
Marianella: He got up.
Teacher: When?
Marianella: At a quarter past seven.
Teacher: Good, João, give a complete sentence.
João: He got up at a quarter past seven.
Teacher: And then . . .?
João: And then he had breakfast.
Teacher: OK. Cristina, a complete sentence.

> *Cristina:* He got up at a quarter past seven and then had breakfast . . . *etc.*

—Write the time adverbials (e.g. *for half an hour*) and sequencing connectives (e.g. *after that*) on the blackboard as they occur so that they can be used as prompts for the following activities.

1.4.5 Written practice/homework

—Decide on a context in which Ss might want to write to someone about a day's activities, e.g. a statement to the police by suspects for a day on which a particular crime was committed. Using the connectives and times on the blackboard as guidelines, Ss then write on their own an account of a day in Tim's life.

With minimal adaptation, this pie-chart material could equally well be used to practise the present simple or *going to* future.

2 Holiday survey: a lower-intermediate level activity

The four graphs below represent the findings of an imaginary survey in a class of 30 students, and the lesson plan which follows suggests some ways in which they can be used. Note that the same form of graph could be used in all four cases.

HOLIDAY SURVEY

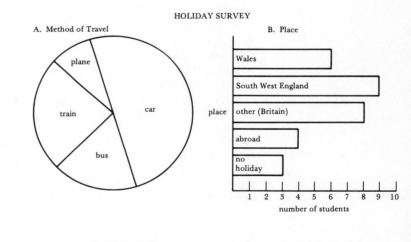

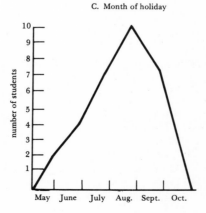

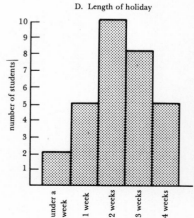

| 2.1 | Aims | —to give intensive oral practice of the past simple—affirmative and interrogative—on the topic of past holidays
—to give guided writing practice |

2.1   Aims   —to give intensive oral practice of the past simple—affirmative and interrogative—on the topic of past holidays
—to give guided writing practice

2.2   Aids   —handout with four diagrams
—handout with comprehension questions on the diagrams
—handout with reading passage

2.3   Procedure

2.3.1   Warm-up

If the Ss' language level permits, discuss what surveys are and and how they can be used. Then hand out copies of the four diagrams and the following questions, which should ensure that Ss understand the diagrams. It can also be useful if Ss indicate which diagram is relevant to which question and note this down in the column on the right.

Questions	Graph
1. How many students were in the survey?	
2. How many students spent their holidays in Britain?	
3. Which form of transport was most common?	
4. How many students spent less than three weeks on holiday?	
5. Which was the most popular month for holidays?	
6. Which different forms of transport did the students use?	
7. How many students spent more than a week on holiday?	
8. In which months did the same number of students go on holiday?	
9. How many students went on holiday before July?	
10. How many students did not stay in Britain?	

Students can check their answers in pairs while the teacher makes a quick random check.

2.3.2   Oral practice in groups

—Tell the students that they are going to carry out their own survey based on their own summer holidays last year.
—Elicit or ask students, individually or in pairs, to decide the questions

they would need to ask to get the information contained in the four diagrams. The questions should be something like the following:

Diagram 1: *How did you travel when you went on holiday last year?*
Diagram 2: *Where did you spend your holiday?*
Diagram 3: *When did you go?*
Diagram 4: *How long did you spend there?*

—Divide the class into four equal groups—A, B, C, and D for Stage One (see diagram below).
—Ss in each group should then ask each other the four questions until they each have four answers from every member of the group. The information can be collected in note form. During this period T should circulate to ensure that Ss are completing the task correctly.
—The class should then be reorganised into groups of four, each group having one member from group A, one from group B, etc. (Stage Two). Thus, in a class of 32, the groupings should be as follows (each letter represents a student according to their original group).

Stage One

A	A	B	B
A	A	B	B
A	A	B	B
A	A	B	B
C	C	D	D
C	C	D	D
C	C	D	D
C	C	D	D

Stage Two

A	B	A	B
C	D	C	D
A	B	A	B
C	D	C	D
A	B	A	B
C	D	C	D
A	B	A	B
C	D	C	D

—Each S then reports to his new group on his survey findings until all Ss have a record of the answers given by every S in the class. They should be saying things like: *In answer to question one, four people went by car, three by train and one by bus in my group.*
—Each of the four Ss in each group can then be asked to construct one of the four diagrams, using the format they feel is most suitable to represent the figures. In the end, each group of four should have a set of charts parallel to those on the original handout but representing their own survey.

2.3.3 Reading and writing

Hand out the following passage, which is based on the diagrams on the original handout.

Holiday Survey

We asked 30 students questions about their holidays in our survey. First of all, we asked the students how they had travelled. Most of them went by car and about 25% went by train. The rest either went by bus or by plane.

The second question was about where the students spent their holidays. The most popular place was the south west of England, where nine students went for their holidays, but a lot of students went to Wales. Most students stayed in Britain for their holidays, but four went abroad and three did not go anywhere.

The third diagram shows when the students went on holiday. As expected, the most popular month was August, when ten students had their holidays. Over three quarters of the students took their holidays between July and September because of the school holiday period. However, a few students had their holidays in May and June.

Finally, the last diagram shows how much time the students spent on holiday. Only two students spent less than a week away. Most of them spent either two or three weeks on holiday.

Ss should be asked to read this passage carefully and to write a parallel passage about the information in their own survey. They should keep to the pattern of the original passage as closely as possible, substituting words where necessary. If, because of seating arrangements, it is not possible for all Ss in each group of four to see all four diagrams at the same time, then the diagrams should be rotated. This will simply mean that each S in a group will have a different paragraph order and have to make the necessary changes in sequencing the expressions *finally, in the second diagrams,* etc.

As a final step, each group's diagrams and compositions can be laid out on large sheets of paper, with decorative embellishments such as postcards, maps or drawings, and put on the classroom walls.

2.4 Alternative activities

The activity described above is only one possible use of the survey graphs and there is a great deal of room for adaptation to focus on particular language items or to make the activities suitable for groups of different levels. For example:

— the graphs could be used for controlled oral/written practice of comparing, producing such language as *More people spent holidays in the south west of England than in Wales.*
— they can be used as an information-gap exercise with Ss in pairs, one S having graphs A and B complete and the other C and D complete, and exchanging the information until both have four complete graphs.
— they can be adapted to practise making plans and arrangements with the *going to* future (*I'm going to travel by plane*) or the future continuous (*I'll be spending a week there*).
— for a more advanced class, the graphs would probably give enough guidance for the final writing exercise without T providing Ss with a parallel passage.

3 Graphs for listening comprehension at an advanced level

(See the end of the article for the graph used.)

3.1 Aims

— to give practice in listening for detail
— to give practice in number discrimination, especially such dates as 1880/1918
— to focus on expressing cause and effect
— to give guided writing practice

3.2 Aids

— handouts
— cassette-player (optional)

3.3   Procedure

3.3.1   Warm-up

Pre-teach any necessary vocabulary (see text below). Discuss what factors cause changes in population (birth and death rates, migration, etc.) and what affects birth rate (living standards, social factors, etc.) Try to elicit sentences such as *The birth-rate changes as a result of changes in living standards*, giving an example if necessary.

3.3.2   Listening comprehension

See text below. N.B. If the text is presented to Ss as a prepared talk of some kind, then T can simply read the script aloud. However, if it is presented as an impromptu delivery, T should improvise from outline notes.

Task 1

—Ss listen to the text and fill in the following table according to whether each period listed was a period of rising or falling birth rate (first two given as examples).

Period	Up ↑ or Down ↓
1850 — 1880	↑
1880 — 1918	↓
1918 — 1920	
1920 — 1940	
1940 — 1946	
1946 — 1950	
1950 — 1962	

(The upward and downward arrows will alternate in this table, but Ss will not realise this until they have completed the task).

Task 2

—Hand out the simplified blank graph (as in illustration (b) below) and explain what Ss should do.
—Play/read the passage again whilst Ss mark the points on the graph according to the information given in the text (see below).
—Play/read the passage again for Ss to check they have completed the task correctly.
—Ss then check their graphs in pairs and join up the crosses to

complete the graph. T can check that the resultant graphs are accurate at a glance.

3.3.3   Reading follow-up
Hand out copies of the text (below) with blanks in place of the expressions in italics; this can be used as a blank filling exercise.

3.3.4   Writing follow-up/homework
After completion of the blank-filling exercise, ask the students to work in pairs to make lists as below under the given headings:

increase/decrease	'because'	cause
rose to went down to jumped up to fell to etc.	due to because of as a result of a consequence of caused by	prosperity changes in society the post-war 'baby-boom' the changing position of women in society

Collect in the completed blank-filling exercise. Ask Ss to write up a commentary on the birth rate during this period based on their completed graphs and the table above.

3.4   The text and graphs used

3.4.1   The text

In the mid-19th century, the birth rate stood at 34 and *rose* slowly to 36 by 1880. This was a time of large families and some people had as many as 10 or 12 children. This mid-Victorian era was a time of great prosperity and economic growth.

From then until 1918, the birth-rate *went down* very rapidly to 18 *because of* economic problems and changes in society. It became normal to have families of only 3 or 4 children and people realized that they could improve their standard of living by having a smaller family.

Due to the post-war baby-boom, the rate suddenly *jumped up to* 25 in 1920. The end of the war brought both optimism and a lot of soldiers back to their wives. However, this optimism did not last for very long and between 1920 and 1940 births *fell* again to their lowest point at 14 per 1,000. Again this was partly *as a result* of the economic problems of the time and also a consequence of the changing position of women in society. More women went out to work rather than spend their time looking after children.

A second 'baby-boom' came with another war and the birth rate increased to 19 again in 1946, but returned to only one more than the 1940 figure in 1950. These lower rates *were causing* a much slower increase in population during this period.

However, with the end of food-rationing in 1950, there was another *increase* to 18 in the early 1960's *caused by* post-war babies starting their own families. Nevertheless, births are never likely to reach the high rates of the 19th century again.

N.B. The words in italics should be omitted.

3.4.2   The graphs

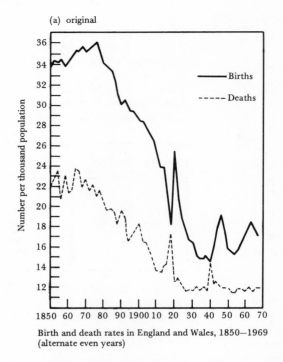

(a) original

Birth and death rates in England and Wales, 1850–1969
(alternate even years)

Graph (a) is the original graph with its source whilst graph (b) is the
graph as it should appear when Ss have successfully completed the first
listening comprehension task. Initially, Ss should be given the bare grid
with no points marked and joined together.

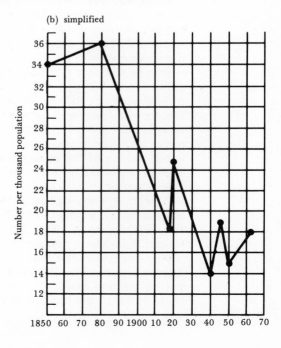

(b) simplified

Section C
Achievement Testing

Background

31

Coming to terms with testing

Eddie Williams

Testing is an area of English language teaching that many teachers shy away from. It is frequently viewed as a necessary evil, a topic where only 'experts' are competent, and where the average language teacher is inadequate. I shall suggest that, far from being a necessary evil, testing can be a positive benefit and, far from being the province of 'experts', it is one where classroom teachers themselves are in the best position to develop their own expertise. I should make it clear at this point that I shall not be talking about testing for placement or general proficiency purposes, but rather about achievement testing, that is to say, the sort of testing that takes place at the end of the term, or at the end of a unit of work, with the aim of checking the learner's learning.

1 Some objections to testing

In general, it seems that those who view testing as a distasteful activity associate it with an older and more authoritarian classroom tradition. While teaching methods and language materials have developed in new directions over the last decade, testing as an activity has not been associated with these developments. It is true that there have been, in recent years, some notable innovations in English language testing techniques, as seen for example in the work of the Royal Society of Arts, or the British Council. I suggest, however, that it is not simply a development of new techniques of testing that will reconcile teachers to the activity, but also some rethinking of the role of testing and how it might contribute more positively to the development of learners and teachers as well as to the relationship between them. In order to work towards this, let us look more closely at why testing is out of accord with the current spirit in English language teaching.

In the first place, testing is associated with competition rather than cooperation. Thus, while classroom activities may involve pair work and group work, such cooperation during a test is condemned as copying, and the individual is expected to work alone. A naive response to this situation is to opt for group tests. While these are perfectly possible, the results of a group test might tell us very little about each individual in that group. If we are concerned, as testers, to look at an individual learner's achievement in a given area, then we must accept that this will not admit of cooperation between learners in carrying out the test task. In the same way, testing does not admit of cooperation between teacher and learner. The teacher who helps and encourages learners with their tasks, and responds to their difficulties in normal circumstances suddenly, in a test situation, withdraws cooperation. The teacher has switched roles from one who guides to one who confronts. This is a change in behaviour that many teachers find disagreeable and perhaps damaging to the relationship that they have built up with the class.

A response to the absence of learner-learner and teacher-learner cooperation in the answering of tests is to introduce cooperation in the preparation for the test. This might range from discussion over what is to be tested, how, when and why, to production of a complete test by the learners. Obviously teachers can decide for themselves how much responsibility for test preparation to hand over to learners; I would also maintain that the teachers' experience and expertise as teachers (a point to be developed below) entitle them to final decisions. Nonetheless, whether it occurs to a high or low degree, such consultation reduces the tension generated by the fear of unknown test content, gives the learners insight into what the teacher is trying to achieve, and sets testing in a more cooperative framework.

The second reason for testing's lack of popularity follows from the first: if testing is viewed as a competitive activity rather than a cooperative one, then there will be a 'winner' and several 'losers'. To be sure, those who were close to winning themselves may not feel too upset, but those at the bottom gain little from the experience, and a succession of such experiences may lead them consciously, and perhaps publicly, to give up the attempt to learn in order to save face. After all, if you're not even playing the game, then you can't lose. The solution to this problem lies in the way in which the tests are marked and the outcome handled. A simple mark or grade may be of little value to the learner. Indeed, since the purpose of classroom achievement testing is not to rank the learners in order, but to give learner and teacher an idea of what has been learned, then we may question whether giving a mark or a grade is necessary. I would not wish to be too dogmatic upon this point; what is certain, however, is that learners will gain more from feedback of a more personal nature which gives credit for what they have got right, as well as help for what they have got wrong.

Apart from the above issues which deal with test preparation and test outcomes—the test framework, as it were—we need to consider further actual test content, i.e. what is to be tested and how. It was suggested above that learners can play an active part in the production of a test. However, this clearly does not mean that the teacher abdicates the role of test producer. There are good reasons for the teacher to retain the right to final decisions here. For example, the learners may have insufficient time to produce a test; the teacher may have to decide on alternative versions; or the teacher may judge that the test proposed is inadequate. Teachers must therefore be capable of evaluating tests and producing tests themselves.

2 The teacher as expert

Unfortunately, some teachers are all too ready to leave test production to so-called experts. Very often the chief claim to expertise of these experts is that they are versed in statistics, rather than the production of achievement tests based on what they themselves have taught. Typically, a 'short testing course' for language teachers, or 'test component' of a longer course, can only touch inadequately upon statistics in a manner which confirms the expertise of the expert, while leaving teachers convinced of their own ignorance and inability. Statistics is guilty of having persuaded many teachers (who are generally trained in the humanities, and whose mathematical knowledge is rusty) that testing is 'not for them'. This is a very regrettable state of affairs since, for classroom achievement tests, I would maintain that many of the procedures of statistical analysis are not appropriate, and that none are essential. (This is not to deny, of course, the crucial role of statistics in standardised tests of proficiency—though even here we should remember that statistics cannot compensate for a bad test.) Achievement tests, however, are not required to discriminate between learners, and since statistical analysis relates directly or indirectly to the differences in the learners' test results, it is not really appropriate to achievement tests. For example, if everyone in a class obtained complete success in an achievement test, this does not necessarily mean that the test was too easy or inadequate because it failed to discriminate; it simply indicates that the learners had learned what was being tested. Of course it is of crucial importance that the achievement test should be a 'good' test, but this is obviously true of all types of testing. I repeat that a bad test can never be redeemed through 'good statistics', and a testing expert cannot tell if an achievement test is adequate or not simply through statistical procedures.

Whether a classroom achievement test is a good one or not is a judgement that the classroom teacher is in the best position to make. Despite this, many teachers make comments such as *I can't test,* or *My tests are awful*. This seems an unjustifiably defeatist, even unprofessional, attitude and for two reasons. Firstly, as far as the content of a test goes, if teachers know what they are teaching, then they must surely know what they can test. Conversely, if teachers do not know what to test, then did they really know what they were teaching? In achievement testing, teachers are obviously the people most qualified to know what they intend to achieve. If achievement testing forces teachers to make explicit to themselves and to learners what they are trying to achieve, then this is surely no bad thing.

Secondly, as far as the methods or techniques of testing are concerned, it is clear that day-by-day teaching in the classroom inevitably involves elicitation and assessment of what learners write or say or do. (Whether the teacher actually corrects the learners' performance or not is another issue.) We may consider testing as a more elaborate and structured form of this elicitation and assessment of feedback, which is an element in any teaching. Teaching without any elicitation or assessment on the part of the teacher is arguably not teaching at all, but simply lecturing where the 'teacher' ploughs on regardless of any reaction from the learners. Any competent teacher must, by definition, be familiar with ways of obtaining and assessing feedback from the learners. It follows that such teachers must inevitably be familiar with techniques of testing.

In short, then, a language teacher knows what to test and how to test. It may well be, however, that the teacher needs to make this knowledge more explicit, to develop it and to discuss it with others; it can also be useful, clearly, to refer to the work of testing experts, though this should be done in a spirit of consultation rather than total reliance. Developing awareness, in this way, of knowledge that one uses rather than analyses in one's day-by-day work is not always easy. However, coming to terms with testing through examining what one is doing in the classroom is an exercise that is likely to have an improving effect on teaching as well as testing.

32

Achievement tests: aims, content and some testing techniques

Mary Spratt

An achievement test is one of the means available to teacher and student alike of assessing progress. It is the aim and content of an achievement test that distinguishes it from other kinds of tests.

1 Aims

An achievement test aims to find out how much each student, and the class as a whole, has learnt of what has been taught and therefore, by implication, to provide feedback on students' progress to both teacher and student, to show how effectively the teacher has taught and to diagnose those areas which have not been well learnt. If an achievement test is well integrated into the learning cycle and into the class perspective on learning, it can also provide an important stimulus for revision.

Achievement tests therefore both look back over the syllabus that has been covered and look forward in that they may indicate directions for future remedial work on the class, group or individual level.

2 Content

The content of an achievement test is indicated by its purpose: clearly, it must test what has been taught. This would seem self-evident, but there are reasons why this goal is not always easy to attain. Firstly, some items are more 'testable' than others, so there is a temptation to test what is easier to test rather than what received greater emphasis in class. Communication, for example, poses problems for testing and, as a result, many courses which state that they aim to teach communication are accompanied by tests whose main focus is accuracy. Secondly, a class may, in the course of a term, have studied a wide variety of functions, vocabulary, subskills, yet the test that aims to assess this learning may last only one class period. This problem can sometimes be overcome by including in the test only those items that make up the priorities in the syllabus. At other times, though, such a solution may be impractical, either because the syllabus contains no obvious priorities or because there is a desire or need to have a more comprehensive picture of the students' progress. In this case, there are two options available: to divide the testing of the items over a series of tests administered within a short time of one another, or to assess only certain areas through the achievement test and others through the continuous assessment of homework and classroom performance.

3 Some testing techniques

Many techniques are available for testing both language and skills, most of which are already familiar to teachers as teaching techniques. What is important is that they should also be familiar to students prior to being used in a test. Otherwise, the student may make mistakes not so much because of difficulties with the language or skills but because of a lack of understanding of what the task requires.

Below is a table outlining a range of these techniques. It is useful to be aware of this range because some items lend themselves more naturally to being tested in certain ways, some methods of testing are better adapted to testing certain aspects of language learning, and some techniques are more suitable to certain age groups and ways of thinking.

Testing focus	*Subjective methods*	*Objective methods*
Listening	Open-ended question and answer Note taking Interviews	Blank-filling Information transfer Multiple choice questions True/False questions Jumbled pictures
Speaking	Role plays Interviews Group discussions Describing pictures Information gap activities	Sentence repetition Sentence responses to cues
Reading comprehension	Open-ended comprehension questions and answers in the target language or mother tongue Summary-writing Note taking	Information-transfer Multiple choice questions True/False questions Jumbled sentences Jumbled paragraphs Cloze
Writing	Guided writing e.g. letter completion, re-writing, information-transfer Free writing e.g. compositions, essays	Blank-filling Sentence-joining

Testing focus	Subjective methods	Objective methods
Grammar	Open-ended sentence completion Re-writing	Expansion exercises Scrambled exercises Transformation exercises Multiple choice questions
Functions	Giving appropriate responses Discourse chains Split dialogues	Matching Multiple choice questions Odd-man-out Listen and match
Vocabulary	Compositions and essays Paraphrasing	Crosswords Classification exercises Matching exercises Labelling

Note that different methods of testing the same skill may well test different subskills. Some of the above techniques test not only the skill or language component mentioned—for example, summary work tests both reading comprehension and summarizing skills.

The techniques in the table above are divided into subjective and objective types, as these two categories involve different kinds of language, language learning and methods of marking. Subjective techniques tend to require students to produce longer stretches of language, i.e. above the simple sentence level, in relatively open-ended situations, and they make demands on the ability to cope with a variety of elements that compose communication and fluency. Objective testing techniques, by contrast, usually require students to recognise or produce a limited range of items in restricted linguistic and situational contexts, thus focusing more on the mastery of receptive skills, accuracy and certain discrete items that make up fluency.

As regards methods of marking, in an objective test there is only one or a limited number of right answers and no doubt about what the answer is. The marker's judgement, tiredness, mood etc. therefore cannot play a role in the assessment. This lack of arbitrariness works in the students' favour as it increases a test's reliability and so guarantees fairness in the assessment of what is tested. In the marking of a subjective test, such as a composition or interview, the marker will often be unsure as to how right an answer is. He may find himself thinking 'well written but poor spelling' or 'accurate but rather unambitious and simple' or 'fluent and communicative but full of grammar mistakes'. In other words, many factors such as grammatical accuracy, spelling, pronunciation, style, vocabulary range, punctuation, or any combination of these may need to be assessed in subjective tests, and there is a risk of the marker doing this inconsistently or even without realising that some of these factors are influencing his judgement. It may also be difficult for a marker to know whether he marked the twelfth composition in the same way as the first, whether he would give the same mark to the same composition if he marked it again, or if another person marking the same composition would give it the same mark. In the absence of pre-established marking guidelines, subjective tests can be significantly less reliable in their results than objective tests.

Another way in which tests may be said to be subjective is in their compilation. If the test content and testing techniques have been selected randomly, this may result in an inaccurate or unrepresentative coverage of the target language or skills. To counter this, test compilation should closely follow the subject matter, syllabus and teaching techniques already employed in the class.

4   Which are better, subjective or objective tests?

Both subjective and objective tests present advantages and drawbacks. Objective tests produce reliable results and focus on accuracy and discrete items, but they provide an assessment of only a limited range of the students' language abilities. Subjective tests can provide information about the students' wider command of communication, but that information may be supplied somewhat haphazardly and is not always easy to assess in a reliable way—though marking guides and/or performance descriptions can go a considerable way towards reducing this unreliability. For examples of actual tests, see articles 37, 38 and 39 at the end of this section.

In an achievement test, the choice of test type will depend on what has been taught, to what extent and how. An objective test is likely to be suitable for an elementary class that has learnt little more than to recognise items, for instance. Similarly, a syllabus that has focused primarily on reading comprehension might possibly be adequately tested by objective testing methods. On the other hand, a writing syllabus that has focused on vocabulary building, composition planning and the use of past tenses might require a subjective test, unless it was felt that students were not yet ready for this less guided format. Many achievement tests contain a mixture of test types in an attempt to cover the syllabus, different types of language learning and differing degrees of exposure to different learning aims.

One final point to consider is that the age, interests and background of students must also influence the choice of test type in the same way as they influence all classroom content and procedure. A student should be able to identify with a test as a measure of progress, and should feel as confident and at home with the test as with the class teaching. An achievement test should never be far removed from the classroom.

33

Writing achievement tests: practical tips

Les Dangerfield

Most language teachers are involved in test writing at some point in their careers. Most commonly, the need is for an end of term or end of year achievement test. This article provides a checklist of the principal points to be considered when writing a class achievement test. The points are not in order of importance but in the order in which they need to be considered when compiling a test.

1 Time

How much can be tested in the time available for the test?
The limitation imposed by the duration of the test, which commonly has to be fitted into one normal-length lesson, necessitates the selection of a valid sample from the structural and/or functional items and skills included in the syllabus on which the test is based. It is important not to ask too much of the students in the time available. To do so can cause them to panic and can penalise students who do not work well under pressure.

2 Coverage

What constitutes a valid sample of the syllabus?
The sample taken from the syllabus is only valid if it accurately reflects the emphasis of the teaching of that syllabus in terms of grammatical and functional items and skills. If, for example, fifty per cent of the test involves letter writing when that activity has not been a major item on the syllabus and has taken up only five per cent of class time, then the test is not a valid one. Care must be taken not to place undue emphasis on an item or skill simply because it lends itself easily to being tested or because it makes the writing of the test easy.

The foregoing raises the question of the inclusion of an oral component in the test. Most language courses have a heavy oral/aural bias during class time and thus an achievement test which does not include an oral component can hardly be said to be valid. However, administrative, personnel and time restraints often rule out the possibility of testing this skill, given that students would have to be tested on a one-to-one or small group basis. This is a problem which has to be left to the individual teacher to solve. One possible solution, if a formalised oral test is out of the question, is to allocate a certain percentage of the test marks to an assessment of oral competence based on the teacher's classroom experience of each student's performance.

3 Format

What form are the test items going to take?
First, it is important to choose formats which test what they are

supposed to test. A listening comprehension test, for example, which requires lengthy (even single-sentence) written answers may mainly reveal the students' ability to write and would thus be invalid as a test purely of the listening skill. Similarly, a written test which involves writing a detailed answer to a given letter may say as much about the students' ability to read as about their ability to write.

Further, students should be familiar with the formats used in the test otherwise poor performance may be due to a misunderstanding of the format rather than to a lack of linguistic competence.

Finally, the teacher has to decide at this point whether to use an objective or subjective format for each part of the test. This choice has important implications for the marking of the test (see 6 below).

4   Difficulty

What is an appropriate level of difficulty for each item or part of the test?
An achievement test assesses the students' learning of a given syllabus, and thus the desired results should be marks clustered towards the top end of the marking scale since one would hope that all the students in a class have successfully learnt what has been taught. The level of difficulty of items included in the test should parallel that of the practice activities done by the students during their course. The kind of variation in level of difficulty of test items appropriate to placement or proficiency tests is not necessary in achievement tests, as it is not their primary aim to discriminate between strong and weak students.

5   Rubrics

Are the test instructions (rubrics) clear and unambiguous?
Complex or badly-written instructions can invalidate the test by misleading students or by turning the instructions into an additional, though unintended, reading comprehension element of the test, i.e. students may complete test items wrongly simply because they have misinterpreted the instructions. The following examples illustrate how easy it can be to give unclear test instructions:

(a) For a cloze or gap-filling test:
Complete the following text by filling in the spaces.

If only one word is required to fill each space, the instructions should state this, otherwise students commonly attempt to write in two, three or even more words in some spaces.

(b) For a multiple choice test:
Indicate the correct option (a, b, c, or d) which completes each of the following sentences.

If the students are not told how the option should be indicated (underlining, circling, writing the correct letter or word(s), deleting the incorrect options, etc.), the test may be completed in such a way that it is difficult for the teacher to see which options the students think are right.

With a monolingual class there are good arguments for giving the instructions in the students' native language, particularly at the elementary level, to prevent students misunderstanding the language of test instructions which can often be quite specialised.

In addition to clear instructions, it is also advisable to provide an example of an answered test item where the format permits (e.g. in the case of multiple choice or sentence transformation items but not, of course, in the case of compositions).

6 Marks

How should marks be distributed between the different parts of the text?

The principal point to make here is once again that the balance of marks allotted to the different parts of a test should reflect the balance of the syllabus. It is impossible to be precise in this, but it should be ensured that important grammatical and/or functional items on the syllabus are well represented in terms of marks and that an appropriate weighting is given to the marks allotted to tests of the skills according to their relative importance during the course.

The weighting of marks must also take into consideration the difficulty of a test item and, to an extent, the proportion of the overall test time that it is likely to take students to complete that item. If a letter-writing item is going to take up a third of the test time, it should not necessarily be given a third of the overall marks, but only to allot to it five or ten per cent of the marks in order to reflect its importance in the syllabus would also be disproportionate and lead to distortions in the test results.

A final point in relation to marks is that, if the test includes an element which has to be marked subjectively, the teacher should give careful thought not only to the overall mark for that element as a proportion of the total marks for the test, but also to the criteria to be used for assessing that element. Even when only one person is marking a set of test papers, it is important for reliability and consistency that marking should be done according to guidelines of one form or another (see *Making extended writing tests less subjective*, page 161).

Techniques

34

Testing functional language

Mary Spratt

This article looks at ways of testing functional language. The methods are listed in random order, and you will notice that they test various aspects of language in use: comprehension, production, degrees of formality, and students' understanding of functions as a linguistic concept. The methods in fact cover a range of testing aims and therefore vary in their applicability to different syllabuses and groups of learners. For discussion of these points, see after the examples below.

1 Some methods of testing functional language

Read and match

Students are given a list of exponents of the same function and a parallel list of degrees of formality e.g. very formal, written, neutral, casual. Their task is to match the degree of formality with the exponent.

Expanding a discourse chain into a dialogue

Students are given a discourse chain and their task is to make up a dialogue from this chain. (See *Discourse chains*, page 28 for an example).

Odd man out

Students have to eliminate one exponent from a list of exponents. This can be done either by eliminating the exponent because it is of a different degree of formality to the others, or by eliminating it because it is a different function from the others.

Parallel texts—degrees of formality

Students are given a dialogue or letter written, for example, in a formal register. Their task is to rewrite this text in an informal register.

Appropriate responses

Students are given an outline of a situation. Their task is then to write what a person would say in that situation. (See example below.)

Rewriting	Students are given a description of a conversation (i.e. a kind of reported speech). Their task is then to write the conversation. (See example below.)
Written role play	(Yes, a strange name, I admit, but I think it gets the point across.) Students are given a detailed account of two people's characters, moods and attitudes in a well-defined situation. Their task is then to write out the conversation that occurred between these two people. (See example below.)
Multiple choice	Students can either choose the best exponent of a function for an outlined situation or choose which degree of formality a given exponent represents.
Split dialogues	Students are given the words of one person in a dialogue. Their task is to read the dialogue, then provide the words of the other person. (See example below.)

2 Some examples of testing functional language

Odd man out	Which is the odd man out in the following: a) Let's go to the cinema. b) Shall we go to the cinema? c) What about going to the cinema? d) How about going to the cinema? e) Do you like going to the cinema?
Rewriting	Read the paragraph below and then write what Janet and Sue said, in the form of a dialogue. In your dialogue you must not use the words in italics. (Janet is Sue's boss and they are both in the office.) Janet *invites* Sue to a party in the evening. Sue *accepts* the invitation and asks what clothes to wear. Janet *suggests* that she wears her new dress. Sue *asks for permission* to leave early to have a bath before the party. Janet *gives her permission.*
Written role plays	These are similar to the rewriting above but students are given more information about the kind of situation and setting that is involved, and the kind of attitudes and relationships existing between the people involved. For example: Mr. Brown is Jim's boss. Mr. Brown is a very formal and authoritarian man and Jim is rather afraid of him. Write the conversation that takes place between them one day when Jim has to ask Mr. Brown's permission to leave work early because he has a doctor's appointment. Mr. Brown refuses him permission and orders Jim back to work. Jim apologises and makes excuses.
Appropriate responses	Read and complete the following by writing what the people would say. 1. You're having a party. Invite a friend. 2. What does a shop assistant usually ask when you walk up to a counter in a shop?

3. You're in the street and you want to find the nearest Post Office. What do you say to a passer-by?

4. You're in a restaurant. How do you ask the waiter for a menu?

5. You and your friend want to go out tonight. Suggest a discotheque.

6. A friend comes to see you. You want to offer him/her a cup of tea or coffee. What do you say?

Split dialogues

Read what Bob says below. Then write what you think Gill says.

Bob: Hello Gill. Is John in?

Gill: _____

Bob: London! But I've been waiting for him to pay me back some money and I need it this weekend.

Gill: _____

Bob: But I need it before Monday! What can I do now?

Gill: _____

Bob: That's no good. I borrowed some money from Peter last weekend. I can't ask him again.

Gill: _____

Bob: Well, it's nice of you to offer. Are you sure?

Gill: _____

Bob: Thanks very much.

3   Some implication of these methods

Three aspects of functional language tested by these methods are:
— the form and meaning of exponents of functions
— the degree of formality of exponents of functions
— the concept of functions.

Students need to know not only the form and meaning of an exponent of a function, the sequence of words it is composed of and its literal meaning, but also its social meaning and appropriateness to different situations. This is important for elementary students as well as for more advanced ones, as the following examples show:

— Would you mind lending me your pen?	v Can you lend me your pen?
— Could you please tell me where the bus stop is?	v Where's the bus stop?
— Shut the window.	v Could you shut the window, please?
— The menu, please.	v Could I have the menu, please?
— Good morning.	v Hello.
— It's great.	v It's very nice.

In many circumstances it would definitely be 'odd' to use one of these exponents rather than the other.

Depending on the age, interests and learning habits of our students and our own ideas of what constitutes efficient teaching, we may find it useful to tell students what a function is doing within a discourse e.g. refusing, thanking, congratulating, disagreeing. To do this we need to teach students the names of the functions. However, particularly with elementary level students, it is important to decide to what degree to adopt such an approach, as learning the names of the functions can, in certain cases, be more complicated than learning the functions themselves, and become counter-productive for this reason.

The table below shows which of the three aspects of functional language mentioned above are focused on by the methods described and illustrated in 1 and 2.

Method	*Aspect tested*
Read and match	(1), 2
Expanding a discourse chain into a dialogue	1, 3, 2 depending on wording of function labels
Odd man out	2 (first way), 1 (second way)
Writing parallel texts in different degrees of formality	1, 2
Appropriate respones	1, 2
Rewriting	1, 2 depending on wording
Written role play	1, 2
Multiple choice	1, 2
Split dialogues	1, 2 depending on wording

KEY: 1 = form and meaning; 2 = degrees of formality;
3 = the concept of functions; ( ) = of secondary importance.

This table can be used to see how suitable each method is for different syllabuses and groups of learners.

35

Three types of objective test

Les Dangerfield

This article will give an overview of three types of objective tests—cloze/gap-filling, true/false tests and multiple choice tests. These test types are commonly used because of the speed with which they can be marked (an important factor for busy teachers), because they involve objective marking, and because of their flexibility. All three can be used to test global and detailed understanding of a text or to focus on specific areas of language such as grammar and vocabulary.

1 Cloze and gap-filling

These are grouped together because they have a basic operation in common, i.e. the substitution by the test writer of individual words in a passage by a space, the students having to write in the missing word or a suitable alternative. This raises the issue of what is and what is not an acceptable word to fill a space, and this can lead to an element of subjectivity in the marking of these tests. One possible course to follow is only to allow the word which originally appeared in the text, marking all the others wrong. An alternative is to establish what the acceptable alternatives are before marking so that only these alternatives are considered correct.

Cloze tests

Conventional cloze tests involve the removal of words at regular intervals, usually every 6–8 words and normally not less than every 5. Consider the following example of a cloze test with every eighth word deleted after the introductory sentence.

'I applied for one of the advertised jobs as a teacher in Lancashire. I wrote a short letter explaining which (a) .... I was interested in and why I (b) .... at that time, I was suitable for (c) .... However, apart from some minor worries, there (d) .... two reasons why I did not send (e) .... the application after having completed the form. (f) ...., and vitally, I had not done any (g) .... before and, what is more, I did (h) .... really want to move to that part of the country.'

Although cloze is primarily a test of the reading skill, the above example illustrates that it can test a wide variety of elements of the language through testing the reading skill. The following table gives the original words of the above text, some possible alternatives and the language point tested (the letters correspond to the spaces in the text):

	Original word	Alternatives	Language point tested
(a)	position	work/employment	vocabulary
(b)	thought	considered/felt	form of the verb / irregular past form
(c)	it	—	pronoun system
(d)	were	—	verb form / agreement with 'two reasons'
(e)	off	in	phrasal verbs
(f)	Firstly	First	use of sequencing connectors and punctuation ('Because' would not be followed by a comma.)
(g)	teaching	work	understanding of the text beyond the sentence that the word occurs in*
(h)	not	—	negation

* This is the kind of global reading skill which can be tested in an extended gap-filling or cloze exercise but not in a single-sentence one.

In the above example, the first sentence is given completely so that the students understand what the passage will be about. Note also that the lines representing the missing words are of equal length in order to avoid providing clues about the length of the word required.

Although cloze tests should not be too short, there is no such thing as an optimum length, since a number of factors will influence length. In particular, the test-writer will need to bear in mind the level of the students taking the test and the amount of time and number of marks to be allotted. For a lower-intermediate class, for example, 20 spaces to fill in 15 minutes can be typical in a one-hour test. Thus, if every seventh word were deleted, the total length of the text would be around 140 words. Note that numbers and proper nouns should be ignored when counting words between spaces except where a number can be deduced from other information in the text.

When using the regular deletion procedure, it is not usually possible to focus deliberately on selected discrete items because cloze is a purely random means of choosing words for deletion. For this reason, cloze texts for use in an achievement test should be carefully chosen so as to ensure that the deleted items all fall within the syllabus followed. The discrete elements tested by cloze are chosen by chance and, if a test-writer wishes to test specific language items, then a gap-filling test, sometimes referred to as a 'selective' or 'impure' cloze, is more appropriate, as in the following 'gap-filling' example.

Gap-filling tests

Consider the following example of part of a gap-filling test in contrast with the cloze test. The example is based on a text from a students' course book (*Starting Out* in the *Access to English* series by Coles and Lord, published by Oxford University Press) and is designed to focus on the past simple form of verbs:

Arthur (a) .... up early on Saturday morning. He (b) .... a shave and (c) .... his clothes on. He doesn't put his suit on when he isn't working. He (d) .... his drawer and (e) .... out his light-coloured trousers. He (f) .... his suit on a hanger and (g) .... it up in the wardrobe, and then (h) .... the wardrobe door.

Note that again the lines representing the missing words are the same length. Only verbs in the past simple have been deleted; the words have not been omitted at regular intervals but the average frequency is every six words.

2 True/False tests

These can be used to test both reading and listening and the understanding of specific elements of the language. The following examples illustrate how they can test such specific elements.
Extract from text:

'On the way to Bath I was delayed by a terrible pile-up on the motorway. After an hour I arrived and had a look around the city. In the afternoon I had my photograph taken and bought three Easter eggs to take home, one for my sister and the others for myself.'

True/False statement	Answer	Point tested
(a) There was an accident on the motorway.	True	vocabulary
(b) The writer took a photograph.	False	understanding of the causative use of 'have'
(c) The writer bought two Easter eggs for himself.	True	understanding of cohesive devices—the pronouns 'one' and 'others'

The following points need to be borne in mind when constructing the true/false test and its marking scheme.

(a) In a listening comprehension test, the points referred to by the T/F statements should be adequately spaced through the text so as to give students time to think, mark their answers and return their attention fully to listening before the next tested point arises.

(b) With only two possible answers—'True' and 'False'—there is always the danger of guesswork distorting final marks: a student could score 50% on the exercise without understanding anything! There are three ways of avoiding or lessening the element of guesswork:

—by subtracting one mark from a student's total for each wrong answer given. However, this has the drawback that it tends to discourage the calculated guess based on a degree of understanding even if it is not complete. If this method is used, it is essential that the students should be told beforehand.

—by adding a third element—'Don't know'—when some of the answers cannot be answered from the text.
For example: *The writer ate two Easter eggs. (T/F/Don't know)*
Answer: *Don't know* (He kept the Easter eggs, but may not have eaten them.)

—by requiring the students to write corrections to the false statements. However, this introduces elements of both 'impurity' and subjectivity into the test. It becomes impure as it becomes partially a test of the writing skill and subjective in that the student's correction may be capable of interpretation in a number of ways. What is more, how do you mark the test if a student correctly answers 'False' but gives the wrong information in the written correction? In this case, a dual-stage marking system has to be used, whereby a student gets some marks for correctly choosing 'True' or 'False' answers and others for the accuracy of the correction of the false statements. Furthermore, if the student's correction is like the following simple example, what proof of understanding does even the correction give to the teacher?
T/F statement: *He went to London* (False)
Student correction: *He didn't go to London.*

In this case, the student's correction is simply a negation of the T/F statement, which does not necessarily imply an understanding of the text. The student may simply have guessed that the statement was false and could negate the original statement without understanding the relevant part of the text.

(c) Negative T/F statements should normally be avoided, as the decision as to whether a negative statement is true or false can lead to confusion.

3 Multiple choice tests

As for the above test types, multiple choice can be used to test either global or detailed understanding of grammar or vocabulary. Furthermore, it can be used to test the understanding of either 'single sentence' utterances or extended texts.

In the examples that follow only single sentences are used, but multiple choice items could equally well be based upon an extended text used to test listening or reading ability. The examples illustrate various possible formats of multiple choice test items as well as ways in which different elements of the language can be tested.

Vocabulary

The right answer and distractors are given beneath the stem, which has a gap in it. For example:

His mother .... him how to make cakes.
A trained   **B** taught   **C** educated   **D** instructed

Reading/listening comprehension

Here the right answer and distractors give alternative completions to the stem. For example:

'The lock was broken and the wind howled through the door every five minutes. He picked up a piece of wood and wedged the door to.' (*Extract from text*)

He kept the door closed by
A putting a brick in front of it.
B holding it with his hand.
C putting something under the door.
D tying the door handle to the bolt.

Appropriateness

Alternative possible responses to the stem are given. For example:

'You're standing on my foot.'
A 'Please, please forgive me.'
B 'Oh! I don't know what to say.'
C 'I'm terribly sorry.'
D 'I apologise.'

Error recognition

The letter above the part of the sentence which contains an error is to be circled. For example:

    A   **B**   **C**   **D**
Yesterday/I bought it/from corner shop/nearby.

Punctuation

Entire sentences form alternatives. For example:

A They asked me where the bank was?
B They asked me where the bank was.
C They asked me, where the bank was.
D They asked me 'Where the bank was'?

Constructing the test

The following points should be borne in mind when constructing a multiple choice test.

(a)   It is normal to have four alternative answers for each item. Any fewer than four means that guesswork becomes an important factor.

(b)   Instructions should make clear how the students are to answer, i.e. whether they should write a word in a space, underline or circle the correct option, or whatever. This operation should be the same for each item within any one section of the test, and an example should be given to make the procedure clear.

(c)   The format of each item within each part of the test should be the same. It is confusing to use a mixture of formats (as in the examples above) in the same section of a test.

(d)   There should be only one right answer. The following example

They .... a cottage for the month of August.
A bought   **B** paid   **C** rented   **D** loaned

is a weak item because, although 'rented' is the likely answer, 'bought' is not beyond the realms of possibility.

(e)   Vocabulary items should be from the same word class, i.e. all verbs, or all nouns, or all adjectives, etc. In the following example

I'm afraid you have no .... but to come with us
A possible   **B** permission   **C** choice   **D** selection

a student knowing that a noun is needed to fill the space would automatically rule out option 'A' and therefore have a greater chance of guessing between the remaining three options.

(f)   Avoid having two distractors with the same meaning, otherwise, if the student is aware of this, the choice will be narrowed to only two options. For example:

He .... the car for £5 a day.
A borrowed   **B** purchased   **C** hired   **D** bought

(g)   Distractors should be approximately the same length, otherwise attention is focused on one option; as in the following:

He stuttered a lot during the speech.
A coughed   **B** spoke with difficulty in pronouncing sounds
C moved around   **D** used emphasis

Once used and found to work well, multiple choice items can be sorted in a test bank, for re-use in varying combinations for later tests of the same syllabus.

36

Making extended writing tests less subjective

Les Dangerfield

'One day I arrived home and found something very strange in my living room'. Complete this story in 150–200 words.

The above item can be considered subjective

—in the way it has been selected by the test-writer as a suitable means of testing the students' ability to write.

—in the way it is answered by the students who are given freedom to choose what to say and how to say it.

—in the way it is marked once the test has been done.

1 Why make writing tests less subjective?

Broadly speaking, subjectivity in tests often makes for unreliability, in that the final marks obtained do not accurately reflect the abilities of the students either individually or relative to one another. Unreliability can be due to various factors:

—the test may unintentionally require of the students imagination, experience or knowledge in addition to linguistic ability. If the test-writer considers these factors to be part of what is being tested, then, in order to make the test reliable, they should be taken into consideration in the marking scheme;

—the tester/marker cannot control the level of language used in the students' answers. Some students may restrict their answers to simplistic language and others may try to express ideas in the target language which it is beyond their ability to express;

—the markers cannot be sure that they will use the same criteria in marking different answers.

2 Making tests less subjective

Most teachers would agree that, to be fair to their students, it would be desirable to find ways of minimising subjectivity in tests. A number of aspects of a test must be considered in pursuit of this aim.

Writing the test item

Test items can only be objective to the extent that they are included on the syllabus and that the formats used are those with which the students are familiar. If the syllabus included the writing of formal letters of request, invitations and responses to these, then, if there can only be one writing test item, it must test one of these. To that extent, this aspect of the test is objective.

Student answers

Guidance of students' answers in the test reduces subjectivity by eliminating the need for students to use imagination or non-linguistic knowledge in their writing and by controlling the linguistic content and organisation of the answers. This guidance can take three forms (N.B. the letters in brackets below refer to examples provided by the writing section of the Elementary (E), Intermediate (I) and Advanced (A) achievement tests on pages 164–176):

Information guidance
This means giving the students information they need to use in their writing, but in a different form from that in which they have to present the information. The information can be provided through: (a) a reading text (I and A); (b) a listening text (A); (c) diagrammatically presented information which the students have to convert into a continuous text (see *Graphs and charts for integrated skills practice* on page 131); (d) a list of points to be included in the students' writing (E); (e) an individual picture (e.g. for description) or a series of pictures (e.g. for narrative).

Linguistic control
This can be provided by:
(a) arranging the information given by means of any of (a)–(e) above in such a way that students are required to use certain language items. For example in E, part 5, paragraph 3, the students are required, by the nature of the information, to use the past simple, the present perfect and a future verb form.
(b) stating explicitly the language which the students should use, e.g. logical connectors (I), or giving the opening words of each paragraph.

Organisational guidance
This can be provided by:
(a) stating the form that the writing should take, e.g. a letter (I)
(b) telling the students how many paragraphs to produce and which information to include in each paragraph (E).

3   Marking the test

The marking of writing tests is likely to be more objective, and thus more reliable, if marking guidelines are provided. These guidelines normally take one of the following two forms.

Dividing the marks between areas

These areas may be some or all of the following:
— grammatical and lexical accuracy
— range of vocabulary and structure used
— appropriateness of style
— layout / paragraphing
— punctuation and capitalisation
— cohesion
— spelling
— inclusion of all necessary information.
The choice as to which of the above elements to allot marks to will depend on the type of task, the level of the students and the content of the syllabus. 'Appropriateness of style', for example, is important when the task involves formal letter writing and would normally only come into play for a fairly advanced test.

Allotting marks according to band descriptions

(See I, note 5.) It is not easy to write such descriptions accurately and this method is more appropriate when a number of markers is involved.
    Both the weighting of the elements and the wording of the band

descriptions should reflect the syllabus and its emphases in order to be valid.

4 An outline example of a guided writing test

The following example shows how informational and organisational guidance can be used in the same test.

(a) The students are given a jumbled list of points about the advantages of living in the country over living in a city and vice versa (informational guidance).

(b) The students then label each point 'Advantage country' or 'Advantage town' according to their own opinions (organisational guidance—ideas).

(c) The students copy the points in order of importance depending on their opinion, into two columns ('Advantages of living in the country' and 'Advantages of living in the town'). This gives the order in which the points will be mentioned in the composition and thus provides the students with a composition plan (organisational guidance—ideas).

(d) The students write a composition entitled 'The advantages and disadvantages of living in the town and the countryside' using the following layout, provided on their test paper (organisational guidance — ideas and layout).

Paragraph 1: The advantages of living in the countryside over living in a town.

Paragraph 2: The advantages of living in a town over living in the countryside.

Paragraph 3: Conclusions—what you think.

Examples of tests

37

An elementary level achievement test

Les Dangerfield

The following is an example of a one-hour elementary/pre-intermediate end-of-term achievement test for a course involving a structural/functional syllabus including the following:
a) The present perfect used with *since, for, already, yet, ever* and *never*.
b) The past simple used to narrate past events.
c) Making and responding to suggestions.
d) Revision of functional items from previous parts of the course:
— classroom language
— introducing people
— making and responding to invitations
— offering objects
— making requests
e) Guided paragraph writing:
— giving information about places/buildings.
— giving information about people.

Test

Part 1   **Listening comprehension***1   *(20 marks: 10 mins**2*)*

(a) You are going to listen to someone interviewing three people about their holidays.
(b) You will only hear the interviews twice.
(c) Look at your listening comprehension answer paper and, when listening, write in the appropriate information to complete the table. Usually only one or two words are necessary for each answer.

Listening comprehension answer paper

Question	Interview 1	Interview 2	Interview 3
Where?	Greece	Italy	Scotland
When?	1.	5.	Late July
How long?	2.	6.	1 ½ weeks
Accommodation	3.	Hotels/camping	9.
Method of travel	4.	7.	10.
Weather	Sunshine/ some rain	8.	Fine/some rain

Part 2

Grammar*³　　　　　　　　　　　　*(30 marks: 15 mins)*

On your answer papers write the correct form of the verbs in brackets.

Example: John _____(1)_____ (like) coffee but he _____(2)_____
not, like) tea.
Answers: (1) likes　(2) doesn't like

　Sue is on holiday in London and, after a few days, she goes to see a friend called Steve.

Sue:　Hello, Steve.
Steve:　Hello, Sue. Come in. I _____(1)_____ (not, see) you for ages.
Sue:　Yes, right. I_____(2)_____ (not, be) in London recently.
Steve:　Well, what _____(3)_____ (you, do) since you came here?
Sue:　Erm, well, not a lot. On Monday, I _____(4)_____ (go) to the Turner exhibition at the Royal Academy and on Tuesday I _____(5)_____ (spend) the day with an aunt of mine.
Steve:　_____(6)_____ (you, like) the exhibition?
Sue:　Yes, it was very impressive. _____(7)_____ (you, see) it yet?
Steve:　Yes, I _____(8)_____ (see) it last week. Look, what _____(9)_____ (you, do) this evening?
Sue:　I _____(10)_____ (not, plan) anything.
Steve:　_____(11)_____ (you, like) to go and see the Razor Blades in concert at the Roundhouse?
Sue:　I _____(12)_____ (never, hear) their music before. What are they like?
Steve:　They're a new punk group. The pianist _____(13)_____ (play) the piano with his toes and they _____(14)_____ (play) their new song tonight. It's called 'I can't bear you'.

Sue: Well, actually, I _____(15)_____ (not, like) punk music very much.
Steve: Oh, well, what about a meal then? . . .

Part 3

Dialogue[4]   *(15 marks: 10 mins)*

   Tom and Margaret are friends; they are trying to decide what to do this evening. Write their conversation, using the following guide.

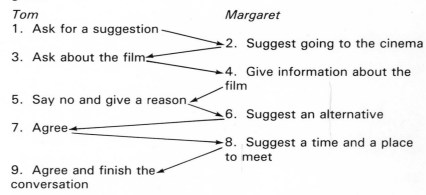

Tom   *Margaret*
1. Ask for a suggestion
                                         2. Suggest going to the cinema
3. Ask about the film
                                         4. Give information about the film

5. Say no and give a reason
                                         6. Suggest an alternative
7. Agree
                                         8. Suggest a time and a place to meet

9. Agree and finish the conversation

Example: 1. Tom: What shall we do this evening?

Now you complete the dialogue.

Part 4

Situations[5]   *(15 marks 10 mins)*

   Write what you would say in the following situations.

Example: You are spending an evening with some friends. What do you say when you want to leave?
Answer: I'm sorry, but I must go now.

1. You don't know the word 'spiteful'. What do you ask your teacher?
2. What do you say when you introduce two friends to each other?
3. You are going to have a birthday party. Invite a friend.
4. A friend is visiting you. You want to offer her a drink. What do you say?
5. You are on a train. You can't lift your suitcase into the luggage rack. How do you ask a stranger in the compartment to help you?

Part 5

Writing*⁶   *(20 marks: 15 mins)*

Write three paragraphs for a tourist brochure about Oxford House using the following information.

Paragraph 1

Name	Oxford House
Type of building	a large country house
Location	near Reading (west of London)
Age	280 years

Paragraph 2

Number of floors	two
Ground floor	a museum of 18th century ceramics
First floor	a private house—seven bedrooms and two living rooms
Outside	large gardens, a farm, a lake

Paragraph 3 (the history of Oxford House)

1720-1800	the Edgerton family home
1800-1920	the Brown family home
1829→	the Richards family home
1955→	a ceramics museum on the ground floor
1990	an extension to the museum

Tapescript for Part 1, Listening Comprehension

Int = interviewer
A = first interviewee
B = second interviewee
C = third interviewee

Interview 1

Int: Excuse me, sir, I'm doing a survey about people's holidays. (Um) Do you mind if I ask you a few questions?
A: Not at all.
Int: Um. Have you had a holiday this year?
A: Er, yes, yes I have.
Int: Where did you go?
A: Well, in actual fact I went to . . . Greece.
Int: Aha. And when did you go there?

A: Erm. It was in May, I think, yes in May.

Int: OK, and how long did you stay?

A: Just for 10 days.

Int: Uh. Where did you stay when you were there?

A: Well, we had a tent and used that most of the time.

Int: Um. And how did you get there?

A: We took a plane from Heathrow to Athens and then went to the coast by bus.

Int: OK. Fine. Erm. Was the weather good?

A: Yes. Most of the time it was brilliant sunshine. It was really lovely. We had a little rain, but not very much.

Int: OK. Good. Thank you very much, sir.

Interview 2

Int: Excuse me. I'm doing a survey about people's holidays. Do you mind if I ask you a few questions?

B: No, of course not.

Int: Have you had a holiday this year?

B: Yes.

Int: Erm. Where did you go?

B: To the north of Italy.

Int: Good. Right and er when did you go there?

B: In the month of . . . in August.

Int: Um. And er how did you get there?

B: I went by train to Milan and then hired a car.

Int: And how long did you stay?

B: Just a month.

Int: OK. When did you . . . Where did you stay when you went?

B: Oh! Lots of different places—hotels and camping most of the time. Er, I think that's . . . I think that's all.

Int: Right. Fine. And what was the weather like when you were there?

B: It was beautiful all the time.

Int: Good. Thank you very much.

B: OK. Bye bye.

Interview 3

Int: Excuse me, I'm doing a survey about people's holidays. Do you mind if I ask you a few questions?

C: Certainly.

Int: Erm. Have you had a holiday this year?

C: Yes, I went to Scotland.

Int: Um. Er. When did you go there?

C: I went there at the end of July.

Int: And how long did you stay?

C: About a week and a half it was, I think.

Int: Erm. How did you get there?

C: Er, car . . . We went by car.

Int: And where did you stay when you were there?

C: You mean what sort of hotel?

Int: Yes.

C: Well . . . stayed in, erm, farmhouses and places like that.

Int: And what was the weather like when you were there? Did you have a good time?

C: Erm. Well, we had some fine days, but it rained a bit, too.

Marking guide

		Marks	*Minutes*
1.	Listening—two marks per answer	20	10
2.	Grammar—two marks per verb	30	15
3.	Dialogue*[7]—three marks each for nos. 2, 3, 5, 6 and 8*[8]	15	10
4.	Situations—three marks per answer	15	10
5.	Writing*[9]	20	15
	TOTAL:	100	60

Notes

These refer to the asterisked/numbered items in the above test.

1.   The listening comprehension is only semi-scripted in that the questions are prepared and then three people are interviewed about their holidays. (See *Listening skills* on page 60 about semi-scripted listening comprehension.) The topic involves the use of and, therefore, the understanding of, the past simple used to narrate past events.

The answers to the first question for each interview are given to allow students time to focus on the task.

Other answers are given where they are considered difficult for the students because of either complexity or audibility of the interviewees' responses.

Only note-form answers are required so as not to make it also a test of the writing skill and so that the students' attention is only briefly taken away from listening to the interviews. The completed boxes provide examples of the kind of answers needed.

Provided that the answers are recognisable, spelling mistakes should not be penalised—this is a test of listening comprehension and not of spelling.

2.   The total mark and a suggested timing are given for each part of the test so as to allow students to pace themselves and therefore finish the test in time, and to see the relative importance of the different parts of the test in terms of marks.

3.   This part focuses both on the reading skill and on the past simple and present perfect (the main grammar points on the syllabus). The dialogue format is used to place the language in a clear context.

4.   This focuses on making and responding to suggestions. It is particularly important here that students should be familiar with this form of testing device and know the metalanguage used. (See *Discourse chains* by Mary Spratt on page 28.)

5.   This tests the revised functional items on the syllabus. Separate situations are used for each point here as it would be unrealistic to include such diverse items in any one conversation.

6.   This tests the guided paragraph writing element of the syllabus. It is given the context of a tourist brochure to make it more meaningful.

The information provided gives guidance on both content and layout and requires use of the past simple and present perfect. (See *Making extended writing tests less subjective* on page 161 for further discussion.)

7.   Test items like the dialogue and situations are open to a wide variety of responses from the students. A scale such as the following could be used to

make the marking of these parts of the test less subjective:

3 marks — appropriate and grammatically accurate.
2 marks — minor inaccuracies which would not interfere with communication.
1 mark — of questionable appropriateness or with a major grammatical inaccuracy.
0 marks — inappropriate or with grammatical inaccuracies liable to inhibit effective communication.

8.   Marks are given only for those parts of the dialogue which are most central to the language of the syllabus. In addition, number 7, for example, would only require 'OK' or a similar response to be acceptable. This system of marking is preferred to a global mark as it is less subjective.

9.   In order to make the marking of this section less subjective, it would be helpful to divide the global mark between the different elements of the writing skill. (See *Making extended writing tests less subjective* on page 161 for further discussion.)

38

An intermediate level achievement test

Marika Szalanczi

The test that follows is for an intermediate group of Portuguese students who are on a course leading to the Cambridge First Certificate examination. The test is written with this exam in mind and some of the techniques used here are similar to those used in the exam.

The test aims to test the following syllabus.

Grammar

— 1st, 2nd and 3rd conditionals
— Reported speech—statements and indirect questions
— *I wish/If only* + past simple
            + past perfect
            + *could*
— *neither . . . nor/not . . . either*

— *It's time* + infinitive
  + past simple
— *Provided, as long as, unless* + present simple
— *In case* + present simple
  + present perfect
  + past simple

Writing

— Narrative (past simple)
— Comparing and contrasting using the following connectors:
  nevertheless, although, in spite of, whereas, however
  Expressing cause and effect using the following connectors:
  as, because, since, so, therefore, consequently

Remedial

— *Think/dream of* (not *in* or *with*)
— Telling the time—especially *half past 5*, not *5 and a half.*
— Simple past of *fall* (*fell* not *felt*) and *drink* (*drank*, not *drunk*)
— Past participles ending in double letter + en (*forbidden, forgotten* etc.)
— Past participles—*writing* not *writting.*
— The difference between *offer* and *give* (*offer* = provide an opportunity to accept something, *give* = transfer ownership to someone else.)
— *A piece of news/information* (*information* and *transport* always singular)
— No preposition, after these verbs:
  answer (not *to*), *telephone* (not *to*), *ask* (not *to*), *enter* (not *in*), *marry* (not *with*), *contact* (not *with*)

N.B. The remedial section concentrates principally on errors typical of Portuguese speakers of English.

Test

Part 1

Gap-filling *(14 marks: 10 mins)*

Read the following passage carefully. For each number there is one word missing. Write the numbers 1 to 14 on the paper provided and then write the word that is missing.

Janice Burton wanted a new camera. ____(1)____ she lived in the country, it wasn't easy to buy one. ____(2)____ , she was really delighted when, ____(3)____ through one of her monthly magazines, she saw an advertisement for a camera with ____(4)____ electronic flash and in a beautiful leather case. She got her cheque-book out and sent off for it straight away. A week later the company returned her cheque ____(5)____ she hadn't remembered to sign ____(6)____ ! She was really looking forward ____(7)____ using the camera. ____(8)____ , when it arrived, she was very disappointed because it was nothing like the one in the ____(9)____ and it hadn't come with a leather case ____(10)____ . They had sent the electronic flash ____(11)____ they had forgotten _____(12)_____ send the special batteries it needed and so she couldn't use it.

She was so annoyed that she decided to return it and write and complain to the Company. She said that _____(13)_____ they returned her money immediately, she would write to the newspapers and tell people not to buy their cameras. A week later her cheque _____(14)_____ returned

Part 2

Sentence transformation   *(16 marks: 15 mins)*

Complete sentence (b) in such a way that it means the same as sentence (a). Write your sentences on the paper provided.

Example: (a) The meat wasn't as good as the fish.
Answer: (b) The fish was better than the meat.

1 (a) She insured her luggage because she thought it might be stolen.
   (b) She insured her luggage in case . . . .
2 (a) 'Why didn't you tell me about it?' she asked.
   (b) She asked me . . . .
3 (a) Bernard arrived late so we didn't go to the pub.
   (c) If Bernard hadn't . . . .
4 (a) How I would love to speak Italian!
   (b) I wish I . . . .
5 (a) 'I was playing football yesterday, so I didn't do my homework', he said.
   (b) He said he . . . .
6 (a) You'd better go to the doctor's.
   (b) If I were you, ...
7 (a) If you don't wear long sleeves, they won't let you into the church.
   (b) Unless . . . .
8 (a) I won't tell the Director, if you put the money back.
   (b) Provided . . . .

Part 3

Error recognition and correction*[1]   *(10 marks: 5 mins)*

What's wrong with these sentences? Write them out again correctly.

Example: What are the latest news?
You write: What is the latest news?

1. He telephoned to the travel agent.
2. The local tourist office will give you informations about hotels.
3. He said me to come back later.
4. He married with Mrs. Robinson's daughter.
5. He has spent the whole afternoon writting letters.

Part 4

Writing*[2]   *(20 marks: 20 mins)*

You decide to enter a competition at a travel agency where the prize is a free holiday for two in one of these hotels in Athens: the Oscar and the Alkistis. Write a short paragraph (60–100 words) saying which hotel you would choose and why. You must use at least four of the following words/expressions: *nevertheless, although, however, in spite of, whereas, therefore, consequently.*

The winner will be the one who, in the judges' opinion, writes the best paragraph.

GREECE ATHENS

Oscar

A 'B' category hotel about 2 miles from the city centre and near to the railway station. There are 9 floors with 120 rooms and 200 beds. All rooms have bath/shower, w.c., balcony and telephone.

- Rooftop swimming pool
- Rooftop terrace
- Lounge
- TV room
- Bar
- Pool bar service
- Air-conditioned
- Lift

Prices shown are per person for half board in twin-bedded room with bath/shower, wc, balcony and telephone.

Supplements per person per night
Single room £2.50

Children's reductions
Apply Category E See page 4

Alkistis

A bright, compact hotel with 120 rooms, all with private bath/shower, w.c. and telephone, on 11 floors with 200 beds. Official category 'C'. A well run hotel fully supervised by the owner. It is in the centre of Athens close to the market and Omonia Square.

- Lounge
- Bar
- Restaurant
- Roof gardens
- Lift

Prices shown are per person for half board in twin-bedded room with private bath/shower, wc and telephone.

Supplements per person per night
Single room £2.00

Children's reductions
Apply Category E See page 4

6 July–19 July

No. of nights:	ALKISTIS		OSCAR	
	Half Board		Half Board	
	7	14	7	14
Prices:	199	249	215	285

Part 5 **Composition*³** *(20 marks: 30 mins)*

Choose one of the following compositions and write between 120 and 180 words. Please write on alternate lines.

1. I had just locked the front door and was leaving the flat/house when . . .

or

2. My most embarrassing experience.

Marking guide

1.	Gap-filling	14
2.	Sentence transformation	16
3.	Error recognition and correction	10
4.	Writing*⁴	20
5.	Composition*⁵	20
	TOTAL	80

Notes

These refer to the asterisked/numbered items in the above test.

1.   This method aims to encourage students to check through their own written work looking for errors and also shows them the most common errors.

2.   The information is taken from a travel brochure. The task has been made more authentic by using the idea of a competition. The words and expressions are in a formal register and this context was chosen as one which would require students to use formal language.

3.   It is recognised that this is a more artificial task than the previous part on writing, with no input and no context. However, compositions of this type are set in the First Certificate exam, and students will have been prepared in class to tackle them.

4.   The majority of the marks in this section are given for the correct use of the connectors and lower priority is given to style and content.

5.   This is marked subjectively but the following guidelines are given in order to standardise the marks as far as possible. The guidelines are similar to those used in the First Certificate exam.

Very good *(18–20)*	Composition contains well-constructed paragraphs with an effective presentation of points. There are very few errors and a wide range of vocabulary.
Good *(15–17)*	Composition contains well-constructed paragraphs and the basic idea is presented clearly. It is free from basic errors and the range of vocabulary is above average.
Pass *(13–16)*	The basic idea is communicated. Grammar and punctuation are reasonably accurate but there are a few basic errors. Range of vocabulary is average.
Weak *(10–12)*	The basic idea is communicated but control of grammar and punctuation is inadequate. Range of vocabulary is below average.
Poor *(9 and below)*	The composition contains badly constructed paragraphs and the basic idea is barely communicated. There are a lot of basic errors and the range of vocabulary is limited.

39

An advanced level achievement test

Mary Spratt

Level: post First Certificate

Syllabus: topic based with skills and language focus

Part of syllabus covered before test:

Topics: —Working Life: value of different jobs, applying for jobs

Skills: —Note taking
—Report writing
—Reading for gist and detail
—Listening for gist and detail
—Oral fluency practice

Revision structures:
—Comparative and superlative of adjectives and adverbs
—Past v perfect tenses
—Present simple v present continuous
—Present v past of *must/ought to/may*
—Gerund v infinitive

Revision functions:
—Exponents of giving advice
—Describing people
—Comparing

Test   The subject of this test is choosing a suitable candidate for a job as a travel courier.

Part 1   **Reading**   *(10 minutes)*

1. Read the following interview form which Mr. Jones, the personnel manager, filled in when he interviewed a candidate for the job of travel courier. Try to decide whether the candidate is suitable for the job or not. Take notes on her suitability if you wish.

Position applied for: **Travel Courier**

Reference: **83/212**

PHOTO

NAME: **Sue Young**   AGE: **20**

SEX: **Female**   MARITAL STATUS: **Single**

QUALIFICATIONS: **5 'O' levels incl. German**
1 'A' level = French

PREVIOUS EXPERIENCE: **a. one year au pair in France**
b. 2 x 6 months = courier with travel company in Spain, France, UK

REASONS FOR APPLICATION: **wants permanent job, likes courier work**

ATTITUDE TO WORK: **bit over confident enthusiastic**

KNOWLEDGE OF JOB: **mentioned need for patience and long hours**

INTERESTS: **dancing, ski-ing, cinema**

IMPRESSIONS OF PERSONALITY: **bit too confident, lively, bright, keen, perhaps bit immature**

PHYSICAL APPEARANCE: **neat**

Part 2   **Listening comprehension**   *(15 minutes)*

You are going to hear a taped dialogue between Mr. Jones and another candidate, Jill Martin. As you listen, complete the interview form as if you were Mr. Jones. You must only write notes. You will hear the dialogue twice.

Position applied for:

Reference:

PHOTO

NAME: AGE:

SEX: MARITAL STATUS:

QUALIFICATIONS:

PREVIOUS EXPERIENCE:

REASONS FOR APPLICATION:

ATTITUDE TO WORK: KNOWLEDGE OF JOB:

INTERESTS:

IMPRESSIONS OF PERSONALITY: PHYSICAL APPEARANCE:

Part 3   **Report writing**   *(25 minutes)*

There is only one vacancy for the travel courier job. Mr. Jones has to write a report to his boss giving his opinions on the two candidates and making a recommendation. Imagine you are Mr. Jones and write the report you would send to your boss, mentioning any relevant information about either candidate (character, experience, attitudes, etc). Your report must be both thorough and convincing as it will be the only grounds your boss has for coming to a decision. You should write 200–250 words.

Marking guide   (Part 2, Listening comprehension—30%, Part 3, Report writing—70%)

Note taking	*Marks*
Students' notes should be:	
genuine notes	10
grammatically correct	5
correctly spelt	5
accurate and complete	10
TOTAL:	30

Report writing	*Marks*
Students' reports should be:	
grammatically correct	30
in appropriate style	15
comprehensive	15
correctly spelt and punctuated	10
TOTAL:	70

Notes

1.   The marks in the listening comprehension give more importance to the quality of the note-taking than to comprehension.
2.   The report writing involves comprehension of the first completed interview form and the listening comprehension, and will also bring in the structures revised in the syllabus.
3.   The recorded material was semi-scripted. The man was given a blank interview form and asked to ask the relevant questions in any order. The girl was given the following information:

Name: Jill Martin
Age: 22
Marital Status: Single
Qualifications: 5 'O' levels — French, History, Maths.,
                                              Biology, English
                              1 'A' level — French
                              Diploma from secretarial college
Present Work: three years in a travel agency
Reason for Application: * present job = monotonous,
                                                            boring
                                      * travel courier = exotic
Attitude to Work: You're not really very interested but fancy
                              a change and need more money. You
                              might not wish to say that, though.
Interests: dancing, watching TV
Personality: bored, indifferent

Section D
Other Areas

40

Teaching at an advanced level

Roger Gower

1 Some common problems

Lack of progress

Although advanced students are able to work for relatively long periods in the target language, they very often feel they are not making progress. After all, apart from less frequently-used vocabulary, there is hardly any new language for them to learn. You, the teacher, know that what they now have to do is to improve the way they speak and write, the way they listen and read. The work is basically remedial and it is not always easy for either you or the learners to discern improvement. In fact, it is often not that easy for learners to realise what their real language problems *are*!

Mixed abilities

Another difficulty in the classroom is, of course, that at this level each student will have different abilities in each of the language skill areas and different deficiencies. One student may speak accurately but not fluently, another may speak fluently but not accurately, another may not understand a native speaker speaking naturally, another may understand everything, another may have a very limited range of expression, another may have great expressive powers, and so on. Yet they are all grouped together in the same class and, in most schools, expected to do much the same thing. This, too, is something that can contribute to a feeling of lack of progress.

Language presentation techniques

The level of language awareness in an advanced class is often quite high, and controlled presentation and practice techniques employed by teachers at the lower levels cannot be employed so rigidly or predictably. You may, therefore think—justifiably—that it is worth working on exercises which explore the language in depth. (A book such as *Discover English* by Bolitho & Tomlinson, Heinemann Educational Books, is excellent for this purpose.) The students can be encouraged to talk about the language and articulate why things are used and when. In some cases, they may feel this is rather abstract and intellectual and nothing to do with improving their own performance, although, in my own experience, this frustration is not so frequent as the contrary frustration of feeling that nothing new is being learnt.

Lack of opportunity for self expression

Advanced students may be advanced intellectually and have definite interests, but their frustration will not stem from the inability to talk about those interests because their English is not good enough; *they* often feel frustrated at the lack of opportunity given in the class to express themselves. In one sense, what interests students matters far more at this level than at a lower level (where the students usually accept that what they are there for is to learn the new language).

Of course an able teacher will, at all levels, exploit a student's general interests, and his or her ability to express them, to the benefit of the class, but it is very much more necessary in advanced classes. (For all these reasons, the idea of a single coursebook at advanced level is, in fact, absurd, although it is a reality in many schools and something many advanced teachers latch onto to give the course a feeling of coherence and the class a feeling of security.)

2 What can be done?

In a school where the students spend all day doing nothing but English, as is the case in many language schools in Britain, many of these problems are intensified. They can be partially solved by:
— providing greater opportunity for individualised work;
— re-grouping the class (or classes) according to language needs and interests;
— providing monitored self-directed learning programmes making use of some kind of self-access system.

Ideally a whole group should do only what the whole group needs to do. If most students in a group need oral fluency practice, they should be able to get on and have a discussion, while other individuals work on, say, a project in the library in order to improve their reading and writing. Of course, to organise a course like this, both the group's individual needs and its group needs have to be diagnosed in advance and a 'scheme of work' for much of the course negotiated with the class. Such a programme takes time, money and resources, and is often not possible in a school where the teacher sees a group of 30 students only twice a week for 1½ hours at a time. There, the teacher is often forced to do more 'whole-group' activities and spend less time on relaxed small-group activities; there too he or she may feel that there is not enough time in class for study and things like 'streamed' remedial work.

I think the ideal should be modified rather than lost, and we should seize upon practical opportunities as we see them. After all, no school is able to individualise completely, no school will 're-stream' everybody, and no school can regroup on every occasion it is desirable. With an advanced general English class in mind, is it not possible to try the following?

Individualisation

Work in a programme of individualised study and individual remedial work (even if it is no more than different students having different homework suited to their needs).

'Streaming'

'Stream' activities in the class so that one group is doing one thing according to *its* needs and another doing something else. (Is it so impossible?)

A 'scheme of work'

Diagnose individual interests, wants and needs well in advance and negotiate a rough 'scheme of work', for perhaps the whole term, with the group. At the very least you could get them to fill out a simple questionnaire to establish these interests. Ideas as to what should be included might be elicited from the whole group, who then decide which ones to include in what order. There are many different ways of doing this but no matter which way you choose, it has to be done in a spirit of mutual co-operation and with a sense of purpose. One simple way is to elicit all the main language skills on to the board (listening, reading, etc.), all the language topic areas (grammar, vocabulary etc.) and as many activities as you can think of (role-play, drilling, etc.). Then there is a discussion, perhaps in groups, of the value and purpose of each of these, e.g. *Why do a role-play in class?, What types of listening are there?, Which is the most important?* In doing this, the students are made more conscious of the reasons behind the methods you are going to use in the classroom and in fact, if the discussion really gets going, how languages are learnt. In my experience this really helps the students understand why they are asked to do certain things in class, which in turn helps to motivate them to do what you want them to do!

You can then continue the process by asking the students to tick those language skills and topic areas they feel most in need of on the course. So you might get as a summary on the board:

Guided speaking practice   ✔ ✔ ✔ ✔
Pronunciation work   ✔ ✔ ✔ ✔ ✔ ✔
etc.

You are then able to distinguish what is an individual need of one or two students and what is a whole-group need.

In general, when you negotiate a 'scheme of work' with a class, it is very important that you give clear guidance about what might be included without determining everything that goes into it. Certainly there is no reason why certain things should not be pushed, even though, as yet, the students may not see their importance. In fact, unless this is done, there is a danger that you might be felt to be abdicating responsibility and not helping them sufficiently, particularly if the group is neither very aware of the language nor of how languages are learnt.

Diagnosing and building on weaknesses

Another way that advanced learners can develop a sense of their own progress is if work on language (e.g. grammar, vocabulary) and on language skills (e.g. practice in skim reading) uses the students' less-than-perfect performance as a basis. In other words, you show the group how important it is to improve by showing them the weakness in what they do. (The emphasis then is very much on your helping them to improve a piece of work rather than your correcting it or your marking it—better that you guide them to correct it themselves.)

For example, you might record the students' performance in a role play, then play it back and try and get them, with or without your help, to improve upon their performance, perhaps after discussion of the main language problems that have arisen. The sort of language problems you might expect will include the usual grammar and pronunciation mistakes, but they may also include such things as use of inappropriate register, dependence on avoidance techniques, poor use of intonation etc. Alternatively you might indicate a general problem area, such as poor discrimination between the past tense and the present perfect, and tell the group you will do remedial practice in the next class. In their written work you indicate where errors have occurred and where communication performance is weak (e.g. by underlining the poor bits and putting a symbol like *G* for grammar or *R* for register in the margin). Students on their own or in pairs or groups then set about improving their production. Of course, you can also set an achievement test at the right time to find out how far the students have improved—or not!

Themes and topics

Many teachers like to give their classes coherence and interest by selecting a topic, or getting the class to select a topic, to act as a theme for several lessons (such themes might include Love and Marriage, Age, Money, Great Events). Other teachers like to get students working over a longer period on a 'subject' like Business, Literature, Science, even Pottery in some cases; English is then learnt through the 'subject', so to speak.

3 Role of the teacher

Clearly, your role as a teacher changes at the advanced level. Since you do not need to introduce new language so much and practise it (it can often be done in a controlled way but it needs to be done more quickly and more spontaneously and relate to an on-the-spot need), you often become more of a study organizer, a planner of work, a source of ideas, language and information, an advisor, a group animator, and so on. While you will also be an on-going assessor of students' progress, you should be seen as more of an improver than a teacher. Of course, talk of such things is only interesting in the abstract—all teachers need to be fully themselves first and foremost, even when they are taking on roles for classroom purposes!

41

Consolidating vocabulary

Mary Spratt

1 The need to teach vocabulary

How many new words do students learn per lesson, on average? This is possibly a question that many teachers have never asked themselves because vocabulary is no longer seen as a very important aim in syllabuses. It is, however, quite revealing to try and work these figures out. There may be lessons in which no new vocabulary occurs, but when working on a reading or a listening text or during a discussion lesson, it is quite common for ten or so new words to occur, and when teaching a new structure or functional exponent, four or five new words may well be needed to build up the situation. These figures do not seem very high, but if they are added up lesson by lesson, week by week, they begin to mount up to anywhere between 150 and 300 words in 30 hours. Not only is this estimate probably a conservative one for intermediate and advanced level classes, but it also does not include all those words that come up unplanned and incidentally during lessons, or all those other words met in listening or reading comprehensions which are left for passive recognition. In this article, however, I want to focus on words destined to become part of the students' active vocabulary.

Focusing on vocabulary

Language teachers are inevitably involved in teaching vocabulary, even though, nowadays, many syllabuses and textbooks state their aims, not in terms of vocabulary, but in terms of skills, functions, grammar or topics. I am not suggesting that these aims are wrong—our aims must be to enable our students to function accurately, appropriately and fluently in the situations they will find themselves in—but one of the tools that enables them to do just this is the ability to recognise and produce a wide range of vocabulary items. I feel there may be a danger in many courses nowadays of vocabulary being used or taught mainly as an instrument on which to hang structures, functions or skills; one result of this may be that, when revision is carried out, it rarely focuses on vocabulary, i.e. on those 150–300 words taught in 30 hours. But my experience of foreign language learning tells me that I rarely remember a foreign word that I have met only once, and I strongly suspect that many students find themselves in a similar position.

In this article I would like to suggest some games and activities which can help students review and remember previously learnt vocabulary items.

Keeping tabs

First, though, some words of advice for the teacher. Before teachers can re-introduce lexical items, they have to know what items have already been introduced. Of course, it is always possible to refer back to the textbook or to lesson plans to know what these items were but, besides being uneconomical from the point of view of time, this procedure cannot keep track of the incidental yet important words that crop up in lessons as students try to say what they want to say.

One way for teachers to keep tabs on all the vocabulary items that arise for active use is to keep a vocabulary list. All this need consist of is a few sheets of stapled paper that are handed out to one student each lesson. The student then simply notes down on the paper any new words that come up during the lesson and then returns the paper to the teacher at the end of the lesson. Next lesson, the teacher gives the sheet to another student to keep a similar record of that lesson, and so on throughout the term. This document can gradually become a most valuable revision aid, can increase students' awareness of the value of vocabulary, and provides a useful tool for the teacher when devising vocabulary revision work.

It is also useful for teachers to remember that the vocabulary items they teach come from limited topic areas. Most elementary and intermediate syllabuses are based on a combination of students' needs and interests and therefore probably cover the following areas: personal identification, house and home, life at home, education and future careers, free time and entertainment, travel, relationships with other people, health and welfare, shopping, food and drink, services, places, foreign languages and weather. These are the topic areas identified for the Threshold Level (see: *The Threshold Level for Modern Language Learning in Schools* by J.A. van Ek, Longman) and they certainly do provide a broad basis for building contexts for vocabulary revision work.

Methods

So far I have spoken about ways in which teachers can group together the vocabulary items they have taught. It is useful now to look at the principal methods that can be employed for vocabularly teaching, as these same methods are most useful for vocabulary revision. Aside from dictionary work and asking students to infer meaning from context, there are probably three main ways of teaching vocabulary:

—showing students the real object or action, or a pictorial representation of these (denotation);

—explaining the new word by relating it to other words in the same lexical field as itself (word families);

—paraphrasing the new word (explanation).

Tools such as vocabulary lists and topic areas, and methods such as denotation, word families and explanation, can provide the teacher with an extremely solid basis for devising a wide range of vocabulary revision activities. All the games and activities that follow have been worked out on these bases. They are also all very simple in design and lend themselves to the devising of similar activities on different word areas. Most of them can be as successfully used at elementary as at advanced levels and they are all fun and (with one exception) relatively brief so they can easily be slotted into the beginning or end of a lesson on the regular basis that revision requires.

The suggested games and activies divide up as follows:

---

1   Revision through denotation
   —labelling   —picture dominoes
   —spot the difference   —picture rummy
   —describe and draw   —Kim's game

2   Revision through word families
   —word thermometers   —odd man out
   —series   —categories 1
   —word bingo   —categories 2
   —associations

3   Revision through explanations
   —'glug'   —vocabulary quizzes
   —crosswords   —vocabulary revision lesson
   —crosswords in reverse

---

2   Revision through denotation

Labelling

Students are given a picture. They have to write the names of objects indicated in the picture. A competetive element can be introduced by making the first student to finish the winner.

Spot the difference

Students are put into pairs. Each member of the pair receives a picture which is slightly different from his partner's. Students hide the pictures from one another and then, by a process of describing, questioning and answering, discover what the differences are.

Describe and draw

Students are put into pairs. One student has a picture, the other a blank piece of paper and a pencil. The student with the picture must tell his partner what to draw so that the drawing ends up the same as the original picture. N.B. The student with the picture must not show his partner the picture until the drawing is completed. At the end, they can compare the two pictures.

Picture dominoes

Students get into groups of 4–6. Each student has 6 picture cards which contain pictures of objects they know, and there is a central pile of 4 cards. (All the students' cards must be different, by the way). The object of the game is to get rid of one's cards before anyone else does. To play the game, one person puts down a card and then the next person puts another card down next to it, if it can be proved that there is some connection or similarity between the two cards and everyone agrees that this similarity or connection exists. After this, it is the next student's turn, and so on. If a student cannot put down any of his cards, he picks up a card from the central pile and tries to go with this card. The first person to put down all their cards is the winner.

Picture rummy

This is similar to picture dominoes in two ways: students have to prove a connection between their cards, and the cards contain pictures of known objects. Students get into groups of 4–6. Six cards are dealt to each player and the remaining cards are put in the central pile. The object of the game is once again to get rid of one's cards as quickly as possible. There are two ways of doing this: either by making up sets of 3 related cards and putting them down on the table, or else by adding to sets of cards already down on the table. Students take it in turns to play and must pick up a card from the central pile if they cannot go. This game involves considerable discussion as students argue over what constitutes a set.

Kim's game

Students are shown a picture or a tray with objects on it, or a series of different flash cards or magazine pictures. They have two minutes to memorize as many of the objects as they can. The cards, picture or tray are then taken away and the students have to say what they saw, or write down everything they can remember seeing, then compare with the rest of the class.

3   Revision through word families

Word thermometers

These are useful for indicating degree in e.g. size, speed, age, distance, emotion. Students are given a list of words in jumbled order. They have to place these words in the correct place on the thermometer.

Series	Construct the following series as in the example.

> *Example*   Cutlery: knife, fork, spoon
> Transport:
> Vehicles:
> Furniture:
> Buildings:

Word Bingo	The teacher thinks of an area of language (e.g. *shopping*) that the students have recently been studying. Students draw 10 squares on their page then put one word connected with shopping in each of the squares. The teacher then calls out, one at a time, words connected with shopping. If the students have the word on their page they cross it out. The first student to cross out all the words on their page is the winner.

Associations	The teacher says a key word e.g. *travelling*. The students then have to write down all the words they can think of connected with travelling. They have a time limit, e.g. two minutes, and the person with the highest number of acceptable words is the winner.

Odd Man Out	The teacher writes words on the board and asks: *Which is the odd man out?* e.g.

cheese   eggs   oranges   bread   soap   meat   (*Answer: 'soap' because you cannot eat it*)

Categories 1	Put the jumbled words in the middle into the right boxes.

Jobs	Countries	Fruit

milk   typist   apples   pigs   shirts   Germany   chickens
Japan   shoes   oranges   pears
butcher   tea   peaches   wine   cows
driver   Greece   socks   Turkey   trousers
plums   pants   baker   dogs
coffee   sheep

Clothes	Drinks	Animals

Categories 2	This is the reverse of the previous activity. The class establishes five categories of things e.g. jobs, animals, countries, clothes, fruit. Each student then writes these categories across the top of a page. The teacher or a student then calls out a letter of the alphabet. The students have to fill in each category with a word beginning with that letter. The student who finishes first shouts *Stop* and his answers are checked. Then another letter is called and the game continues. This game can also be played in groups.

4   Revision through explanations

'Glug' (sometimes known as 'Coffee Pot')

Someone thinks of a particular verb. The rest of the class then have to find out what that verb is by asking questions in which *glug* represents the verb they are looking for. So, for example, they might ask questions like: *Do you like glugging? When do you glug? Is it difficult to glug? Can you glug by yourself?* until they find the right verb. This game can also be played in groups.

Crosswords

You are no doubt familiar with crosswords, but do not forget that you can easily devise crosswords round topic areas. Mary Glasgow Publications produce some very useful books of crosswords for EFL learners, called *English Crosswords, 1, 2,* and *3.*

Crosswords in reverse

Give the students a small and simple completed crossword and get them to write the clues. If this is done in groups, the groups can pass on their clues and a blank version of the crossword to the next group who can then fill in the answers.

Vocabulary quizzes

Divide the class into groups of 4 or 5 students and give each group a different list of words that have recently occurred in their English lessons. Each group then has to write questions that would produce those words (e.g. if *hot* were on the list a question might be: *What's the opposite of 'cold'?*). When each group has completed their questions, they take it in turns to ask them to all the other groups. The first group that gives the right answer to a question gets a point, and the winning group is the one with the most points at the end. It is a good idea if the teacher writes each vocabulary item up on the blackboard after it has been given and then, when the quiz is over, has a quick pronunciation drill from the words on the board.

Vocabulary revision lesson

(N.B. This can easily take 1½ hours with an advanced class.)
—The teacher makes a list, in two columns, of new words that have occured in recent lessons. (Be careful not to include too many words—40, for example, is quite enough for an advanced class.)
—The teacher copies this list and hands out a copy to every member of the class.
—The students read through the list and individually underline each word whose meaning they cannot remember.
—All the students mingle in a free space in the class and ask one another the meaning of all the words they have underlined. Both the questions and the answers must be in English, of course. N.B. The teacher must not help at this stage.
—The students return to their seats and go through their lists in pairs, checking with one another, and with dictionaries if necessary, to see they have the right meaning for each word. The teacher at this stage can make sure that everyone is on the right track.
—The students get into groups and each group becomes responsible for a section of the list. So, for example, if the class were divided into two groups, one group could be responsible for column 1 and the other for column 2, or, with 4 groups, the first group would take charge of the first half of column one, etc. It then becomes the task of each group to write definitions or crossword-like clues for each word on their part of the list.

—All the students turn over or hide their original word lists.
—*Quiz:* Each group takes it in turn to read out a definition or clue. The first group to guess the word correctly wins a point. It is useful to put a limit on answering time, and essential if there are only two groups. The activity continues until each group has read out each of its definitions. Scores are counted up and the winner is announced.
—*Pronunciation practice:* During the quiz, the teacher can write each answer up on the blackboard as it is given. At the end, a very simple choral repetition drill can be given on each item, to reinforce and clinch pronunciation, meaning and memory.

Follow-up lesson (optional)

Word Bingo (see above): Each student puts words from the original list into the squares on their bingo card.

Acknowledgments: Word Thermometers in an article by Francis Curtis, Vol. III, no. 2 of *Newsletter for Portuguese Teachers of English.*
Picture Dominoes and Picture Rummy in *ELTI Games*, British Council, London.

42

Using songs

Sheila Ward

1   Why teach songs?

Many teachers cannot see the point of teaching songs and tend to think of it as a frivolous activity suitable only for five minutes on Friday afternoons. Below are some of the valid reasons for teaching them.

Authentic activity

Many of us spend a fair amount of our spare time listening to songs and many people, especially youngsters, enjoy joining in, so by using songs in the language class we are getting the students to do something that they would do in real life. Many of our young students may never have the opportunity to visit an English-speaking country but they are very much involved with British and American pop music.

Authentic language

Most English songs we hear on the radio or television have not been produced for EFL learners and have not been recorded by people with Received Pronunciation, so they are a good way of exposing our students to authentic language.

Motivation

As people tend to find songs enjoyable, we can liven up the language class by using them to stimulate the students' interest.

Repetition	Repetition can be very boring for students but they will happily repeat the same structure over and over again if it is contained in a song.
Rhythm and stress	As songs have a very marked rhythm, we can help our students to use the correct rhythm and stress by reciting and singing songs.
New vocabulary	Songs provide a means of learning new vocabulary in context, and words learnt this way are rarely forgotten. Most of us can probably still remember words from songs learnt in our foreign language class when we were at secondary school.
Group activity	Singing a song is a great way of unifying a group. We can see this from the way songs are used in politics, at football matches, etc. It can foster co-operation among students and give the shyer ones a chance to join in. Students who have more difficulties than others will have an opportunity to make a contribution to the corporate effort without worrying about getting it wrong, and this may increase their self-confidence.
Practising alone	Our students may have few opportunities to speak English to other people outside the classroom, but they can always sing a song when they are alone. No one will take much notice if you walk down the road singing to yourself, but if they hear you talking to yourself they may think there is something wrong with you! Thus songs are a means of oral reinforcement outside of the class.

Bearing all these reasons in mind, it is a pity that so many teachers either relegate songs to a five-minute slot on a Friday afternoon, or, even worse, do not exploit them at all. In my opinion, songs should be an integral part of any language programme.

2 Choosing and using songs

When choosing a song we must keep in mind our aims and choose one that will help us achieve them. Below is a list of possible aims and suggestions on how to choose and use the songs.

Structural consolidation

Several collections of songs have been commercially produced to provide practice in certain structures and, in addition to these, good examples can be found on many traditional and pop records. When choosing a song for this purpose, it is better if the song contains plenty of examples of the target structure and focuses mainly on one grammatical point.

It is advisable, especially at beginners' level, to teach the song after the structure has already been presented and practised in class. A song could be exploited as follows:

Step 1:   pre-teach the new vocabulary.
Step 2:   recite the chorus line by line, getting the students to repeat each line.
Step 3:   say the chorus together.
Step 4:   sing the chorus together.
Step 5:   follow the procedure of steps 2, 3 and 4 with the verses.
Step 6:   sing the whole song together.

With elementary classes and children, it is preferable if they do not see the text, as their reading can hinder their listening and they may not hear the correct stress and rhythm, not to mention pronunciation. But it is advisable to check, perhaps by individual repetition, to make sure the students are saying the words correctly and not merely saying what they think they hear.

Learning new vocabulary	Teachers should decide which vocabulary they wish to teach and then choose a suitable song. For example, *There's a hole in my bucket* contains everyday words like *bucket, stone, knife*, whereas *Yellow Submarine* contains words connected with the sea: *sea, waves, aboard, sail*.
Listening comprehension	Almost any song can be used for listening comprehension before the students learn to sing it. Below are three ways in which *There's a hole in my bucket* could be exploited:

—Listening for gist. One or two questions could be asked such as: *Who are the people?* (A man and a woman) *Is he happy or unhappy?* (He's unhappy)
—Listening for specific information. This could be a True/False exercise, e.g: *He has got some water in his bucket.* (F) *She tells him to mend his bucket.* (T)
—Listening for the precise wording of songs, e.g. through gap-filling the lyrics of a song while listening.

Reading comprehension	The same techniques can also be used to practise reading comprehension with the lyrics of songs. This seems less natural as we are more likely to listen to a song than to read it, but it does provide a change from always treating the song as a listening comprehension.
Phonology	*Pronunciation*

Try to analyse which sounds your students have difficulty with and find suitable songs that contain examples of that sound. Do not choose a song that is too complex, however, or the whole aim will be lost. For example, many nationalities have problems with the initial /h/, so a good song to practise this is: *He's got the whole world in his hands*.

Stress and rhythm
It is important, especially at elementary level, to choose a song in which the accented beats of the music fall on words which normally carry strong stress, so that the students will learn to associate content words with strong stress and grammatical words with weak stress. A song such as *My bonnie lies over the ocean* employs very natural rhythm and stress.

Discussion work	This can take place before the listening as a warm-up session or afterwards in the light of what the students have heard. A song which could be used in this way is the Beatles' *She's leaving home*. The teacher can lead into the theme by asking the students if they think children should go on living with their parents after they are grown up, what problems exist between generations, etc. This arouses the students' interest in hearing the song. Alternatively, the discussion could take place after as exploitation of the song. A written follow up could be the letter that the girl left explaining why she was leaving home or the parents' letter to 'Problem Page' asking why their daughter has left home.
Cultural background	Whereas literature is by and large the product of an educated elite, songs, especially folk songs and pop songs, are the natural expression of the people who created them and reflect the life and mentality of those people. By introducing our students to songs, we help them to understand the culture of the people whose language they are learning and, consequently, to understand the language itself better. If we take

the example of Portugal, we could say that its folk-songs generally reflect an agricultural or sea-faring community, the 'Fado' of Lisbon an urban community and the 'Fado' of Coimbra a university community. By combining the three we can begin to understand something about Portuguese culture.

It is very difficult to give guide-lines as to which songs to select to provide a cultural background to Britain. A combination of folk songs, pop songs, musical and light opera would certainly give a varied picture of British life.

Singing for enjoyment

In mentioning the five-minute Friday afternoon slot at the beginning of this article, I was in no way intending to criticise it. There are times when students are tired, when they have been subjected to intense mental activity and they welcome the singing of songs for enjoyment.

43

Homework and correction

Les Dangerfield

1 Why set homework?

To extend and consolidate classroom practice

Commonly, students have no more than three hours of classes per week in the target language, divided, perhaps, into three one-hour sessions during the week. In this case, two homework tasks per week involving, say, half an hour of student time each, will increase the time spent practising the language by 33% and increase the frequency of contact with the language from three to five occasions per week.

Further, homework can focus on reading and writing, which are innately solitary activities, thus freeing more class time for practice of the listening and speaking skills.

To allow students to work at their own pace

Classroom tasks usually have to be done within a fixed time-limit set by the teacher, which may mean that faster students have to sit doing nothing whilst the slower students face the possible embarrassment of not finishing the task in time. Homework, however, can be done at a student's own pace, allowing more time for reflection and lessening the pressure to finish the task quickly.

2 Important pre-requisites for homework tasks

The following apply largely to writing activities, as homework tasks will normally involve writing rather than the other skills.

Validity

Tasks must be valid in terms of the aims for which the teacher is setting the homework. If, for example, a teacher wants students to practise the *use* of the passive, an active-to-passive transformation exercise would not be a valid way of practising this as, although it ensures that students know how to manipulate the verb forms, it cannot conclusively show whether they understand its use.

Guidance

At a simple level, this means clear instructions with examples of what the students are required to do. However, beyond that, it has implications for the amount of control that the format of the task has over what the students can produce. The degree of guidance can be divided into four general categories:

Controlled: where the student is given little or no room for error, for example in an exercise involving simply the choice of alternative words to fill each space in a given text where each of the chosen alternatives for each space is acceptable. This level of guidance produces what is little more than a copying exercise.

Cued: in which the language of the exercise is given, but the student has to perform a task such as joining given sentences with given connectors.

Guided: in which details of content are given but students have to formulate their own way of expressing that content. For example,

Write a letter of application for a job saying:
Paragraph 1:   which job you are applying for
　　　　　　　　where you saw the job advertised
Paragraph 2:   how old you are
　　　　　　　　what qualifications you have
　　　　　　　　where you worked before
Paragraph 3:   why you want the job
　　　　　　　　when you are available for interview.

Free: in which students are provided only with a subject for their writing, perhaps in the form of a composition title, and, ideally, a purpose for which they are writing.

Guidance has a number of functions and the relative weight of these varies according to the nature of the task and the level of the students.
— It means that students can produce extended pieces of written work from a very early stage and this has motivational value.
— It limits the students' scope for error. If, as in the guided category of task above, details of content are given, students are not tempted to express ideas which they are not capable of expressing in the target language.
— It can ensure that students use certain items of language or an appropriate range of items in their writing. An example of this can be seen in the writing section of the *Elementary level achievement test* on page 164, in which the guidance given for the third paragraph ensures that the students use the simple past, the present perfect and a form of the future. One of the drawbacks of unguided composition is that

students can write answers using only simplistic language which can deceptively appear better than an answer by a student who has attempted to use a wider range of language.

— It helps to make the task purely linguistic in that it lessens the demands made on the students' imagination or on their knowledge in other fields.

Meaningfulness

Grammatical exercises should involve thought on the part of the student rather than a mechanical operation which can be carried out without necessarily understanding the language involved. For example, instead of using the following transformation exercise:

Exercise item	*Student answer*
a) I've broken a cup.	I haven't broken a cup.
b) I've seen John.	I haven't seen John.

the task would be made more interesting, and also made to require thought, by using the following instead:

Exercise item	*Student answer*
a) Did you like the new John Fowles book?	I haven't read it yet.
b) Did you like the new Fellini film?	I haven't seen it yet.

The second exercise is more meaningful in the following ways:
— the student response forms part of a realistic conversational couplet;
— it is related to the real world of films, books, etc.;
— it requires understanding in seeing the semantic relationship between the noun *book* and the verb *read*.

Extended writing tasks can in turn be made more meaningful through contexualization. In other words, the students are told not only to write but also why they are writing. In each of the examples below, (a) is a typical composition topic and (b) is the same topic given both a context and an imaginary audience:

(a) Describe someone you know.
(b) It is your first month at University. Write a letter to your parents describing a friend you have got to know there.

(a) What are the arguments for and against capital punishment?
(b) You are an M.P. Write a short speech, which you are going to make in Parliament, either for or against capital punishment.

(a) When you arrived home last night you found that your home had been broken into. Describe what you found.
(b) When you arrived home last night you found that your home had been broken into. Write a report to the police about what you found.

These are typical compositions given to advanced language learners. At lower levels, it is likely to be necessary to provide more guidance, but the idea of contextualisation still applies. At advanced level, knowledge of context and reader are particularly important for determining an appropriate register for the composition.

Motivation

Much of what has been written above in connection with meaningfulness applies here. If an exercise requires thought, or if the relevance to the real world of a writing task can be seen by the students, then they are likely to find the homework more interesting and thus more motivating.

An awareness of the interests of the students is also important. Teenagers are more likely to enjoy writing the sleeve notes for a new record by their favourite pop group than a letter of application for a job, even if they are more likely to do the latter in real life. This can also be an argument for setting alternative tasks to satisfy the heterogeneous interests within a group of students.

3 Correction techniques

The first point to look at here is what the teacher wishes to achieve by reading and correcting the homework. The answer, in brief, is to find out what the students have or have not learnt and to *communicate* that to the students. For the student, the effectiveness of this communication depends, in practice, largely on the system of correction used by the teacher. Correction of homework can take a number of forms.

Full teacher correction

By this is meant the full written correction of all mistakes by the teacher, after which the homework is handed back to the students. This is by far the most common correction technique used, but the question arises of exactly how much attention students give to their mistakes thus corrected and, even if they make a brief mental note of mistakes at all, how much learning takes place as a result of this effortless process of glancing over the homework.

Student-student correction

Students check each other's homework in pairs, discussing it and making any necessary alterations before handing it in to the teacher. This requires them to think carefully about what is and what is not acceptable, and thus learning is more likely to take place. However, this method does have a disadvantage in that students may wrongly identify mistakes and, as a result, reinforce mistaken ideas. Further, in many teaching situations, teachers are required to build up an assessment of individual students, part of which is usually based on homework, and such co-operation between students conflicts with this requirement.

Indication but not correction

In *Problems and Principles in English Teaching* (Pergamon, 1980), Brumfit discusses a number of approaches of this kind, but this article will restrict itself to two. First, the mistake can simply be underlined by the teacher, leaving the student to identify the nature of the mistake and to correct it. Second, as well as underlining the mistake, the teacher can indicate why it is wrong by using a code such as the one given below.

If a marking code is used, then it is, of course, important that the students are made familiar with it beforehand and that they are able to understand the terminology used. For obvious reasons, it is also advisable for teachers in the same school to use the same code.

Symbols for Indicating Errors

Number or agreement, e.g. *he want* #   *3 dog*

∧   Something is missing, e.g. *I went ∧ school yesterday*
        morning.   I am ∧ student.

[ ]ʷᵒ   Word order, e.g.   *Where Paul [does] wo work?*

WW   Wrong word, e.g. *I didn't buy something.* ww

wf   Wrong form, e.g. *His English is very well.* wf   *I didn't saw her.* wf

T   Tense, e.g. *I saw a nice sweater and I buy it.* T

[⌐]   This needs to be reorganized, e.g. *The city grew in*
        such a way that the old centre, outlined in a
        time that [there is no automobiles and bus . . .
        and now is different in dealing with so much
        traffic.]

?   What do you mean? e.g. *[I am glad as if I had slept.] ?*

ʃ   Spelling, e.g *broʃther   coʃfortable*

P   Punctuation, e.g.   *What is it.* P

VF   Verb-form wrong, e.g.   *I gived him my coat.* VF

ø   Not necessary, e.g.   *I saw a man and ø asked him*
        the way.   an old ⊘and blind man

N.A.   Not appropriate in this context, e.g.   *Dear Sir,*
        How are you? ... N.A.

[*Acknowledgement:* This marking code was compiled by Marika Szalanczi]

Once the homework has been returned to the students, they can be asked to correct their own work individually or in pairs, returning the corrected form to the teacher for a second check. This system has the advantages of:
— requiring the students to think about and learn from their mistakes;
— providing the teacher with important feedback on whether the mistakes were made simply as a result of a lapse or due to misunderstanding what had been taught;
— still allowing a teacher to evaluate and allot marks for each individual's work for assessment purposes.
Opposite is an example of this marking code put into practice.

10, Oxford Road,
Cambridge
8th April

Dear Anne,

\#   How **is** Fred and the children?
              You know Anne, I've moved to a new
ww flat, **it's** nice and friendly. There is a fantastic
ww fireplace and the flat has plenty of **place** **to** my
furniture.

VF   Do **you can** guess where I've put my desk?
In a corner between two windows because, as
ʃ you know, I need   sunligʃ to work on my
ʃ books. Can you also gʃess where I've put my
armchair? Just in front of the fireplace.

            Oh! I forgot. There is a big wall just
wo behind the door and I've put [there] my bed and
the wardrobe.

            Well, I hope that you and your husband
\#T and **that** beautiful children of yours **could** come
wwʃ and **know** my flat one day. It's a little one but
ww there is enough **place** for me and my things.

                    Best wishes

                        Betty

In practice it is necessary to use Pit Corder's distinction between
mistakes and errors (*The Edinburgh Course in Applied Linguistics* Vol. 3,
Ed. J.P.B. Allen and S. Pit Corder, published by OUP) to make one
further refinement to this system. Here, a mistake refers to slips of the
tongue or lapses which may equally well be made by a native speaker or
by a learner of a language and which can therefore readily be self-
corrected. An error refers to incorrect language produced as a result of
an imperfect competence in the language. Teachers can make use of the

marking code to deal with mistakes but not errors, and they must use their knowledge of the students and the syllabus they have followed to decide which of these two categories applies. In the case of an error, teachers have to correct in full themselves.

| 4   Remedial work | For the teacher, homework should confirm, or otherwise, the effectiveness of the teaching strategies used so that any necessary remedial teaching can be carried out. The form that this takes will vary according to the importance of the misunderstanding in linguistic terms and to the number of students involved. For errors made by a large proportion of the class, the teacher needs to use class time for considerable further practice. Where smaller numbers are involved, directed remedial group-work may be possible. |

These 'remedies' however, can only seriously be applied to errors which have been made by enough students to warrant further class time being spent on them. The majority of mistakes and errors usually apply to individuals, and time constraints do not allow for considered action involving class time in each case. These mistakes or errors, therefore, must be communicated to the students by other means, and it is in this area that the teacher must select the most appropriate of the correction techniques outlined above.

44

Should we use the L₁ in the monolingual FL classroom?

Mary Spratt

For many years, under the influence of behaviourist thinking, it was considered anathema for either the student or the teacher to use the student's native language in the classroom. This was particularly true at elementary and intermediate levels, where it was feared that this use would encourage L_1—FL (i.e. first language—foreign language) interference and laziness, and slow down the process of FL sound-word association. The types of activity that took place in the classroom also did much to exclude the students' need to use the L_1, as their exposure to language was mainly confined to accuracy practice in the controlled contexts of different kinds of teacher-centred work, e.g. drilling, reading or writing. The teacher's need to use the L_1 was also restricted by the nature of such activities and language, by the use of visual aids to communicate meaning, and by the limited and constantly recurring kinds of task that restricted the range of the language of instruction.

Nowadays, the language, activities and roles of the EFL classroom are considerably different from those sketched above. From early on in the language-learning process, students are given not only accuracy practice but also fluency practice, in which they have to cope with such varied aspects of communication as discourse signals, unpredictable language, information gaps, broken sentences, hesitations, cohesive devices and discourse itself. The grading of language has also changed: it is no longer mainly lock-step and linguistic, but also takes students' needs and wants into consideration. Activities have also become more varied. As well as drills, there are mingles and information-gap activities; as well as multiple choice readings, there are jigsaw readings, jumbled paragraphs and cloze tests, to name but a few. Students also communicate much more with one another than before, whether in group work, pair work or mingles, and are encouraged to take initiatives in their learning strategies. Teachers too have taken on a new role. No longer are they mainly initiators and correctors of speech, but they are also monitors, encouragers and consultants.

This new classroom climate may well invite the use of the L_1, because students may struggle to say or write things they do not quite know how to and, with the teacher out of earshot, they now have ample opportunity to use the L_1 if they are not motivated or able to use the FL. Teachers, too, may well consider using the L_1 to explain things to students, for example, to give instructions or even for comprehension work on authentic texts.

Unlike in behaviourist times, there now seems to be no clearly defined line on whether the L_1 should or should not be used in the classroom, and for this reason teachers can easily find themselves wondering about the following:

— *Can I stop the students using the L_1 in the classroom?*
— *Do I always want to stop them using it?*
— *When could it be useful for them to use the L_1?*
— *Why do students use the L_1?*
— *Are there any means I can provide students with to stop them using the L_1?*
— *Should I ever use the L_1?*

The rest of this article will consider some of the issues these questions raise by looking first at student use of the L_1 and second at teacher use of the L_1.

1   When should students use the L₁?

Observation of FL classrooms shows that students often use the L_1 in the following situations:

— when they do not know the required FL;
— when they are unsure of what they have to do, particularly at the beginning or end of an activity;
— when they want to release tension.

Imagine, for example, a group of students embarking on a production-stage activity. To function solely in the FL they will need:

— to know the language of the role assigned to them;
— to be able to enquire of others, or establish with others, what is required of them i.e. task management language. For example:
  Whose turn is it now?
  What are we meant to be doing?

Who's meant to start?
It's my turn.
Who's chairman?
Are we meant to be writing anything?
You should be writing down my answers.
Wait a minute.
Who am I working with?
One point for me.
Wait a minute, let X speak.
— to be able to cope with unknown language, e.g.
How do you say X in English?
What does that mean?
I don't understand (what you're saying).
A thingamejig/a wadjamacall it.
X, could you | *(come here a moment, please).* |
    | *(tell me how to say X).* |
— to be able to comment on the activity or on one another's
performance e.g.
How boring!
Great idea!
What a crazy suggestion!
You must be mad!
Lovely!

N.B. The above are just a few exponents of these functions.

In many classrooms, teachers carefully teach students the language required for the activity in hand but not the language of task management, of talking about unknown language or of commenting on performance. Yet what is common to these latter kinds of language is that they are the language of social interaction, of organization, of expressing feelings and doubts. They are also the kind of language students need to know to be able to function fully as students in the FL. Much language teaching these days concentrates on students' needs and wants in the impersonal sense of doing things in the outside world; it concentrates less frequently on providing them with ways of expressing their excitement, dilemmas or organizing capacities either as students or as people. All these functions are, however, very common in the speech of native speakers—a basic need, in fact.

Role plays, pair work, group work, games etc., provide excellent authentic opportunities and contexts for the teacher to feed in or teach precisely this kind of language. Clearly, not all the exponents can be taught at once, nor would one want to teach everything to every level of student. It is necessary to select, grade and recycle these exponents throughout the elementary, intermediate and advanced programmes.

Students equipped with the above language will undoubtedly be better armed to cope with pair and group work activities. These activities can nevertheless still put a strain on students, particularly at the elementary level. To function solely in the FL can be very exhausting, as most of us probably know from our own experience. Students may sometimes need to use their L_1 simply to release tension and to let off steam.

2   When should the teacher use the L_1?

Let us look at three occasions on which teachers might want to use the L_1:
— for instructions and classroom management;

—for explanations and justifications;
—for communicating meaning or checking comprehension.

Instructions and classroom management

Although the language of instructions and classroom management may sometimes seem long and complicated, it can in fact, usually be reduced to certain basic elements that repeat themselves from one class to the next, e.g.
— *Get into pairs.*
— *Don't show your papers to one another.*
— *I want you to read this very quickly.*
— *X, could you go and sit next to . . .*
— *I want you to write a letter . . .*

This language, like the language exponents listed previously, forms an integral and recurring part of classroom interaction and an opportunity for genuine teacher-student communication. For these reasons, the teacher can aim to give the students at least a passive understanding of this language.

Various things can be done to help the elementary student in particular to cope with this language, and it is mainly the elementary student we are concerned with on this point. Firstly, teachers can be consistent, at least initially, in the exponents of management language that they choose to use. Secondly, they can reinforce the meaning of that language through the use of mime, gesture, visuals and even dummy runs of activities with the collaboration of better students. Thirdly, they can be careful to use the beginning of an activity to check that students have actually understood. It may sometimes be useful at this stage to say in the L₁ what has already been said in the FL if difficulties or strain seem apparent.

Explanations and justifications

Teachers may wish to explain the concept behind the use of a particular language point (e.g. the present perfect) or explain to students the reason for doing a particular activity or using a particular participation pattern. Depending on the language level and attitudes of the class, it may sometimes be more effective for the teacher to do this in the L₁.

Communicating meaning or checking comprehension

When teachers communicate the meaning of an FL item (e.g. text, structure, vocabulary) through the FL, they are involving the students in an authentic learning activity, that of trying to understand what the speaker is saying and possibly trying to relate the concept of what they are saying to one they already know.

Language learners outside the classroom, e.g. in shops, meetings, conversations, are constantly involved in this process, which can sometimes also become one of negotiation as they ask for further clarification of something they are dimly beginning to understand. This authentic activity and the language that accompanies it surely form a part of a learning strategy that any language student requires and thus must be encouraged in the FL class.

This having been said, many teachers remember very well those situations in which they felt that their paraphrasing in the FL of the meaning of an item or the concept behind it was at best approximate or ambiguous. This is particularly true with abstract vocabulary items and concepts. In this case, once the above-mentioned negotiating process has taken place, a useful check for students and teacher alike, particularly at elementary level, is provided if the teacher simply asks the students for the L₁ equivalent of the point in question. However, where vocabulary is concerned, teachers must check prior to the class that there is such an equivalent and also, depending on the level of the class, point out what the collocations and connotations of that word are, so as to be able to anticipate misunderstandings. One of the well known dangers of translation is, of course, that there may not be a one-to-one correspondence between two languages in a given area.

3   Conclusion

This article has attempted to give teachers some guidelines for deciding what role, if any, the L_1 can play in the monolingual FL classroom. To make such a decision teachers must consider the following:
— what needs the L_1 is filling;
— whether students should master the expression of these needs in the foreign language to be able to function fully either inside or outside the classroom;
— what affective role the use of the L_1 may be playing;
— how important that affective role is.
On answering these questions, they can decide whether or not to use or to allow the use of the L_1.

45

Choosing the best available textbook

Alan Matthews

In most teaching situations, the textbook plays a crucial role because it is the main teaching and learning aid. This is especially true of teaching in primary and secondary schools, where the textbook represents the core of the syllabus to be covered throughout the school year and where the vast majority of classwork and homework will derive directly from it.

During term time, school teachers are very busy people whose working hours extend well beyond the 'normal' working days. In most countries, the majority of teachers of English are women who usually have a large number of additional time-consuming commitments to husband and children. However desirable it may be to prepare extra 'home-made' teaching materials, in reality it is all too often impossible to find the time. Any material that may be produced will always supplement the textbook, never replace it substantially.

Given, then, the centrality of the textbook, it makes sense to ensure that the best choice is made from the ever-increasing range available. I am concerned that decisions should be based on well-thought-out criteria and not simply on an attractive cover, the name of the author(s) or the liberal use of 'in-words' such as 'communicative' or 'functional' which superficially promise great things!

First, though, a warning. I am definitely not wanting to encourage teachers to change textbooks for the sake of it. If you and your students are generally satisfied with the books you have been using this year, then it is probably best to stick with them for next year. A change from one book to another inevitably involves a great deal of extra work for you as you gradually familiarise yourself with the new book. An annual change can often be unsettling to the students, too, as they sense your dissatisfaction.

However, if you are considering a change, what procedure might you adopt in order to reach a well-informed decision? Basically you have to analyse (a) your specific teaching situation and (b) the competing textbooks and, as a result of this analysis, discover which textbook fits your situation most exactly. Here are a number of questions you could ask yourselves to help you in this analysis.

1 Defining your own teaching situation

Syllabus

What exactly does the syllabus consist of? What are the teaching objectives of the syllabus in terms of structures, functions, topics, vocabulary, relative importance of the four skills, etc? Does the textbook under consideration do them justice?

Time available

How many teaching hours are available in the school year? At first sight there always seem to be considerably more teaching hours available than in fact there are. In secondary schools, teaching time is usually lost for a variety of reasons—national and local holidays, end-of-term tests, beginnings and ends of terms, teachers' absences through illness, elections held in the school buildings, sports day etc. It would be unwise—and needlessly expensive—to adopt a textbook which provides too much material for the teaching hours available.

Students' age

What is the age of your students? Are the social settings, the topics, the vocabulary areas etc. suitable for the age of your students or are they too juvenile, or too sophisticated? Textbooks which are designed for use with students in their upper teens are often chosen for younger students and predictably fail to live up to expectations. Also adult students are often obliged to use textbooks written with children in mind.

Students' interests

What are the interests of your students? Whatever their interests may be—and these may well vary according to whether the students are from a large city or from the country—are they reflected in the textbook? It is important that the textbook is used with pleasure and does not provoke a bored groan from the students.

Students' background

What is the social and cultural background of your students? Are they from fairly sophisticated middle-class families or largely from working-class families? Are they from urban centres or rural areas? Or a mixture of all these? Are the social and cultural situations portrayed in the textbooks familiar, welcome and motivating or are they alien, confusing and off-putting to the students? The action of many textbooks is understandably set in Britain, partly because the authors wish to teach something about everyday British life and customs, but also because many such books are aimed at foreign students who follow a language course in Britain. This type of book may not be particularly appropriate in your teaching situation.

Class size

What size are your classes? Most school teachers throughout the world labour with classes of at least thirty students. Most textbooks are written by people who are not teaching in such circumstances (if they are teaching at all, that is!) Many textbooks seem to be written with the private language schools in mind (this is, after all, where many EFL authors are employed) where classes of between 10 and 20 are the norm. It is sometimes difficult successfully to adapt textbooks written for use with smallish classes for use with groups of thirty or more students.

Students' level

What level are your students? Unless you teach beginners, this is no doubt an impossible question to answer in a simple way because each of your classes will be characterised by mixed ability and mixed aptitude. Ideally the textbook should cater for the range of levels in your classes and should be neither too demanding nor too easy for most students.

2 Assessing the merits of available textbooks

General impression

What is the general impression of the book? Does it 'feel right' in terms of appearance, design, size, lay-out, etc? Does it pass the 'flick test', i.e. are you impressed when you flick through it briefly for the first time?

Methodology

What methodology is implicit in the organization of the book? Is it structurally or functionally organized or topic based? Or a mixture? Very importantly, would teachers in your school be able to handle the book and teach reasonably well (and happily) with it? Does this also apply to the older teachers trained some years ago as well as to the younger and probably as yet untrained teachers? Or would the methodological approach adopted by the textbook confuse and alienate them?

Grammar

How well is the grammar of the language covered? Many functionally-organized textbooks tend to skate over the surface of the grammar. I think this is dangerous: one of your main aims should still be to teach students to communicate, both orally and in writing, with a fair degree of accuracy. Communication without regard for grammatical accuracy should not be our aim.

Four skills

How well are the four skills covered? If you teach in a secondary school, you have little or no way of knowing the purposes for which your present students will need to use their school English—or indeed whether they will ever have reason to use it at all. It seems sensible, therefore, to aim to lay a solid foundation in all four skills from which the students can later proceed according to their individual needs. Many elementary textbooks concentrate heavily on oral and aural skills and neglect the development of reading and writing. It should not be forgotten, however, that in all examinations the students are tested on their ability to read and to write.

Grading	How well has the textbook been graded? How much new material is introduced per teaching unit? Is it overloaded? Is the grading too steep, i.e. is too much covered too quickly? Unlike structurally-organized textbooks, which are finely graded according to the supposed difficulty of the structures, functionally-organized books often seem to be graded fairly arbitrarily.
Lay-out	Is the general lay-out of the book clear and attractive? Are the units well labelled, with subdivisions clearly marked and easy to follow? Are the pages cluttered and therefore off-putting and difficult to use? If students are expected to write in their books (in boxes, tables, etc.), has sufficient room been provided?
Presentation and practice of new language	Have the new teaching points been clearly presented within a reasonably convincing context? Have sufficient exercises been provided for the students to do, or has the teacher been left to make them up? Are there both controlled exercises for accuracy practice (probably of the more traditional type), as well as freer, more creative ones for fluency practice? Are there enough for some to be set as homework? Has provision been made, by the deliberate recycling of items, for revision of language already covered?
Variety	Is there variety from unit to unit or does each one monotonously follow the same predictable sequence of exercises? The nature of the materials in each unit should determine the number and type of exercises, and thereby naturally provide variety.
Illustrations	What pedagogic purpose do the illustrations have? Or are they mainly intended as decoration? Many textbooks appearing these days make lavish use of colour but few exploit it systematically for pedagogic purposes. The main effect of colour—other than as a superficial eye-catcher—is to push up the price of the book very considerably. It is often not worth the extra money. Are the illustrations, whether colour or black and white, pleasing to the eye or are they grotesque? Do they portray clearly what is intended pedagogically or do they serve to confuse?
Story-line	Is the backbone of each unit a story-line? If so, is it interesting and well written or is it embarrassingly trivial and inane? A story-line usually forces the teacher to work through the book unit by unit in the order in which they are presented and, however interesting at the beginning, the story may well flag as the book progresses.
Series	Is the textbook part of a series? If so, are the other books also suitable? If not, does this matter?
Sexism	How does the textbook portray the sexes? Does it, like most, present a highly unflattering 'music-hall joke' type of image of women? (Most women teachers throughout the world still happily use such books and thereby help to perpetuate this stereotyped image!)
Ease of use	How easily can you find your way through the book? Is there a helpful Contents Page, an Index, a summary of grammar and/or functions covered? Are the instructions on how to use each exercise clear and simple?

Culture bias

Is the textbook too British (or too American), i.e. are the topics and situations included of little relevance and of even less interest to students at school in your country (for example, opening a bank account, hiring a car)?

Extras

What extras exist to make up the total package? Is there an accompanying Teacher's Book? If so, does it provide you with real help or does it confuse you? Many courses also contain audiocassettes, videocassettes, recorded songs, workbooks, wallcharts, testpacks etc. Would any of these additions substantially help you to use the basic textbook? (Often the only really essential extra is the audiocassette, i.e. recordings of the dialogues without which the textbook would be much the poorer.)

Pre-testing

Has the textbook been properly and extensively pre-tested, i.e. has the material ever actually been used before finding its way into print? This is of course extremely important. Look carefully at the Acknowledgements section: if the textbook has been tried out this will certainly be mentioned; if there is no mention of trialling, you can fairly safely assume that none took place.

Availability

When you have finally chosen your textbook, with the help of the above criteria, you must ensure it will be available in the local bookshops in good time for the start of the school year. The extensive use abroad of imported books from Britain has sometimes led to problems of availability, with teachers forced to teach for several weeks without any textbooks. It is better, I think, to have a textbook for the whole of the school year—even if it is not your first choice—than to be waiting for weeks for your first choice to arrive.

Price

Last—but far from least—the price of the book. By choosing an imported book teachers impose an extra financial burden on students or on their parents. This may be justified, however, if you are convinced of the advantages of the book. Remember also to look at the price of the cassette.

Summary

Finally here, for quick easy reference, is a summary of the main criteria for assessing the pros and cons of textbooks:

- general impression
- methodology
- coverage of grammar
- four skills
- grading
- lay-out
- presentation of new language
- accuracy and fluency practice
- variety
- illustrations

- story-line
- series of books
- sexism
- finding your way around
- too British/American
- extras
- pre-testing
- availability
- price

Contributors

Eunice Barroso has taught English as a foreign language for eighteen years. She completed the RSA Dip. TEFL course at the British Council Institute in Lisbon where she has been teaching for four years. She is involved in teacher training with Portuguese state sector teachers.

Mike Beaumont trains teachers at the University of Manchester. His classroom experience includes the teaching of both children and adults, and he has worked within the state system in Britain and for VSO and the British Council abroad. Overseas assignments have taken him to India, Iran, Portugal, Morocco, Colombia, the Philippines and Spain. His current interests include the development of graded tests of reading ability for secondary level pupils.

Donn Byrne has worked as a teacher and teacher trainer in Europe, East Africa, India, South America and Canada. From 1960 to 1977 he served with the British Council as an English Language Officer and from 1976 to 1977 was Visiting Associate Professor in Applied Linguistics at Concordia University, Montreal. He is the author of a number of handbooks and teaching materials, including *Teaching Oral English* and *Teaching Writing Skills* (Longman Handbooks for Language Teachers).

Carmelita Caruana has been working in Egypt for the past three years after spending three years at the British Council in Lisbon. She is currently Deputy Director of the English Teaching Centre in Cairo, where she is also responsible for teacher training.

David Cranmer graduated in music at Sidney Sussex College, Cambridge and successfully completed his M.Mus. in musicology at King's College, London. He became an EFL teacher in 1977. Since that time he has taught at various institutions in Britain, Iran, Holland and Portugal. He has been teaching at the British Institute, Lisbon since 1981.

Les Dangerfield graduated in Economic History at Exeter University. He taught EFL in England and Germany before beginning work, in 1980, as a teacher and teacher trainer at the British Council Institute in Lisbon, Portugal, where he is now Assistant Director of Studies.

Ian Forth was educated at Hatfield Polytechnic and the University of Leicester. He has taught EFL for seven years in England, France, Cyprus and Portugal.

Sue Gaskin has a B.A. in English and the RSA Dip. TEFL. She spent seven years teaching English in Portugal and has also taught in Greece, Japan and the Soviet Union.

Roger Gower is the Principal of the Bell School of Languages, Cambridge. He has extensive teacher-training experience, and has taught in London, Italy and Mexico. Before working for the Bell School, he was Director of International House, London. He is co-author of *Teaching Practice Handbook* with Steve Walters (Heinemann, 1983).

Rob Hirons is Director of Studies at the British Council, Kuwait. He has taught EFL in Greece, Iran, Portugal and Kuwait. He is an experienced teacher trainer on the RSA Dip. TEFL and Preparatory Certificate and is an assessor for both schemes. He is interested in classroom interaction and the management of learning.

Alan Matthews has taught in secondary schools in France, Senegal and Turkey and in British Council centres in Brazil and Portugal. In Lisbon he directed an RSA Dip. TEFL course and ran courses for Portuguese teachers of English. Currently he is working as a teacher trainer for the British Council in Spain. He is co-author of a number of textbooks.

David Palmer, who was Assistant Director of Studies at the British Council, Lisbon from 1979 to 1980, is currently Chairman of the Department of Modern Languages at the Ecole des Cadres, a Paris business school. He holds an M.Phil. in English and Education from the University of London and is currently developing video materials for the teaching of management English.

Carol Read is a teacher, teacher trainer and co-author (with Alan Matthews) of *Themes, Pyramid* (both Collins) and *Tandem* (Bell & Hyman). She has taught in France, Venezuela and Portugal and is currently living and working in Madrid.

Mary Spratt is Assistant Director of Studies (Teacher Training) at the British Institute, Lisbon. She is responsible for teacher training within the British Institute and for the British Council's teacher-training programme in the state school system in Portugal. She is co-author of *Longman Proficiency Skills* and has worked previously in the UK, Italy, Cyprus, Algeria and Belgium.

Marika Szalanczi studied at Hull and Manchester Universities. She has taught English in Nigeria, the UK and Portugal, where she was also involved in teacher training. She is currently lecturing in English for Academic Purposes at Middlesex Polytechnic.

Sheila Ward studied Modern Languages at Leeds University and Portuguese at Lisbon University. She has taught EFL in several countries including England, Spain, Somalia, Greece, Cyprus and Portugal. Her main interests are singing and playing the guitar. She is the author of *Dippitydoo* (Longman, 1980), a collection of songs and activities for young learners of English as a foreign language.

Ron White has worked in Fiji and Papua New Guinea and has been to many parts of the world as a visiting lecturer. He taught at the University of Manchester before going to the Centre for Applied Language Studies, University of Reading, as Director of Courses. He is interested in the developing of composition skills in writing.

Eddie Williams works at the Centre for Applied Language Studies in the University of Reading. He has worked in TEFL in Cyprus, Malta and France, and has undertaken teacher education tours for the British Council in Europe, Latin America, and North Africa. His current interests include reading, classroom testing, bilingual education, and the use of video in language teaching.

Glossary

David Cranmer and Alan Matthews

Only terms used within this book are listed. Cross references are printed in bold type.

accuracy   The production of correct instances of language, particularly language **form**. (Cp. **fluency**.)

accuracy practice   Classroom activities which give the students opportunities to produce correct instances of language, e.g. **drills**, written exercises.

achievement test   See **test**.

appropriateness (also **appropriacy**)   The use of correct *register* in a particular context. It would be *inappropriate* if, for example, while receiving a decoration, a young woman greeted the Queen of England with 'Hi there, gorgeous!' Although a feasible greeting in another context, it does not take into account the formality intrinsic to the situation, the Queen's social position, her age and sex, nor the relationship between the speaker and the Queen.

authentic texts/materials   Texts or other materials originally intended for use by native-speakers but used subsequently also to teach the language to non-native speakers.

backchaining   In a **repetition drill**, initially repeating only the last part of a phrase/sentence, progressively extending backwards what is being repeated until the whole phrase/sentence is included, e.g. in a repetition drill of *Let's go to the cinema*, first drilling *cinema*, then *to the cinema*, next *go to the cinema*, and finally *Let's go to the cinema.*

blank-filling (also **gap-filling**)   An exercise/test in which students are required to think of suitable words to put in spaces where words have been taken out of a text. Unlike a **cloze exercise/test**, the spaces do not occur at every nth word, but wherever the exercise/test writer wants them, e.g. in order to focus on a particular language point.

brain pattern   A diagram in which notes are laid out visually, with the main topic in the centre and sub-topics radiating from it and from each other, the relation between them being shown through lines linking them. See page 75.

choral drill   See **drill**.

closed pair   See **pair work**.

cloze exercise/procedure   A completion exercise in which every nth word has been taken out of a text, or the procedure by which every nth word is taken out. (See also **blank-filling**.)

coherence   The logical relation of sentences forming a text. A student may, for example, produce a composition in which all the sentences are grammatically correct, but which lacks *coherence*.

cohesion (also **cohesive devices**)   The overt relating of one sentence to another or one part of a sentence to another through the use of **reference devices** and **logical connectors**.

communication gap   A situation in which one speaker/writer knows information not known by another (**information gap**) or there is a difference of opinion between speakers/writers (**opinion gap**).

communicative activity   An activity which fills a **communication gap**, i.e. through the transfer of information to fill an **information gap** or the exchange of opinions aimed at resolving an **opinion gap**.

competence   A native-speaker's/learner's theoretical knowledge of a language system (Cp. **performance**.)

concept checking   Making sure a student has properly grasped the meaning behind an item that is being presented/explained, e.g. when presenting/explaining *used to*, checking that students realise its meaning involves being (a) past and (b) habitual.

concept question   A question which a teacher asks a student in the process of **concept checking**.

connectives   See **logical connectors**.

contextualise   Put in a situational and linguistic context, i.e. **elicit**/indicate what kind of text or linguistic context something is drawn from, and elicit/set the scene.

cue (also **prompt**)   A word/phrase/picture/gesture etc. used to stimulate a response from a student, especially in **drills**.

cue cards (See also **role cards**)   Cards with pictures/words used to cue or prompt students in **drills** and **role plays**.

discourse   A stretch of language used for a communicative purpose, i.e. not simply as a language model.

discourse chain   A visual representation to show the logical progression between one **function** and another and/or to **cue** such a progression, usually in a dialogue but sometimes in a written text. See, for example, page 28.

discrete item   In a test, an item or question which focuses on only one specific teaching point; for example, in testing verbs, *one* from among tense, number, person, *not* a combination of these.

distractors   In **multiple choice questions**, the incorrect choices.

drill   A type of highly controlled oral practice in which the students respond to a given **cue**. The response varies according to the type of drill.

  choral drill   Any type of drill in which the whole class speaks simultaneously.

  individual drill   Any type of drill in which students speak one at a time.

  meaningful drill   A drill that can only be performed if its meaning is understood, e.g. using the **cue** *This is a good book* to stimulate the response *I'd like to read it*, and *This is a delicious cake* for *I'd like to eat it*. In order to respond, the learner must understand the relationship in meaning between *book* and *read, cake* and *eat*. (Cp. **mechanical drill**.)

  mechanical drill   A drill which the student can perform without understanding what the language item means, i.e. mechanically (Cp. **meaningful drill**.)

  repetition drill   A drill in which the item being practised is repeated with no change.

  substitution drill   A drill which is varied by substituting one word/phrase for another, as determined by a **cue**.

transformation drill   A drill which requires the learner to *transform* a sentence in response to a **cue**, e.g. from affirmative to negative, statement to question, active to passive, present to past, or the reverse.

elicit   Encourage students to suggest a vocabulary item, structure etc. rather than providing this language.

exponent   The actual language used to express a **function** or a **notion**. For example, the function of *asking for directions* can be expressed by the exponents *Where is . . .?* or *Can you tell me how I get to . . .?* or *How do I get to . . .?* etc.

extensive reading/listening   Reading or listening to relatively long texts, usually for one's own pleasure, where the aim is global rather than detailed comprehension, e.g. reading an extract from a novel or a simplified 'reader', listening to a fairly extensive radio broadcast. (Cp. **intensive reading/listening**.)

filler   A non-silent pause, e.g. a hesitation when speaking filled by *er, um, ah, you know, sort of* etc.

fluency   The production of language which flows well, both because it is free from undue hesitation (oral fluency), and because it is natural in terms of the use of vocabulary/idioms etc., i.e. does not seem stilted (oral and written fluency). (Cp. **accuracy**.)

fluency practice   Classroom activities which give the students opportunities to produce language within a less guided framework in order to encourage **fluency**.

form   The phonological and grammatical characteristics of an utterance, e.g. features of pronunciation, word order, morphology, rather than the meanings conveyed by these forms. The formal system of a language.

function   The communicative purpose to which an utterance is put. e.g. *Have you got a pen?* is likely to be expressing a request rather than asking about possession.

functional approach   An approach to the teaching of languages which emphasises the communicative purposes of utterances. Thus a functional approach will have teaching units labelled *describing people, asking for and giving directions, giving reasons, requesting things* etc., all of which are examples of language functions. (Cp. **structural approach** and **notional/functional approach**.)

gap-filling   See **blank-filling**.

grammar   The rules that govern the form of a language.

group work   Work performed by the class in smaller units, usually of between 3 and 8 students, on a given task. The main aims of group work are to give greater opportunity to each student to participate actively in order to foster a co-operative (rather than competitive) spirit among the students and to encourage them to work independently of the teacher. (See also **pair work**.)

individual drill   See **drill**.

individualisation (also **individualised work/study**)   The provision of learning materials which meet the *individual* needs of the students, e.g. self-access materials, materials for study at home.

information gap   See **communication gap**.

information transfer   A practice activity which involves the students extracting relevant information from a reading or listening text and reproducing it in diagrammatic or semi-diagrammatic form; or the reverse procedure.

integrated skills　Any combination of the four **skills** used to perform interrelated activities.

intensive reading/listening　Reading or listening to a text in order to understand it in detail. (Cp. **extensive reading/listening**.)

interference (also **L₁** or **mother-tongue interference**)　The errors made by students in speaking or writing the foreign language (L₂) as a result of the influence of their mother tongue (L₁). For example, the incorrect sentence *I am here since 5 o'clock* uttered by a French student would probably be due to the French *Je suis ici depuis cinq heures.*

jigsaw listening/reading　A classroom technique whereby the class is divided into groups—usually 2 or 3—and each group is given only part of a situation or story. After listening to or reading their respective parts, the groups discuss them in order to build up the whole situation or story (often to solve a set problem). Each group represents one piece of the jigsaw which can only be completed by communicating with members of the other group(s).

jumbled sentences/paragraphs/pictures etc. (also **scrambled**)　Sentences etc. which are deliberately given to the students in the wrong order, the task being to provide the correct order.

learner-centred (also **student-centred**)　An approach/activity which takes as its starting point the needs and/or interests of the learners and involves them as fully as possible in the learning process. (Cp. **teacher-centred**.)

lock-step grading　A way of organising a syllabus in which the order of items to be taught is determined strictly by what has already been taught, e.g. the present continuous tense can only be taught after the present of the verb *be*, because the present of *be* is used in forming the present continuous. Similarly the past continuous must come after the present continuous and the past of *be*, and the past perfect after the past simple.

logical connectors (also **connectives**)　A feature of textual **cohesion**—words and phrases that serve either as links between different parts of a sentence, or between sentences, and which indicate the relationship between what they are linking, e.g. She was sick during the night *so* she didn't go to work next day. (= Result)　He was very impatient with his mother. *Not only that but* he said some very rude things. (= Addition)

marker sentence (also **model sentence**)　The first example of a newly presented structure or exponent that students focus their attention on and subsequently use as a model for producing other similar sentences.

meaningful drill　See **drill**.

mechanical drill　See **drill**.

metalanguage　The terminology used to describe language, e.g. *verb, simple past, subjunctive, noun phrase, dative, consonant.*

mingle (also **mingling activity**)　A classroom activity in which students stand up, move round the classroom and talk to or interview a number of their colleagues, in order, for example, to carry out a survey or questionnaire. (N.B. a coined term, not widely used.)

mode　The language medium, either speech or writing.

model sentence　See **marker sentence**.

morphology　Grammar at or below the level of the word, i.e. involving 'endings', prefixes, suffixes and internal changes within a word, e.g. in irregular verbs (*drink, drank, drunk*) and when changing parts of speech (*deep→depth*). (Cp. **syntax**.)

multiple choice questions See **questions**.

multiple choice test See **test**.

needs analysis The analysis of the linguistic needs of a student or group of students in terms of **skills, structures, functions, notions,** vocabulary items etc. *Needs analyses* are most frequently carried out for ESP (English for Specific/Special Purposes) groups to ensure the relevance of the teaching materials. Some students do not have easily identifiable needs, e.g. school children.

notion An abstract concept, e.g. time, duration, frequency, quantity, space, weight, size, futurity, possibility etc.

notional/functional approach An approach to language teaching which is organized and labelled in terms of **notions** and **functions**. (Cp. **functional approach** and **structural approach**.)

objective test See **test**.

open pair See **pair work**.

opinion gap See **communication gap**.

pair work Work performed by the class in pairs in order to give students maximum opportunity to participate in an activity.

    closed pair Two adjacent students working together (Cp. **open pair**.)

    open pair Two students in different parts of the classroom responding to one another, usually in dialogue. Typically this occurs prior to work in **closed pairs**, to act as a model to the class and to enable the teacher to check whether the students have grasped what is being taught well enough to work by themselves in closed pairs.

performance The language as actually used by a native speaker or learner (Cp. **competence**.)

placement test See **test**.

pre-questions Questions which are set before the students read or listen to a text for the first time. The purpose of pre-questions is to help students focus on the main points of a text.

pre-teach To teach vocabulary items, structures etc. immediately before the students meet them in a reading or listening text.

productive skills Those skills which involve the production of language, i.e. speaking and writing. (Cp. **receptive skills**.)

proficiency test See **test**.

prompt See **cue**.

questions

    multiple choice questions 'Questions' consisting of a number (usually 3 to 5) of statements/questions only one of which is correct. The student must indicate which one is correct.

    true/false questions 'Questions' consisting of a number of statements about a text. Students must indicate whether each is true or false.

    wh-questions Questions which begin with *who, which, when, where, why* and *whose*. Questions beginning with *how* are also included. (Cp. **yes/no questions**.)

    yes/no questions Questions which elicit from the students a *yes* or a *no*, often followed by a short verb form. For example, *Did you go out last night? Yes, I did* or *No, I didn't*. (Cp. **wh-questions**.)

realia   Real objects taken into the classroom as aids, either to clarify concepts or to provide a more realistic setting, e.g. toy vehicles, things to eat or drink, bus tickets, menus.

Received Pronunciation (R.P.)   The non-regional accent in British English originally associated with the socially prestigious public schools. It was adopted by the BBC for its announcers, hence the almost synonymous term *BBC English*.

receptive skills   Listening and reading, i.e. those skills which involve receiving language. (Cp. **productive skills**.)

redundancy   In a given utterance not all features, whether phonological, grammatical or lexical, are essential for the meaning of the utterance to be clearly understood, e.g. in the sentence *Yesterday I walked all the way to school* the notion of past time is established by *yesterday*, thus making the past tense ending *-ed* (or /t/) *redundant* as far as meaning is concerned.

reference devices/words   Words which refer backwards or forwards to other words and phrases in the same or a different sentence, e.g.
- Joanna used to live in Lisbon but *she* left *there* last month
- Joseph rather fancies port wine. So *do* I.
- Look over there. *That's* the house that Jack built.

reference skills   The skills needed by students to use available reference sources efficiently, e.g. using dictionaries, encyclopaedias etc, understanding and using a library system.

register   Variation in the choice of vocabulary, structure, accent etc. used to express an idea, e.g. degress of formality, degrees of intensity (in apologies, complaints etc.), the social position of and relationship between speakers, age, sex, how specialised an audience is being addressed and in what field. (See also **appropriateness**.)

remedial work   Specially devised work to help students remedy errors they are still making in previously taught language.

repetition drill   See **drill**.

role cards   Cards used to define a person's role, e.g. in terms of their character and/or the opinions they are asked to represent in a **role play**. (See also **cue cards**.)

role play   A classroom activity in which students play parts or roles, and often work in pairs or in groups. The precise content and roles are often determined in advanced by the teacher, usually by providing the students with **role cards**. Role plays aim to prepare students for the 'real world' outside the classroom by giving them **fluency practice**. (See also **simulation**.)

scanning   Running one's eye over a reading text in order to locate a specific piece of information as rapidly as possible, e.g. locating someone's telephone number in the directory, finding out the time of the next train from a railway timetable, looking up a word in the dictionary.

scrambled   See **jumbled**.

self-access materials   A range of learning materials from which the individual student can select tasks or exercises according to his/her specific needs and preferences. These can be done at the student's own pace and corrected from keys provided, with little or no help from the teacher.

simulation   An activity in which students are set a task, e.g. to put together a newspaper front-page or a 5-minute radio broadcast. The students are assigned the necessary roles to perform the task but, unlike some **role plays**, the students always retain their *own* personalities.

skills   Listening, speaking, reading, and writing, often referred to as *the four skills*.

skimming   Very rapidly looking through a reading text to get the gist or general idea of its contents. (Cp. **scanning**.)

split dialogue   Students are given one person's half of a dialogue and, with the help of the contextual clues, are required to write or say the other person's half.

structural approach   An approach to the teaching of languages in which the basic **structures** are taught. They are graded in difficulty and taught one by one until the whole grammatical system is covered. (Cp. **functional approach** and **notional/functional approach**.)

structure   A grammatical form, e.g. a verb 'tense', the use of gerunds after certain verbs, participal phrases, conditionals.

student-centred   See **learner-centred**.

study skills   The skills needed by students to enable them to study effectively, e.g. listening to lectures and note-taking; reading books, articles etc. and note-taking; writing essays, dissertations etc.; participating in tutorials and seminars; using reference materials efficiently.

subjective test   See **test**.

substitution drill   See **drill**.

syntax   Grammar above the level of the word but not beyond the sentence, e.g. word-order and the use of multi-clause sentences (conditionals, clauses of cause and effect, contrast, time etc.) (Cp. **morphology**.)

teacher-centred   An approach/activity in which the teacher determines what is to be taught and directly controls the teaching of it. (Cp. **learner-centred**.)

test   A task, typically unaided, in which students are required to answer questions so as to show what they know and do not know.

  achievement test   A test aiming to discover how much and what a student has learnt over a given period. End of term/year tests are normally of this kind.

  cloze test   A test using **cloze procedure**.

  multiple choice test   A test composed of **multiple choice questions**.

  objective test   A test which can be objectively verified, i.e. which will produce the same result irrespective of the markers and the conditions under which they mark.

  placement test   A test aiming to place students in rank order or into groups of similar level.

  proficiency test   A test designed to show whether a student is capable of performing certain given tasks.

  subjective test   A test for which the mark given depends on the subjective judgement of the marker, e.g. a composition.

  true/false test   A test composed of **true/false questions**.

time lines   A visual representation of time consisting of a horizontal line moving from left (earlier) to right (later), on or parallel to which are indicated points or periods of time, and the relationship between them in terms of verb tenses. Below is a time line demonstrating the meaning of the present perfect continuous with *for* and *since*.

Example of a time line

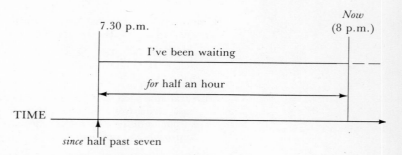

usage   The manifestation of our knowledge of the **formal** system of a language. (Cp. **use**.)

use   The way we use the **formal** system of a language to achieve some kind of communicative purpose. (Cp. **usage**.)